OUT OF
THE BLUE

OUT OF
THE BLUE

The inside story of the unexpected
rise and rapid fall of Liz Truss

Harry Cole and James Heale

HarperCollins

OUT OF THE BLUE

The inside story of the unexpected rise and rapid fall of Liz Truss

Harry Cole and James Heale

HarperCollins*Publishers*

HarperCollins*Publishers*
1 London Bridge Street
London SE1 9GF

www.harpercollins.co.uk

HarperCollins*Publishers*
Macken House, 39/40 Mayor Street Upper
Dublin 1, D01 C9W8, Ireland

First published by HarperCollins*Publishers* 2022

1 3 5 7 9 10 8 6 4 2

A catalogue record of this book is
available from the British Library

ISBN 978-0-00-860578-0

Printed and bound in the UK using 100%
renewable electricity at CPI Group (UK) Ltd

For our mums and dads – thank you!

'It was always hard to see the aim of it all,
or where it might lead, except that she
would be at the centre of it.'

Julian Glover on his fellow student
Liz Truss

'Politics is just like show business. You have a
hell of an opening, coast for a while, and
then have a hell of a close.'

Ronald Reagan

'I'm someone who has always acted with
integrity, I have always been clear about what
I will do and followed through on my promises
and been honest about the situation, and
that is what I would do as PM.'

Liz Truss, 24 August 2022

CONTENTS

CONTENTS

AUTHORS' NOTES

This is not an authorised biography. While we were pleased that Liz Truss agreed to be interviewed by us, we had no access to her papers, letters or any other communications beyond those acquired through journalistic endeavour. Conversations or communications reported were told to us first hand, by witnesses, or in some cases by somebody with direct knowledge of discussions. Some of Liz Truss's family, colleagues and friends declined to talk to us, but many of them agreed and for that we are extremely grateful.

Plenty of those we spoke to are named in these pages, but many more insisted on anonymity. It was a delicate time for any upwardly mobile MP, adviser, official or friend to be speaking candidly about the Prime Minister. We are particularly indebted to those civil servants who have risked their jobs to do just that. Some sources have been known to the authors for years, others literally came out of the blue. As ever in politics, there are bad-faith actors whose attempts to rewrite history make them unreliable witnesses. In those cases their public utterances may have been included, but private comments were either not sought or were disregarded.

We decided to write this book quickly, so those of you expecting Robert Caro will be disappointed. Politics is as much about personality and plotting as it is about policy. We hope to provide the reader, and voter, with some clarity on the least-known incumbent of the highest office in recent times. It was written during the turbulent tenure of Truss's premiership, when the judgement of history was yet to be passed. But the clues were always there, as this book will make clear.

We could not have even attempted this without the brilliant team at HarperCollins – with particular thanks to Imogen Gordon Clark, Oliver Malcolm and Simon Gerratt. And thank you to our day-job editors Victoria Newton and Fraser Nelson for being so understanding during a rather brutal writing schedule. A massive thanks also to our *Sun* and *Spectator* colleagues who picked up the slack.

Harry would like to thank Ian McEwan – who even in retirement from a brilliant teaching career will not let slip how he votes; Paul Staines, Tom Newton Dunn, Glen Owen, James Slack, Christian May, Kate McCann, and his sisters Olivia and Georgina for their wise counsel over many years. And thank you to beautiful Margaux, who, despite a front-row seat, will never tell him what actually went on in the room where it happened.

James thanks David Sorley for inspiring a love of politics; Robert Vilain, Ben Lazarus, Katy Balls and James Forsyth for their mentorship. Thank you too to Brittany Davis for her endless patience. Shahryar Iravani, Helena Kelly, Hannah Dawson, Emily Webber and Hannah Tomes for their support. And Clare, Martin, Ellie and Georgie: I owe it all to you.

Harry Cole and James Heale
Blackheath and Richmond
October 2022

Introduction

'THE GEEKS WILL INHERIT THE EARTH'

Not many politicians get to play Wembley, but Liz Truss was standing in the wings of the vast concert venue in West London on 31 August 2022. After a brutal seven weeks of Conservative Party civil war she would take to the stage resoundingly the bookies' and pollsters' favourite to be Britain's next Prime Minister. While the crowd was not exactly roaring, over the noise of 5,000 London Tories and some cheesy dance music, an aide said: 'How surreal is this? You're about to be PM.' 'My whole life has felt surreal,' she replied.

While a relentless focus lasting over 20 years got Truss to the cusp of power, even that day her rise was still baffling to many. A gawky Liberal Democrat, who joined the Conservatives. A nerdy policy wonk, who plunged the Tory Party into a sex scandal. A passionate Remainer, who was put in the highest office of the land by the most devout Brexiteers in Parliament. The party loyalist who became 'the disruptor in chief'. A free market-eer, overlooked and dismissed for decades, while openly flouting a radical alternative. A one-woman 'think tank' so sure of her views that she did not hesitate before pulling the levers of power. Dismissive of emotion, and possibly too logical for the delicate art of politics, she told a Cabinet rival: 'The geeks will inherit the earth.'

Within a week of the last leadership hustings at Wembley, the one-time teenage republican was kissing the hand of Queen Elizabeth II. Two days later, the beloved Monarch was dead; Britain had a new Prime Minister and a new King. Nothing could have prepared the 47-year-old career politician for her first few weeks in office. Part fate, part self-inflicted, not since Winston Churchill and the fall of France in 1940 had a new leader experienced such a baptism of fire. A different war on the European continent left Britain teetering on the brink of recession, with families facing a winter of misery as the soaring price of energy left millions risking destitution. The champion of the small state would oversee the largest peacetime market invention on record. But it was Truss's own tax cutting that sparked a run on the pound and the biggest self-enforced City meltdown in British political history.

Truss had promised to be the 'disruptor in chief'; unfortunately for her, almost all of that disruption occurred for the financial markets, among high-street mortgage lenders and within her own party. The Tories' poll ratings tanked quicker than the pound as the briefest of truces after 2022's leadership election exploded into a fresh bout of internecine warfare. When a member of Truss's campaign team accidentally tweeted that she would be ready to 'hit the ground' on day one of her premiership, most people saw the funny side of the typo. In reality, it took just 44 days for the new Prime Minister and her 'kamiKwasi' tax plans to disintegrate on impact. The self-immolation of her administration was historic by any standard. The fall-out of her mini-Budget sparked comparisons to Suez, and Britain leaving the Gold Standard, as one of the worst errors of the past 100 years in British policy making. 'Take away the ten days of mourning after the death of the queen', jibed the *Economist*, 'and she had seven days in control. That is the shelf-life of a lettuce.' As her old friend and mentor Baroness Shephard remarked, 'she certainly started with a good bang'.

1975

'SMART ALEC'

In the summer of 1975 Britain overwhelmingly voted to Remain. The Prime Minister Harold Wilson insisted his government was 'Yes' to Europe but would 'accept your decision – whichever way it goes'. In reality his Cabinet was heavily split; seven secretaries of state backed 'withdraw', as Leave was called then. Some 17.4 million Brits voted for the UK's continued membership of the European Community, in a result that was said to 'put the uncertainty behind us'. The new opposition leader Margaret Thatcher claimed that the stonking 67 per cent victory could not have happened without the support of her Conservatives. It was a strange summer of sunshine, strikes and strife. And within the year it was Wilson who was leaving.

Amid the now familiar turmoil, his successor – but nine – was born to John and Priscilla Truss, both devout fans of Europe that summer. After the brutal loss of a little boy, Matthew, just a year before, baby Mary Elizabeth's arrival at Oxford's John Radcliffe Hospital on 26 July 1975 was a blessing for the heartbroken couple. Christened Mary but known always to her father as Elizabeth, she, rather appropriately, burst onto the scene amid a blazing row about Europe. Like their daughter 41 years later, mum and dad were passionately on the side of staying 'in' during that first referendum.

Despite several generations of Bible-bashing in the family, by the time baby Mary arrived it was a house that had turned from Christianity to the embrace of left-wing politics. John was a maths prodigy who won a place at Cambridge a year early and was once 'pretty religious' but was said to have never forgiven God for the loss of his first-born son. Beyond school hymns, faith seems to have played little role in his daughter's upbringing, who said in 2022: 'I share the values of the Christian faith and the Church of England, but I'm not a regular practising religious person.' While his brother Richard became a priest, John Truss ploughed his unquestionable talents towards classical music and his free-wheeling academic career. In the first 11 years of his daughter's life, the family would migrate on the whim of his fellowship from Oxford to Warsaw, Kidderminster, Paisley, eventually settling in Leeds – bar one year in Vancouver, Canada.

Leeds was almost a homecoming for Priscilla, who was born in 1946 in Bolton, just 50 minutes away in 1975 via the newly opened M62. Her parents George Grasby and Joan Spencer had married four years earlier in Cleveland, Yorkshire. The daughter of successful Lancashire paper manufacturer Harold Spencer, by any metric Joan was well-off. The Spencers lived at Hampsons House with a domestic servant named Aranka, according to the 1939 census. With more than four acres of gardens and woodland, the secluded five-bedroom country manor, seven miles north-west of Bolton, is worth more than £2 million today. It seems the family wanted for little in Joan's early years too, with a full household staff in 1911 including Margaret the cook, Kate the governess, maid Rose and a nurse named Marie. George Grasby, however, hailed from more humble beginnings as the son of a bootmaker from Driffield, Yorkshire. He would read classics at The Queen's College, Oxford, before a brave career in India as an intelligence officer in the Second World War. In the mid-1950s he moved to Bolton School, where he spent the next 25 years as head of classics. He was later described as an 'inspirational teacher remembered fondly by many of his former pupils'. Former pupil Jonathan Boardman describes Grasby as one of his childhood heroes, the man who 'planted in me his own love of Latin'. He told *The Times*: 'Many of his students adored him and he remains my favourite teacher. He was very clearly a post-Second World War socialist, a very Attlee minded sort of person.' Friends say Priscilla was sent to 'a Catholic school run by nuns which she hated', while her paternal grandfather, also called George, was on the extreme fringes of the Church as a devout Christian Scientist. Eventually she would attend the fee-paying Bolton School where her father taught.

While John Truss was born in Watford, his family also hailed from the north. His father Clifford was an insurance clerk and son of a travelling ironmonger who married clergyman's daughter Joyce Mary Birtwistle in Derbyshire on the eve of the Second World War. In 1959, after 20 years of marriage, and when John was 12, Joyce died suddenly at Guy's Hospital; Clifford Truss never remarried. While there is scant evidence that John's upbringing came close to Priscilla's family privilege, his mother left effects of £8,021 2s 4d – almost £175,000 in modern money – suggesting a degree of comfort unknown to many in post-war Britain.

John Truss met Priscilla Grasby at Cambridge University in the late 1960s. They found common cause as 'not exactly communist sympathisers but certainly socialists', according to one who knew them well. Priscilla was something of a pioneer, reading history at what was once called New Hall, the all-female college founded in 1954. Set up to counter the fact that Cambridge had the lowest proportion of female undergraduates of any institution in Britain at the time, New Hall was boosted around the time of Priscilla's matriculation by a very large cheque from the Darwin family. So vast was the endowment that it allowed the college to expand to more than three hundred women; the Queen Mother even turned up to cut the opening tape in 1965.

John arrived in academia as a precocious teenager and does not appear to have ever left. After marrying Priscilla in Farnworth, near Bolton, in 1969, John took a junior research fellowship at Oxford, followed by a post at Paisley College of Technology in Renfrewshire, before he became a professor, now emeritus, of pure mathematics at Leeds University. Priscilla was a nurse and a teacher, before later joining academia herself. In 2016, at the age of 69, she submitted her PhD thesis to Leeds University's School of History. Its title, 'Primitive Methodism in the Yorkshire Wolds, c. 1820–1932', is a nod to her family's northern roots.

In spite of her upbringing as the privately educated grand-daughter of a capitalist mill boss, Priscilla was clearly sympathetic to the Marxist cause. After spending time in Prague in the early 1960s, and with a babe in arms, she upped sticks to 'try out life under the communists' in 1977. Soviet tanks had rolled into Prague less than ten years before John Truss accepted a contro-versial posting at Warsaw University. His daughter was just two when she uttered one of her first words: *zeger*, meaning 'clock' in Polish. While pictures exist of a young Liz Truss playing in the bitter Warsaw snow, friends say her parents found the whole experience 'quite grim' in reality. It ended up 'disabusing them of the notion communism was a good thing,' one said, 'mainly because they spent a year in queues.'

As the family travelled, it grew. When her father's junior research fellowship at Oxford ended, he spent a couple of years as a teacher at King Charles I High School in Kidderminster, where Truss's younger brother Chris was born in 1978. Then he found employment at Paisley College of Technology, and in 1979 he took the family on the long journey up the M6 to Glasgow. Two more boys arrived here; Patrick in 1980, and Francis in 1983. By her own admission Elizabeth, as she was nearly universally known by then, was a 'bossy' elder sister, 'always the doctor operating on them', but she resented the male-dominated environment from an early age. She later recalled often feeling 'that with having three brothers, there were assumptions made about me that weren't made about them ... I just think everyone should have an equal chance and I resent being typecast.' Low Road, where the Trusses lived in Paisley, was described by *The Times* as 'a bourgeois haven amid council estates and main roads'. The family moved between two houses on the street, 'one a capacious detached villa, the other a sturdy semi-detached'.

While money was tight in childhood, with holidays more likely to be a Youth Hostel in the Lake District, on one rare aeroplane flight, a young Elizabeth noticed that her 'brothers were given "Junior Pilot" badges and I was given "Junior Air Hostess". That just really annoyed me,' she told the *Mail on Sunday* decades later. Often the family stayed with their parents' friends arounds the country, something attributed to their 'frugal' father. Such preferences were matched in John Truss's eating too; one family friend recalled the young family 'eating a lot of lentils'. They also abhorred food waste, as did their only daughter.

'Fun, very bright, questioning and determined' was how the young Elizabeth was described by her uncle, Richard Truss, to *The Times*. 'Swotty' is how Truss puts it herself. She was taught from a young age to know her own mind. One of her earliest memories is of being given a name badge with her birth name – Mary – on her first day at school. She claims she marched up to the teacher and demanded it be changed. The family took the *Guardian* in the 1970s and 1980s, branching out to the *Independent* when it was formed in 1986, and they would discuss the papers around the kitchen table. Truss and her brothers were always taught to question the way things were, planting the seeds of rebellion that would blossom as she got older.

One such early rebellion came as a brush with hardline unionism, Truss begging her parents to let her join the Orange Order's Majorettes on account of a fascination with their twirling batons. Banned however, she turned instead to the more mainstream Brownies and Girl Guides.

Education in early 1980s Scotland was traditional in a way that seems extreme now. West Primary School still boasted the cane for unruly kids, with the future Prime Minister later recalling how she witnessed one girl being spanked in front of the entire class. Christian songs were a staple part of daily life; the curriculum focused heavily on the 'traditional' subjects of Maths and English. The self-proclaimed 'child of the Union' was possibly the only English girl in a school of hundreds at a time of heightened national feeling. She attended West Primary from 1979 to 1985: the year she began, Scotland had voted for devolution but was thwarted by a turnout threshold. Anti-English sentiment was in the air: the Thatcher government was deeply unpopular in Paisley, one of the few constituencies to have never elected a Tory to Parliament before or since.

The Truss family shared such feelings. As she would endlessly recall in her later career, Truss's first political activity was being taken on a CND march through the streets of Scotland 'aged seven or eight' chanting 'Maggie, Maggie, Maggie, Ooot, Ooot, Ooot'. 'My mum's always been a bit of an activist; she was concerned about the world and wanted to get involved. So I guess that's why I first got involved in politics,' Truss said in 2018.[1] The family regularly hosted a stall outside the Paisley Piazza shopping centre and ran CND jumble sales and ceilidhs where she and her brothers gamely joined in the Scottish dancing. Nuclear disarmament was Priscilla's 'big thing', with mother and daughter attending the anti-nuclear protests outside the Greenham Common RAF base in Berkshire where American cruise missiles were sited. 'We did a number of things like marches, protests', Truss reflected in the *Daily Telegraph*. 'On one occasion when we went down to London in a bus, we had made some "nuclear bombs" out of carpet rolls – ours didn't quite work because it had floral wallpaper on it.' Priscilla harboured wistful thoughts of being arrested but always said she could never allow that to happen while she had children. A picture from the Paisley *Daily Express* in October 1985 shows a ten-year-old Liz with her mother and brother Chris holding aloft a homemade CND banner, created on their kitchen table, ahead of a planned protest trip to London.

Despite her upbringing, Truss says she had an early 'fascination' with Margaret Thatcher, even agreeing to play her during a mock election to mark the 1983 contest at her Paisley primary school. She later recalled in the *Scotsman*: 'I jumped at the chance, and gave a heartfelt speech at the hustings, but ended up with zero votes. I didn't even vote for myself … even at that age, we knew it was simply unpopular to be a Tory in the West of Scotland.'

After six years in Scotland, the family returned south when John became a lecturer in mathematics at Leeds University in 1985. The family home has remained here ever since, aside from a brief spell in the late eighties when John's work took them abroad to Canada for a year in British Columbia. Truss would compare her hiatus there favourably against the education she received in the UK, later using it to highlight Britain's educational divide. 'The whole culture was people wanting to do well and succeed. People wanted to be at the top of the class, going home and working on your homework was a good thing. While the school I was at in Leeds was the opposite.'[2] Family friends recall how much Truss enjoyed the patriotic and upbeat Canadian culture; 'O Canada' was sung every day in assembly. Decades later, in July 2022 Truss posted a picture on Instagram of her class at Parkcrest Elementary School in Burnaby, a suburb of Vancouver. The caption read: '30 years ago I spent a year in Canada that changed my outlook on life #pioneerspirit #optimism.' Brenda Montagano, now a teacher at the school, was a classmate of the girl she knew as Elizabeth. 'I remember her accent and I remember her being very smart,' Montagano told the *Sunday Times* in 2022. 'Now that I'm a teacher, I recognise that it's no small feat to change schools, never mind countries, at that age. She came in and was confident, chatty, tried to get to know everyone. She made her mark.'

In contrast to her time in Canada, Truss has few fond memories of her education in Leeds. Upon arriving at Roundhay comprehensive school from Paisley, she was dismissively told by teachers that 'things in Scotland are very old-fashioned – we're much more modern here in England'. Such innovations as 'environmental studies' were regarded by Truss as little more than 'claptrap'. One lesson seared into her memory was a history class at the age of 13 in which the students were supposed to be learning about Elizabethan explorer Sir Francis Drake. The height of the educational endeavour was standing on their desks, pretending they were on the deck of *Golden Hind*. The classes, in her mind, were insufficiently stimulating. The picture Truss paints is of a 'right-on politically correct' institution stuffed with 'bolshie' teachers, eager to preach their views as 'card-carrying' Labour members. When standing for the leadership 30 years later she said that 'while we were taught about racism and sexism, there was too little time spent making sure everyone could read and write'. She even claimed in one debate that 'the reason I am a Conservative is that I saw kids at my school being let down in Leeds'. One Roundhay teacher who overlapped with Truss told *The Times* that 'The fabric of the school was crap, really awful. There were ceilings collapsing, water leaks, gas leaks. The GCSE pass rate would have been 40 per cent A–C.'

But the sixth form was markedly better than the rest of the school, with reports that, to help her gain acceptance to Oxford, Truss received extra maths lessons (in addition to nearly daily extra maths with her father). Martin Pengelly, an ex-Roundhay pupil and *Guardian* journalist, quoted one peer: 'She made it to Oxford, so how bad can it have been?' Few contemporaries, moreover, recall such an emphasis on progressive causes as Truss suggests, or that it came at the expense of academic rigour. Nathan Hull, a Tory member of North Yorkshire county council who was in the year below Truss at Roundhay, said it was 'the best state school in Leeds by a country mile and has been for donkey's years'. He pointed to the fact that each of his seven siblings went on to gain postgraduate qualifications as being 'pretty typical of the school'.[3]

What is clear is the anger many feel at Truss's vocal and repeated criticisms of the school. One man who has known the Truss family since the 1990s said 'pupils who were her contemporaries' now regard Truss a 'a traitor'; former teacher, Bernie Haynes, who taught at Roundhay when Truss was a pupil said her comments were 'a kick in the teeth'.[4] Others went further, with one neighbour of John Truss describing his daughter as a 'lying bitch' who told 'lies about our local school'. For her part, the former pupil is unrepentant, regarding such criticisms as a desperate rearguard effort to defend a failing system. 'They're all lefties, they would say that,' Truss told friends of the criticism.

Her efforts to paint Roundhay as being 'at the heart of the red wall' also sparked much local amusement. Leeds North East, the constituency that contains both Roundhay school and the tall stone houses in which Truss grew up, was Conservative from 1955 to 1997. The Truss family home was a five-bed, late Victorian terrace on Ingledew Crescent. 'It was very, very middle class,' one friend told *The Times*. 'Very Posy Simmonds.' The house itself was packed and lively, with Priscilla and John keen to host friends for sports events and New Year's parties. While her brothers were sportier than Truss, she was a regular on the tennis courts by her house and witnesses say she was an extremely competitive child. Her younger brother Francis reflected on Radio 4: 'She was someone who had to win.' On board games, 'she created a special system to work out how she could win. And then if she was losing she might sort of disappear rather than lose.'

For an unashamed nerd, childhood can be tough at the best of times. And while Liz Truss herself seems to have made little impact on the locals or her classmates, her parents were certainly well known in the neighbourhood. Her mother's habit of dressing in a bright yellow homemade banana costume certainly made her a local talking point. Priscilla had signed up to the World Development Movement, campaigning for fair trade against the exploitation of developing countries: an ironic twist given her daughter's subsequent vocal support for free trade. One Leeds resident vividly recalls Priscilla handing out bananas in the high street in protest at the exploitation of Third World farmers. Years later Truss would laugh to tears remembering how schoolmates used to shout: 'I saw your mum in Tesco's, dressed as a banana again.' Truss describes her mother to friends as 'quite innocent, but quite earnest but also quite fun at the same time'. Her father was similarly unbothered about what others thought, regularly riding an ancient Victorian-era bicycle outside Roundhay school. Pupils would delight in that almost as much as in the banana outfit.

A contemporary of Truss clearly recalls a GCSE school trip to Sellafield in Cumbria, where pupils were given a tour of the nuclear reprocessing site before a Q&A. Truss did her best to ask a barrage of anti-nuclear questions and 'probably won some kudos from the teachers by showing that she could debate well with adults', according to *The Times*. Not all though were so impressed: Truss herself suspects that some of her teachers thought her an obnoxious smart alec who thrived off the attention. By her own admission she was 'a bit of a geek … a mainstay of my school computer club, and I was happy to spend time programming in BASIC, and whiled away many a contented teenage hour doing so'. One Leeds friend says she 'absolutely loved' computers and recalled being told of her excitement at seeing one wheeled in at her Paisley primary school. At secondary school Truss relished using early systems like the Commodore 64 and ZX Spectrum, and regularly went round to friends' houses to do programming to escape learning German verbs and maths equations enforced by her father. Music practice was a must too, given John Truss's interest in the field. 'I always wanted to be top of the class,' she would recall to friends years later. And with an A in Maths at A-Level alongside a B in English Literature, a C in German and an A in General Studies she was not far off.

Outside her copious studies, a young Truss could be found drinking cider underage in her favourite pub, the Stables, or the Mansion in Roundhay Park. In later years she later claimed her political philosophy was based on the slogan of a local take-away at Briggate, saying in a 2015 speech: 'I would look at the Chinese restaurant over the road and the sign in the window, which said: "Enjoy life. Dine here often." That just struck me; it's the philosophy I have now adopted for the way I live.'

In her later teens, Truss began to think about party politics for the first time. In 2012, in her first major *Times* interview, she said that 'Growing up as I did, I never met a single Tory.' Her family's politics, in her words, were 'to the left of Labour'. But by the late 1980s, Truss had begun to question her parents' views for the first time, debating with her mother the merits of America and the capitalist West against the communist USSR. Truss vividly recalls the collapse of the Berlin Wall when she was 14 years old: at home Thatcherism was triumphant and abroad the Soviet Union was crumbling. 'Aren't these farmers going to starve?' enquired Truss one day as her mother condemned the iniquities of free trade. Dinner-table discussion from teenage Liz was more often prefaced by the question: 'Don't you think that America is actually better than the USSR?' Rebellion was brewing in the Truss household.

But it was a chance encounter ahead of the 1992 General Election that saw Truss break from her parents and join a polit-ical party. The local Liberal Democrat candidate for Leeds North East, Christopher Walmsley, visited Roundhay school to give a speech to Truss and her fellow sixth-form students. Truss was impressed with what Walmsley said and decided to go canvassing with the Lib Dems, or what she called the 'acceptable face of right-wingery in Leeds'. She joined up shortly thereafter and began attending Lib Dem conferences. 'My parents were fine with the Liberals,' she says of her days in the early 1990s canvassing for Paddy Ashdown's party. One veteran from the Lib Dem youth wing recalled in the party's *Liberator* magazine: 'She was always older than her age even at 17 when we first met. Always very ambitious and confident and displays the same mannerisms as she did all those years ago.' It was Truss who introduced her mother to the party, eventually leading Priscilla to stand, unsuccessfully, for Leeds city council in 2004.

But why the Liberal Democrats? Truss would tell the BBC years later: 'I was sceptical of the sort of politically correct chat I heard and the fact that it felt like no other opinions were allowed, and I rebelled against that by joining the Liberal Democrats. Now you might think, "Well, that isn't very right wing", but in terms of Leeds politics as it was at the time, that did feel like a step away from where I'd come from. We didn't really know any Tories; my parents' friends worked as teachers or they work for the NHS. So I didn't really have much exposure to what a Conservative was.'

1993

LIBERAL YOUTH

In September 1993 a young brunette from Leeds arrived to take up her place at one of Oxford's grandest colleges. The post-Thatcher consensus ruled supreme but the winds of change had begun to blow. The same month that Liz Truss arrived at university, a fringe Eurosceptic party called UKIP was launched, following the Maastricht rebellion that summer. John Major would shortly be launching his 'Back to Basics' crusade while a Labour frontbencher called Tony Blair had won plaudits for his promise to be 'tough on crime, tough on the causes of crime'.

But such matters held little concern for Truss the fresher, whose priority was enrolling in the Oxford University Liberal Democrats (OULD). She threw herself into the cause, recruited within days for a coach trip to London to campaign against the skinheads and racist thugs of the British National Party in the Millwall by-election. She wrote about the experience in the *Oxford Student* to mark anti-racism week, decrying the 'odd political environment where nobody knows what anybody stands for, where slanging matches win elections and where councils have so little power nobody gives a damn anyway … It is vital that the politically apathetic population make an effort. I urge anyone who is reading this to do something, even if it only involves writing a letter. General non-involvement got us into this mess. Participation gets us out of it.' And participate she certainly did, quickly becoming one of the better known faces on the Oxford political scene – if one that was a little baffling.

Truss's parents had made it their life's work to see her enrolled at one of the great universities. Having met at Cambridge, the pair desperately wanted their daughter to go there too; but in a regular bout of teenage rebellion she ignored them and deliberately chose Oxford instead. Applying to read Politics, Philosophy and Economics, she did not enjoy an easy ride in, having tried to 'game' the collegiate system. Teenage Truss opted to apply for Merton College, one of the oldest and wealthiest, which only began admitting women in 1980. Her logic, as she later told friends, was to apply for the richest college so it would have the nicest facilities and cheapest accommodation. Summoned before the intimidating 'five don grill', in an interview process that ended up lasting days, Truss faced a barrage of eclectic political, philosophical and economic questions from the quintet of Oxford tutors. One of her challenges included writing an essay about Greek philosophy, about which she knew nothing. To her dismay, she was then pooled to the all-women St Hilda's to be interviewed – a sign that the dons thought Truss wasn't good enough for Merton.

Rather than meekly accepting this slight, Truss 'kicked up an almighty stink' and complained to Merton, querying why she had been sent to St Hilda's instead. College staff urged Truss to go ahead and see what she thought of St Hilda's. A disheartened Truss duly turned up for her interview, whereupon she launched into a ferocious interrogation of her own. She demanded to know why the college was still all women. St Hilda's baulked at the pushy girl from Yorkshire, so Truss found herself being recalled to Merton, where it appears she had grown in confidence by her third round of interviews. Two and a half decades later she would regale aides with the story of how she 'talked my way in' to Oxford.

Like many an unleashed hot-housed swot, Truss relished that first year of freedom away from parental control. She preferred pubs to clubs, and was a regular at Merton College 'bops' or drinking pints of scrumpy at the Turf Tavern. She was chastised by tutors for not doing the work properly, particularly in her first year. In her first seminar, she listened motionless as her new tutor addressed her. After talking to Truss for some time, the academic stopped and demanded to know, 'Why are you not writing all this down?' Truss retorted that she had no idea that that was what she was supposed to be doing. Her socialising and activism were blended; campaigning, drinking and finding boyfriends all in the same circles. Friends recall her barely working in her first year and then doing virtually nothing but in the third.

Cool Britannia was on the rise but there was little sign of that in Truss's crowd. Contemporaries recall her as 'grungy', arriving on campus in flowery trousers and desert boots. One described her set as 'young fogeys' who 'embraced being uncool'. Another remembered Truss for being mousy-haired in long skirts and scarves – 'sort of' like Hermione Granger.[1] Fellow student and future *Guardian* journalist Tanya Gold recollected her as 'a library-bound anorak, with no lingering smell of depravity about her small, neat form'.

Merton was an eye-opening experience for Truss, who had 'never met anyone like' the students she found at Oxford. She recalls being perplexed by the number of men walking around in blazers and chinos, though she enjoyed some of Merton's more eccentric traditions like the 'time ceremony' involving port and gowns. The college also offered her a different philosophical perspective and enjoyed a 'pretty right-wing' reputation for the standard of the time. It was here that Truss, the keen maths student, would learn more about commerce and finance for the first time. She would later explain to colleagues that what 'really made a difference' to her outlook was studying economics, and described her PPE course as 'a real sort of penny drop moment' for how the economy works and shapes politics. 'I believed in personal freedom by that stage, but I hadn't understood how business works, how money works really that much,' she would say years later.

Oxford in the mid-1990s was not the hotbed of political activity that it had been ten years earlier. The charismatic orators of the Oxford Union like Boris Johnson and Michael Gove had left; the battles over the miners' strike and communism had concluded. Much as in Westminster, the economic debate was largely a settled one at Oxford. Alternative fault lines, such as Europe, divided the political societies instead. Dominating the opposite side of this debate was a group of notorious Eurosceptics a few years above Truss, who included Daniel Hannan, whom Truss later appointed to the UK's Board of Trade, and Jacob Rees-Mogg. The latter left Oxford in 1991 but Hannan, an early Brexiteer, had set up the 'Campaign for an Independent Britain' with his friend and future MP Mark Reckless.

Truss joined the rival and devoutly Europhile Oxford Reform Club, which championed Eurofederalism. It was established by Mark Littlewood, then a fellow Liberal Democrat who would later rekindle his friendship with Truss when they reunited in Westminster. The black-tie dinners focused on attracting the less stuffy elements of the Oxford political societies. Alongside Truss was a future pillar of the Whitehall establishment, Olly Robbins, who later became the UK's chief Brexit negotiator under Theresa May. Littlewood recalls: 'The Oxford Reform Club was basically the counterattack on Dan Hannan's CIB, it was pro-EU. But Oxford politics was much more social: it was basically a refuge for people who were not conservatives. There were a few Tories in it, but it was basically people who didn't like the Labour Club and the Liberal Club because those clubs were all activist orientated.' One member told *The Times* that Truss was someone bristling with ideas. 'She was the person you wanted to sit next to. She was quick-witted and sharp. She enjoyed the repartee.' Both Truss and Littlewood were also members of

Oxford's Hayek Society, a student group advocating free trade. Littlewood recalls: 'Margaret Thatcher and Liz Truss are not intellectuals: they are gut-instinct free-marketeers. She's not going to quote Von Mises chapter 17 at you.'

Unusually for one so active in Oxford politics in the 1990s, Truss largely shunned the Oxford Union, a traditional breeding ground for future PMs and Cabinet ministers. Instead she preferred to focus her energies on the far less glamorous Oxford University Student Union. Having been elected to the executive in her first term, she quickly became known for 'holding dissenting opinions on various OUSU issues', according to an article in the *Cherwell* student newspaper, which noted how she had 'publicly disagreed with the position of Women's Officer'. Another article recalls an incident in Truss's first term in which she was admonished for insensitively handling a call from a 'distressed' gay student. Truss loudly shouted about the call across the room, prompting an admonishment from the council. She told the paper: 'It is a shame that people have to use such a petty device because they disagree with me on other issues. Unfortunately, many people at council were afraid to speak out, as is often the case.'

She had little time also for the university's notorious Oxford University Conservative Association (OUCA), which was then dominated by a 'wet' faction of Tory moderates, but still ended up usually voting with the Tories at OUSU council. A friend remembers: 'She hated those Tory-wet, Tufton-Bufton, rah-rah sing-song, pass-the-port types who ran it.' Pointing out that two more moderate future colleagues on the Conservative benches were involved, they added: 'The Oxford Union in the 1990s was totally Nigel Huddleston: Damian Collins was the president. Absolutely dripping wet, Tory boy stuff.' Another contemporary was equally scathing of the Oxford Union: 'All the hacks were nauseating, baby-kissing, kind of campaigners who pretended to have 1,000 friends and would take notes on you and keep it in a book. You needed smarminess to get on.'

21

Truss was clearly a lively student. Marc Stears, who tutored Truss at Oxford and later served as Ed Miliband's speech-writer, recalls her as being 'a libertarian Liberal Democrat'. 'In our tutorials, Truss demonstrated an unnerving ability to surprise. No other student matched her mischievous ability to read out essays on any number of the main events in British political history which always managed to say something new; not always accurate, but definitely new.' Stears wrote that his student's essays were 'creative and self-consciously unconventional' and when pressed in debate 'she almost never backed down'. He wrote in *The Times*: 'She insisted her judgement mattered just as much as anyone else's. Older tutors were probably more frustrated by how she was happy to deviate sharply from the textbook.' Another told the same paper: 'She was definitely a memorable student – full of original ideas and energy. Open-minded and creative, not given to just accepting orthodoxies.'

But outside of tutorials, Truss threw herself with some vigour into the political social scene, blending debate with heavy drinking. She was recognisable enough to appear regularly in *Cherwell*'s infamous John Evelyn gossip column. Littlewood points out that her inclusion in such scribblings was an honour itself. 'It sounds pompous but that means you were a society figure. Anyone in politics would know "Oh that's Liz Truss."' With regards to an upcoming party, the pseudonymous columnist sarcastically teased that no one 'at all sensible' would want to sit 'within a hundred feet' of 'Liz "PC's her middle name" Truss'. In an article entitled 'Ugly Couplings', the column celebrated the relationship between Truss and another student, Malcolm Hutty: 'Evelyn couldn't fail but notice some of the more unpleasant combinations [with] which Cupid has pricked his prophylactic arrows', he wrote. 'Merton College is in danger of dying laughing at the sight of Talculm Smutty and Liz "popular" Truss whining and deigning [sic].' Like Truss, Hutty had a keen interest in politics. Though he has declined to discuss his relationship with Truss, he still regularly attends events at the Institute of Economic Affairs (IEA) and stood as a Brexit Party candidate in the 2019 Election. The pair were a couple, with one friend suggesting Hutty's 'eye-watering' libertarian views would have gone some way towards 'radicalising' the young Truss. A source who knew them both well said Malcolm was 'the hard-core libertarian nutter on campus. The libertarian equivalent of the one bloke with the socialist worker party sign: but his sign would say legalise everything.'

Both Truss and Hutty were on an invitation-only mailing list called Hacks, where a handful of thrusting undergraduates debated everything from major political issues to 'the world's best pick-up lines'. An analogue version of an internet chat forum, the group included Sheridan Westlake, who has served in every No. 10 administration since 2010 as a special adviser to Cameron, May, Johnson and now Truss. Westlake was a key player in the Oxford politics manoeuvrings of the 1990s. Chris Philp – a future Tory MP and Truss's first Chief Secretary to the Treasury – was among those profiling his shenanigans in the pages of *Cherwell*. Westlake tried to get Truss to run for the sabbatical women's officer on an abolition ticket; an entreaty she ignored. She did though agree to serve beneath him on the Oxford Union's consultative committee alongside Hutty. Philp was later suspended and fined by the Union for selling a transcript of OJ Simpson's address at the society to national newspapers; Westlake was the Union press officer at the time.

The 'Hacks' group of Truss, Westlake, Hutty and others would often row, branding each other 'twatface' and 'tosser'. At one point in the messages, some of which were published in *The Times*, Truss got into a row with another student called Paul Martin, who was also involved with the Lib Dems. After Martin mocked some points made by Hutty, an enraged Truss shot back: 'I hope you drown in Nuffield Pond.' 'She was always at the centre of some sort of crisis for her views on things,' said Martin. 'She was like an early "anti-woke" person, she was constantly fighting the students' union.' Martin recalled how Truss would get into 'incredibly intense fights about issues', such as her defence of pro-life groups, even though she herself was pro-choice. 'It would wind people up. People thought that was kind of an attention-seeking thing,' Martin said. 'But looking back on it, it was an incredibly male-dominated world and she was probably the only visible woman Lib Dem activist. Maybe some of it was driven by the compromises of having to try and get ahead in that world.'[2] Julian Glover, another Tory adviser and former journalist, said of Truss the student to CNN: 'It was always hard to see the aim of it all, or where it might lead, except that she would be at the centre of it.' Another friend adds: 'It sounds such a boring thing but she has not changed a jot.'

While she enjoyed debating with her fellow students, it was party politics that held the most appeal for Truss. Former contemporaries from the Oxford University Liberal Democrats said her arrival 'felt like a big deal' because of her already established involvement with the party at a national level. At that point she was said to have been in a relationship with an activist from outside the university, Wyn Evans, who was about four years her senior. He would go on to become a Lib Dem councillor. Evans is clearly no longer a fan of his former girlfriend, tweeting in April 2022: 'Biggest war in Europe for 75 years and our Foreign Secretary, in a major speech, can barely utter the word Europe.'[3] Truss became president of OULD in her first year and quickly took aim at OUCA at the 1994 Freshers Fair, calling her rivals 'sad' after they issued a series of flyers featuring an image of a glamorous woman in a low-cut dress and the slogan: 'You've Never Had It So Good'. 'It is very sad that OUCA had to resort to such tactics to recruit new members,' she told the student press. 'They obviously had no real policies to promote.'[4] Truss's own tactics were hardly more subtle: one eyewitness recalls her running around the fair, telling students: 'Join the Lib Dems! We'll legalise cannabis!' Her stand was bedecked in posters bearing the slogan 'Free the Weed!' to the consternation of more moderate members.

Truss's views at this time were a mix of social liberal, political radical and economic conservative, which fits with her self-conscious anti-establishment bent. In the summer of 1994 she penned a piece for the *Free Radical* – the then-newspaper of the Lib Dem youth wing – making an impassioned case for the lowering of the voting age. She decried 'the right-wing authoritarian lobby' and suggested that 'the age of criminal responsibility should come to us with the right to vote'. Truss bemoaned 'the lack of respect and trust' that teenagers commanded in society and insisted that 'one day discrimination against the young will be acknowledged as the last great barrier to true liberty'.

Roger Crouch succeeded Truss as president of OULD. His memory of Truss was someone who – even as a student – was 'determined, single-minded and willing to challenge orthodox and prevailing, often male, wisdom'. He told CNN that, far from a political transformation, 'Liz was always more of a privatising, libertarian liberal so there is a consistent thread of thought there. I remember a student discussion group in which she advocated privatisation of lamp posts.' He said, 'she was determined, slightly eccentric and challenging ... and had an acerbic sense of humour, which I think is why we got on'.[5]

But while her views helped her to stand out, they were not always popular with other students, who accused her of 'attention seeking'. One said: 'I thought she was personally obnoxious and obsessed with "radical" causes like decriminalising drugs rather than the issues that actually were relevant to the local elections.' Another student recalled an 'incredibly close' election in the Oxford Central ward where other Lib Dem students put in hours of work delivering leaflets. 'I remember Liz doing nothing except turning up to the thank-you drinks afterwards,' they said. 'It puzzled me at the time how she was such a committed political activist and yet she seemed so disconnected and uninterested in the "boring" bits of politics.'[6]

In September 1994, Truss took her unique brand of provocation to a national level with a speech to the Liberal Democrat Conference in Brighton. The unpopularity of John Major's government gave leader Paddy Ashdown hopes of making inroads into traditional Tory areas. But his attempts to present his party as respectable were somewhat hindered by the efforts of his own youth wing. The Liberal Democrat Youth and Students (LDYS) were determined to support two controversial motions: one calling for the abolition of the monarchy and the other the legalisation of cannabis. Truss supported both. Having been filmed for *Newsnight* canvassing activists in Brighton, Truss was called to the stage as a delegate to make her case for a referendum on the introduction of a republic after the Queen's death. Her four-minute speech began by noting the 'close interest' the press had paid to the amendment before also taking a swipe at Labour: 'this party will not duck and weave the issues that people are interested in debating'.

With a confidence beyond her years, the 19-year-old explained to the conference how she had been outside the Royal Pavilion and had, ironically, been unable to find supporters of the Royal Family. The mannerisms were the same as those of the future politician; only a higher-pitched squeak and darker hair reveal the age gap. Turning on a statement by Ashdown that everybody in Britain should 'have the chance to be somebody', she replied that 'only one family can provide the head of state. We Liberal Democrats believe in opportunity for all. We believe in fairness and common sense ... we do not believe people are born to rule.' But though she won applause for her speech, 'the controversial and potentially electorally damaging move was defeated on a show of hands, to the great relief of the leadership', the *Guardian* reported that day. At that result, loud cheers and a rousing chorus of 'God Save the Queen' swept around the hall, with pro-monarchists waving Union Jacks in delight.

The antics of Truss and her peers even inspired a Lib Dem ditty for its infamous but odd 'Glee Club'. When the sun goes down at their conference, the sandals-wearing activists gather around a piano for a sing-song with famous tunes adapted to suit the news from Westminster. Sung to the tune of 'Day Trip to Bangor', Truss's speech led to the song: 'The week we went to Brighton'. It concludes: 'Didn't we have a lovely time / Upsetting Paddy Ashdown / Making him hot at the thought of pot / Available at sweetie counters / "No, not at all," he was able to call / "We'll have a Royal Commission"' / So wasn't he lucky / We didn't go on / To abolish the Queen!'

That conference was far from Truss's only clash with Ashdown; the following year she criticised him for being a hypocrite about green issues, prompting a friendly rebuke from the then-leader after a summons to his office for a meeting. After he died in 2018, Truss recalled how much she 'enjoyed debating with him'. Neil Fawcett, one of those who canvassed with Truss at the conference, told *The Times*: 'I got the impression that she was more concerned with grabbing the limelight and being seen to be radical rather than believing in it.' Truss herself has admitted to the BBC's Nick Robinson: 'in my youth, I was a professional controversialist' but insists that she should not be 'held accountable for things I said when I was nineteen'.

The experience of Brighton only encouraged Truss to stand for the executive of the national body for LDYS. Underneath a headline that proclaims 'Elizabeth Truss for Treasurer', it lists her skills as an 'experienced community campaigner' and a 'founder member of the Leeds North East Young Liberal Democrats'. It notes her maiden speech 'calling for the party to practise what it preaches' at the Torquay Federal Conference and even boasts an endorsement from the bruised Paddy Ashdown: 'Elizabeth is a good debater and is utterly fearless.' Long-time Lib Dem activist Kiron Reid also predicted that 'Liz will be a determined treasurer and lively member of the executive.'

She lost but Truss subsequently won election as a 'Policy Development Officer' in early 1995. In her manifesto, Truss gave her republican speech pride of place, writing that 'Everybody has the right to be treated with respect as a person, without discrimination, favouritism or patronising paternalism. That is why I campaigned against the monarchy and prohibition of cannabis. It is also why I want decentralised decision-making.' Her erstwhile colleague Alex Wilcox, who served as the national youth chair when Truss gave her republican speech, did not remember her time on the executive fondly. She 'kept attacking me when I was chair of the Liberal Democrat Youth and Students because I wasn't left-wing enough,' he recalled; she was an 'utter egomaniac pain in the backside, incapable of working in a team'.[7]

Truss was certainly keen enough to attend training for Lib Dems who wanted to be MPs or candidates. Future leader of the party Tim Farron recalled attending one session, at which he joked: 'It would be a good time to join the Tory party because they were in such disarray you could probably climb quite high. It was tongue-in-cheek and I'm not sure if Liz Truss was present but who knows, perhaps she took my words seriously.'[8] Reid later told *The Times* that back then Truss came across as 'gawky … but still outgoing, confident, happy to speak out and argue and debate things. I think she always liked the attention from being a little bit outrageous.' The pair were photographed together holding a Liberal Democrats flag during a mass trespass at Twyford Down in Hampshire in protest at a motorway project. Despite vowing to pursue deregulation and liberalisation for infrastructure projects in later life, she also protested against the M11 expansion at the time.

But Twyford Down was to prove seminal to her political journey. Her emotional break from the Lib Dems took place in the passenger seat of Simon Hughes's car, the party's future deputy leader, when he gave her a lift to the protest in July 1994. As often with Truss, on the way the two had an argument about economics. Hughes asserted that the person who earns the most in a company should only be paid a maximum multiple more than the person who earns the least; Truss took the opposite view. The pair debated vociferously, until eventually Hughes groaned: 'Oh, Liz you're just a Tory.' And she thought, well 'actually maybe I am'. Truss would later tease Hughes that he was responsible for her conversion when they worked in the Coalition government.

The formal break came during her final year at Oxford, when she quit her post on the Liberal Democrat's youth wing. In her words: 'During my time there I gradually moved to the right of politics because I realised that the Tory Party was saying quite sane things.'[9] Though the exact date of her defection is unclear, by November 1995 she had certainly shown signs of frustration with her party. Another student on the Lib Dem mailing list noted that the university's Labour Club had 'thrashed' the Lib Dems in an election in which Truss did not turn up. She replied: 'I thought it was best not to come, bearing in mind that I was feeling more inclined to shoot members of my own team than that of the Labour Club.' 'In those days the party was going through a particularly soggy social-democrat phase,' a contemporary says. 'I think she was appalled both at how shambolic it was and how many Trots there were.'

Of her resignation from the Lib Dems, Truss later remarked: 'I saw the light. I studied economics. I realised that they got it wrong when they talked about putting a penny on income tax and they also wanted to join the Euro at the time, which I thought was a bad idea.'[10] Alan Renwick, a fellow Oxford student, recalled on Radio 4 meeting Truss years after university and asking if she held to those anti-monarchy views of old. 'She simply said that those sorts of issues were no longer what were most important to her and she now was mostly focused on the economy.'

Certainly many of her one-time Lib Dem colleagues are fairly understanding about her switch to the Tories. Kiron Reid told *The Times*: 'Liz was always a social liberal and an economic liberal. I think that has been consistent throughout.' Mark

Littlewood says that while Truss is no longer a republican, she kept her anti-establishment streak. He told the BBC: 'I don't think there was a kind of road-to-Damascus experience, where she suddenly changed her mind'; instead it was 'more a judgement about what was the best, most successful, most likely vehicle to succeed in politics'.[11] At Oxford in the 1990s economic issues simply 'weren't the meat and drink of political debate'. Political identity centred more on 'matters of social freedom or civil liberties and the Conservatives were broadly on the illiberal side of these debates'.[12]

Truss certainly has kept consistent in these areas; though never a raver or smoker herself, she supports the right to be so and raised eyebrows when she voted against the plain packaging of cigarettes in 2015. She says she loathed the posturing and social conservatism of John Major's government, later describing the 'back to basics' agenda as a 'suicidal set of public announcements'.[13] Branding the party she would one day lead as 'really homophobic, old-fashioned', she would tell friends she had to 'hold her nose' for much of the 1990s. Truss herself believes the Tory Party has changed out of recognition. 'The Tory Party came to her, not the other way round,' an ally insists.

Principle was one thing; ambition was quite another and Truss certainly had that in spades. According to friends, spending a lifetime in opposition as one of a handful of Lib Dems simply did not appeal. In the mid-1990s, life in the Liberal Democrats in Oxford University 'wasn't the sort of place where you found ambitious students who expected to be ministers one day,' one contemporary admits. Truss confessed more frankly to friends that she thought the party was simply 'shit' and that she had 'outgrown them' having enjoyed the fun of the protesting, student activism and drinking in her salad days. Still, at least it gave her a good line to use for years thereafter: 'Some people had sex, drugs and rock 'n' roll – I joined the Lib Dems.'

Forward-thinking, ambitious and a social liberal: with her left-wing background, why didn't Truss join Tony Blair's rebranded party? 'I just thought they were a bunch of automatons,' she told the *Spectator* in 2018. 'People having more freedom, people having control of their own money – the Labour Party seemed to want to junk those ideas.' In private she described her Oxford contemporaries in Blair's new model army as simply 'awful people'. Her fundamental rejection of the left has been described as being 'deeply held and almost personal ... she has no friends on the Labour benches'.[14]

Instead, the teenage radical became a Tory in her final months at Oxford. As her university contemporary Rafael Behr wrote: 'It wasn't a choice any twentysomething of our generation made to be cool.' But, as he added in the *New Statesman*: 'maybe it was a shrewd political investment, buying shares in a blue chip institution at the bottom of the market on the bet that they will eventually rebound'. John Major may have been certain to lose the next Election but Truss was perfectly placed to rise with the party's fortunes when they returned, as they always did. She left Oxford with a 2:1 in PPE and a job at oil giant Shell. A satirical Lib Dem society newsletter called *The Focush* lacerated her choice of employer, suggesting she would end up working 'as an executioner for the Nigerian government'.[15] The reality was somewhat more prosaic ...

1996

THE GREASY POLE

The newly blonde graduate that arrived at Shell PLC's imposing HQ in 1996 was unrecognisable from the grungy 'greenie' of a few years earlier. The card-carrying Conservative joined the oil giant's finance department ready to climb the corporate ladder. And she might have gone far. Each recruit took a 'Current Estimated Potential' survey that pinpointed where you might reach in the firm by the age of 55: Liz Truss had been ranked a 'B+'.

On that high-flying trajectory, Truss took her accountancy qualifications and moved into the spare room of a fellow Shell graduate's boyfriend's flat in Lewisham, before settling in nearby Greenwich. Despite this area of London being rock-solid Labour territory, Truss quickly sought out some local kindred spirits. Friend Jackie Doyle-Price, a future colleague in the Commons, is credited with introducing Truss to the local Lewisham Deptford Conservatives. It was not long before Truss was effectively running things, and within two years she was chairing the branch at the age of just 23. Truss enjoyed the day job at Shell but those who knew her then could see that her real love was for politics. As the rest of the country debated Oasis or Blur, she was more likely to be found arguing the intricacies of mortgage interest tax relief with fellow Tories like Robbie Gibb and other members of the National Association of Conservative Graduates. Cutting their teeth there were Dan Hannan, Mark Reckless and David Gauke; all would later sit as Conservatives in Parliament. Truss remembers begging her bosses for time off to attend the Tory Party Conference. In 1997, she and her fellow Lewisham activists attended that year's event: her abiding memory was how much better the food was than at the Liberal Democrat equivalent. She also gave a short speech on the case against raising National Insurance.

Attending a drinks reception one evening, Truss was introduced to members of the neighbouring Greenwich Tories. Among them was Hugh O'Leary, a former London School of Economics (LSE) graduate embarking on a career in accountancy. Truss has told friends it was 'not love at first sight', though, unlike many Tory boys at the time, O'Leary was not wearing one of the blazers she despised. Like Truss, O'Leary was raised in the north, in the affluent Liverpool suburb of Allerton before a move to Heswall on the Wirral. His father, John, was a lecturer and solicitor who married Susan, a nurse, in 1972. Hugh was born in 1974, the oldest of three. A former neighbour of the family told how 'Hugh was much more serious' than his siblings. They told *The Times*: 'He was very studious and whenever I saw him he would have his face in a book. He was very earnest and very quiet but a lovely boy.'

While Truss was campaigning as a Lib Dem at Oxford, O'Leary was a staunch Tory at the LSE. Like his future wife, he was a fixture in various student elections between 1992 and 1995, running against the Tories' future *bête noire*, the self-styled 'money saving expert' Martin Lewis. Lewis, a frequent critic of the Tory government during the 2022 cost-of-living crisis, was a left-wing rival to O'Leary three decades earlier as they slugged it out in the National Union of Students elections of spring 1993. O'Leary triumphed against Lewis – a candidate of the 'Democratic Socialist Group' faction – though both attended the NUS Conference that autumn.

Like Truss at Oxford, O'Leary regularly appeared in his student newspaper, replete with endless political manoeuvrings. He was cruelly mocked as a 'Tony Blair grin-a-like ... however hard he tries, Hugh is unfortunate in that he still looks like a Care in the Community case emitting a sad, desperate whine as he is exposed to the ridicule of the masses.' He also had a run-in with miners' leader Arthur Scargill after the latter likened Tory attacks on pits to the persecution of the Jews by the Nazis; O'Leary called the remarks 'offensive'. Standing for Financial and Services Officer in March 1993, he bemoaned in the *Beaver* how 'the LSE Student's Union has been dominated by special interest groups which are very vocal but very small'. And he blasted 'left-wing heroes' on campus for the 'personal abuse targeted at anyone who dares to offer a dissenting opinion'.

In February 1994 O'Leary, standing for the LSE union's post of Welfare and Equal Opportunities Officer, issued this eyebrow-raising statement to his fellow undergraduates: 'For too long, we have been told that "Equal Opportunities" means sacrificing our individuality to whichever left-wing clique chooses to speak for us. We have allowed scrounging work-shy communists to set the agenda. We have sat idle as their "centrist" fellow travellers kow-towed to their ridiculous demands in the name of political correctness. Well, enough is enough. It's time for a system that allows each individual to prosper on their own merits. That rewards the true virtues: charity, courage, decency, honesty and good old-fashioned hard work. That's equal opportunities and that is what I stand for. P.S. Socialist Workers Party? More like Socialist Shirkers Party. P.P.S. Anti-Nazi League? Take out the "anti" and the "league" and you have got a fair description of the sort of people who beat up black police officers for being "traitors".' With such outspoken views, it's hardly a surprise that O'Leary and Truss clicked so quickly.

After that initial Party Conference encounter, Truss was invited to stand in the upcoming council elections, attending a meeting of the West Greenwich Ward Conservatives at O'Leary's flat, where the pair signed each other's nomination papers. Graeme Coombes, who was the deputy leader of Greenwich Conservatives, was on the panel that selected Truss to run for councillor. 'She was very intelligent and articulate. She said at the time she was hoping to stand for Parliament,' he said. 'It was clear that the council was probably a small pond for her and actually she was destined for bigger and better things.'[1]

From there, romance between Truss and O'Leary grew as the pair spent their weekends together traipsing around no-hope Labour wards of south-east London, door knocking and leafleting together. On their first proper date, they went ice-skating: O'Leary slipped and sprained his ankle. There was no more skating after that but plenty more dates. But neither of them were very successful at politics; both lost in the 1998 council elections, though she was to secure more votes. One account suggests Truss accelerated the relationship after being evicted from her flat for being too messy, moving in with Hugh instead. After two years of courting, the couple got married in front of around a hundred friends and family – including a good handful of young Tories – on a hot summer's day in 2000.

They wed under Hawskmoor's baroque splendour in St Alfege Church in Greenwich and held the reception at the nearby Trafalgar Tavern – a mirror-image of the wedding of Bella Wilfer and John Rokesmith in Charles Dickens' *Our Mutual Friend*. Truss's uncle Richard officiated at the marriage, and the reception was a political affair at a venue soaked in history. The Trafalgar was the home of nineteenth-century 'Whitebait Dinners', where politicians from Pitt the Younger to Gladstone and his followers would travel by barge from Westminster for the local delicacy and all-night political debates. In 1867 the Tavern featured in a *Punch* cartoon of Lord Derby flanked by Disraeli, urging Gladstone to dine with the Tories rather than with his fellow liberals; a fitting nod to Truss's own political journey. As budding politicians, it was no surprise that both Truss and O'Leary gave rival speeches, or that Truss joked that hers was the better. The wedding was just half a mile from their current London home, a townhouse that they bought in 2006 for £751,500; the labour of love has been slowly renovated over many years, and is now estimated at £1.6 million. Their two daughters Frances and Liberty followed in 2006 and 2008.

The couple have been extremely private about their relationship, beyond Truss joking that their shared love of economics 'means whenever I want a late-night discussion about supply side reform, there's always someone on hand'. Keen to shield her children from the public glare, Truss has claimed that they were educated in the state sector, which is true to some degree. While both daughters did attend a selective state senior school, they also first went to Colfe's, a respected south London private co-ed all-through school close to Greenwich. 'Frances is maybe a bit more centrist and Liberty is maybe slightly more Conservative but they are both very supportive of me,' Truss claims. 'I remember carrying Frances round in a baby sling when I was campaigning to be a councillor, so they've been brought up on politics, and they're very involved in what I do, they come campaigning, they're involved in this campaign, although sometimes they complain that I talk too much about politics.'[2]

According to family friends, O'Leary has been a great asset to Truss in her political activities too. One describes him as 'quiet, self-effacing, sardonic, with a very dry sense of humour'. A life-long Conservative, he has always been happy to let her have the limelight, being mobbed for selfies by younger activists, while he melts into the background. His unassuming nature means few strangers at drinks parties are aware of his more famous partner, allowing him to pick up gossip and unvarnished political opinions about the subjects of the day, including his wife. 'He's very intelligent, very interested,' said one local Conservative who knows the pair well. 'He never appeared to harbour his own political ambitions.' A keen activist, O'Leary unsuccessfully stood three times for Greenwich Council in the 1998, 2002 and

2006 local elections. He now serves as the President of Lewisham Deptford Conservative Association, the local branch that his wife chaired nearly a quarter of a century earlier, and still canvasses with the Greenwich Tories at weekends.

Curiously, when running for leader in 2022, Truss avoided all reference to her husband's service in the voluntary party. Her most public display of affection prior to entering No. 10 was in 2019, when she shared a photograph of them to mark Valentine's Day, captioned: 'Love of my life'. O'Leary has been happy to promote the image of a house-husband there to support his wife's career in private and by taking more of the burden of childcare than many men of his generation, while continuing his career in accountancy. Truss certainly didn't let family life distract her from her career ambitions – her waters broke prior to the birth of their first child during a work meeting, but she returned to work shortly afterwards. Family friend, cookery writer Mallika Basu, said: 'They are a great team. Both are keen cooks and very good cooks. She does lovely roasts, he does a good curry.'[3] A friend of the couple says: 'Denis Thatcher's model was "always present, never there". Hugh has taken a leaf out of that book.'

A source close to Truss praises O'Leary for being 'incredibly supportive of her' even though he 'never really wanted her' to hold the highest office in the land. 'On a lot of things he's adviser number one. He is incredibly political, very right wing, unbelievably right wing – he's almost as right wing as her. He loves the Tory party.' Having met his wife at a Conservative party conference, O'Leary proved to be a regular at the annual gathering. He was spotted in the bars of the 2022 event, moving anonymously through the crowd, meeting friends and collecting gossip. 'He constantly gives her advice,' says a No. 10 aide who served under Truss, who suggests O'Leary was a model political spouse: engaged, informed, supportive but not interfering. 'He was very influential, not in like a meddling way – "Oh, give this person a job" – but if asked to give an opinion he would.'

While their marriage remains private, Hugh O'Leary's accountancy career is something of a mystery too. As of 2022, his only publicly declared work involves an obscure company – Arrakis Investments Ltd. Liz Truss's ministerial declaration of interests claims he has been employed by the company since 2017. But declarations published on Companies House suggest he is not an employee. Arrakis undertakes little trading activity and appears primarily to be a vehicle for holding unlisted investments. In the five years for which accounts are available it appears to have acquired new investments on just one occasion. Most of the transactions that can be seen from the company's accounts consist of loans given by the director, Jonathan Raymond, to the company and some very small loans between Arrakis Investments and a separate company, Arrakis Trading. Raymond is the godson of and former assistant to tycoon Jack Dellal, with whom he had close financial ties. A billionaire property dealer, 'Black' Jack was investigated by the Department for Trade and Industry in 1989, but was cleared of any wrongdoing.

The turn of the millennium saw a dramatic escalation in Truss's political fortunes, while O'Leary took a back seat. Tory MP Nick Gibb agreed to put her forward to become a candidate after she agreed to read and study Ayn Rand's libertarian tome *Atlas Shrugged*. It wasn't all plain sailing though: at her Parliamentary Assessment Board selection meeting she encountered long-time Tory blowhard Sir Roger Gale MP, who didn't think too much of Truss. Fortunately for her, Gale's colleague Eleanor Laing fielded the follow-up interview and quickly approved her application. It meant she could now stand for parliamentary seats, ahead of the looming general election in 2001.

Early knock-backs included being rebuffed from Islington North by the then local chairman and future Commons colleague Andrew Mitchell, denying her the chance to run against future Labour leader Jeremy Corbyn. Truss was instead duly selected as the candidate for Hemsworth in West Yorkshire. She also opted to leave Shell, having concluded that life in the oil industry was rather less exciting than she had first envisaged. The job had given her a grounding in business, with her work on liquid natural gas shipping allowing her to travel through much of Asia and the Middle East. Instead, the former ZX Spectrum devotee opted to join telecoms giant Cable & Wireless, reasoning that it was best to learn more about the still-fledgling internet industries despite the pop of the dot-com boom.

At the following year's general election, Truss fought hard but it was a hopeless cause. The *Guardian* ranked her eleventh from bottom in women candidates who 'drew the short straw' for unwinnable seats. The constituency had been Labour since it was created in 1918, and at one time had been the party's safest seat, with 85 per cent support. But she was only 25 years old; a candidature like this was the apprenticeship a potential high-flyer should expect. And while Conservatives weren't popular in the former mining town, the 'Save the Pound' stall that she manned on Hemsworth High Street proved to be a hit. In later years, Truss remarked to friends that the gains she and other Tories made in seats like this were to prove an early indicator of the Labour Leave voters who secured Brexit in 2016.

A number of Truss's immediate family came to canvass with her, including her mother, who channelled her years of experience protesting to bear on the aforementioned stall. But it wasn't an easy decision for Priscilla Truss, according to a former neighbour, after Liz stood again in 2005. 'She said she was quite torn. She'd agonised over whether to support her because she was her daughter, or not to support her because she was a Tory. In the end, she decided that family ties should win out.' 'For the children, Priscilla has always been there for them,' a family friend said. 'The fact is Liz is proud of her politics but she is also proud of her mother's political views, too.'[4] Liz's father, however, declined to go campaigning. When Liz Truss stood to be Tory leader, John spent much of the campaign abroad in Finland, almost certainly to avoid being a distraction to his daughter. His colleagues at Leeds University were sent an email warning them not to speak publicly about her.

Liz Truss lost the 2001 Election but managed to achieve a 3.2 per cent swing: some way short of the 26.4 per cent needed to oust the incumbent, Jon Trickett, though more than double the national average. The overall result was another Labour land-slide of 412 seats, with the Tories, under William Hague, winning 166, a net gain of just one. It prompted much soul-searching and head-scratching for party chiefs at the scale of defeat. Most had expected to make significant inroads into Labour's 179-seat majority; instead they had barely dented it. That defeat – and the subsequent election of Iain Duncan Smith as leader – prompted a series of initiatives aimed at making the Tory Party electable again. 'The old right-wing think tanks weren't particu-larly helpful to the Tory modernisers,' says Tim Montgomerie, the co-founder of ConservativeHome, 'so they built their own.'[5] The vanquished supporters of Michael Portillo set up Policy Exchange; Andrew Haldenby and Nick Herbert of the David Davis campaign went off to create Reform, to improve public services. Montgomerie and Duncan Smith launched the Centre for Social Justice three years later.

Truss shared in this spirit of modernisation: she supported Portillo's failed leadership campaign and helped launch Conservatives for Cities, a short-lived effort to win more seats in inner-city areas by generating fresh ideas. A mix of think tank and pressure group, it had a website, hosted events and had various branches around the country: one attendee recalls it was about 'Projecting ideas around and creating a platform for herself.' Ambition and ideology in equal measure were Truss's justification for the project, according to friends, as she tried to help make her party electable again. It was the kind of organi-sational, promotional challenge that Truss relished, though her early efforts were not helped when party spokesman Theresa May failed to turn up to an event. MPs Alan Duncan and Steve

Norris – both noted champions of more relaxed social attitudes – were early supporters of the initiative, with future Tory MPs Justine Greening and Alec Shelbrooke also involved. Ahead of the 2001 Party Conference, the *Observer* profiled the pressure group, which wanted to soften Duncan Smith's 'hardline image on blacks, gays and single people'. It argued 'for more liberal planning and licensing laws to encourage economic growth in inner cities. It signals that liberals in the party have not given up the fight, despite Michael Portillo's defeat.'[6] At the time the embattled leader was considering tax breaks to reward married mothers who stayed at home to look after children – the antithesis of Truss's efforts as childcare minister a decade later. The following year, another Conservatives for Cities conference event hit the headlines after comedian Jim Davidson made a joke about asylum seekers as waiters, which offended Tory MP John Bercow and his then-fiancée Sally so much that they walked out.[7]

Truss's third tilt at office was back in Greenwich in Blackheath Westcombe, when she ran for the council in 2002. She lost again, coming sixth with 1,360 votes in a three-seat ward. Alex Grant, a Labour councillor who defeated her in the two local contests, thought little of Truss: 'If you'd said to anyone in Greenwich in 2002 that Liz Truss was going to become the Conservative Party leader in 2022 we'd have all fallen off our chairs with laughter and surprise. You often meet young politicians, and immediately sense that the person has star quality and is going to go far. But with Liz Truss that just wasn't apparent.'[8] He added that she seemed to show little interest in Greenwich politics. Of her 1998 bid Grant said: 'I don't think I ever met her until the count'; four years later 'again, Truss was largely invisible during the campaign'.

Others suggest that interpretation is ungenerous: fellow former Labour councillor Gary Parker says his impression of Truss was that she 'certainly knew where she was going'.[9] Running alongside her in 1998 was Douglas Ellison, who later won a seat on the council. 'She was definitely resilient,' he recalled. 'I don't know how many selection processes she went through. There was this enormous self-belief to keep on getting up in front of these audiences and voters to eventually try and get that break. She was a sucker for punishment. She's adaptable, a pragmatic chameleon,' he told the *Sunday Times*. 'To me, she came across as upper-middle-class, but she didn't exactly wear a T-shirt saying it.'

Truss's battles were not confined to her political life. Her parents divorced in 2003, a devastating blow to the children, who have always been intensely close. While she was greatly pained by the split, Truss herself told friends that she was not surprised, given how badly the pair were getting on. It came after John Truss declared his love for another woman; Priscilla now reportedly lives in another Leeds suburb.[10] Elsewhere, Truss carried on working at Cable & Wireless, where she was part of a two-woman government team. Labour peer George Robertson joined the firm in early 2004 and recalls speaking to her about her ambitions before a lunch one day with the Panamanian ambassador: 'She had a passion for politics, was seriously interested in it and I encouraged her to go for a seat. She did strike me at the time as being fresh-minded, enthusiastic and the Tory party needed people like that.' He says that he didn't think she would end up in the Cabinet, adding: 'I know she was ambitious but I don't think she'd ever imagined she'd be in No. 10.'

Truss ended up taking voluntary redundancy from the firm in March 2005, citing a 'number of reasons' for her decision to quit. Her departure was part of a 'staff exodus' that saw eight of a 35-strong communications team leave, following an internal merger.[11] Truss instead went on to a similar post with PR consultancy The Communication Group, where she served as managing director of the political division. Here she was more likely to be found in *PR Week* than *Prospect*, warning in November 2006 about the dangers of a Gordon Brown-led government for lobbyists: 'Public affairs directors will need to have well-prepared strategies to influence government and not just rely on contacts.'[12]

Outside work, Truss spent many of her weekends encountering numerous future Cabinet colleagues at successive selection hustings. This included being defeated in 2003 by her fellow former Conservative graduate David Gauke for the seat of South West Hertfordshire. In 2004, she lost out three times: in Kensington & Chelsea to Malcolm Rifkind, Surrey Heath to Michael Gove, and Broxbourne to Charles Walker. More than two hundred and twenty hopefuls applied for the plum seat of 'K&C' in January 2004; that Truss at 28 was among the favourites – alongside future ministers Kit Malthouse and Jacob Rees-Mogg – shows how seriously she was already being taken.[13] Six months later she was pipped by Gove at the Surrey Heath selection; Truss later recalled being unnerved by a future Cabinet colleague at the meeting. 'I think Jacob Rees-Mogg was running for that, me, Andrea Leadsom,' she said in 2018. 'All I remember is that he slightly unnerved me by bringing *The House at Pooh Corner* along and I remember thinking "Where have I gone wrong?"'[14] Having lost again, Truss was billed by the *Telegraph*'s diary as the 'favourite' for Broxbourne in November. But Truss and Andrea Leadsom were defeated by Walker. 'The fire was burning and it would not be put out,' Truss says of her decade-long efforts to find a winnable seat. 'I just really, really, really wanted to do it. And almost, the more I got knocked back, the more determined it made me because I thought why shouldn't I do it?'

Truss's break came instead two months later in Calder Valley, West Yorkshire, where an unexpected vacancy arose. The sitting candidate, Sue Catling, was forced to quit over an affair with the local association chairman, Barrie Henderson. Her final demise came at a bitter selection meeting in January 2005 – the third attempt to unseat her after a furious two-year battle with activists suspicious about her private life. Catling maintained throughout that the party's 'old guard' were still rooted in the past in their attitudes to gender, declaring, 'I was accused of everything except murder and paedophilia.'[15] Despite her denials, the affair was confirmed in court a year later after Henderson admitted a 'violent and unprovoked attack' on Catling after a row that left her with a partly severed finger; he was sentenced to community work for actual bodily harm. While the seat lacked the super-majorities of Kensington, Surrey and Broxbourne, it was certainly winnable – though it was Labour-held, it had returned only Conservatives prior to Tony Blair's 1997 landslide. It was the Tories' 41st target overall and the 24th most winnable against Labour.

Into the breach stepped Truss, a rising star at Cable & Wireless and hailed as one of the party's 'brightest young candidates'.[16] She triumphed over a field that was, unusually for the party, entirely female. The local association were taken aback to be presented with a single-sex list, but Calder Valley was dismissed as a 'very special case'. 'It wasn't an all-woman shortlist,' explained Central Office. 'It was a shortlist that just happened to be all women.' Truss's reaction to being chosen in February was workmanlike: 'It is vital for the new candidate to raise their profile immediately.'[17] Truss told local journalists that she was 'really, really, pleased to have been chosen', adding that she was a 'hardworking Conservative', citing experience canvassing in local, parliamentary, European and general elections. Her relative youth meant 'I have plenty of energy to fight this campaign when we are pretty close to the election.' She promised to leave behind both her home and job in London and moved to the 'beautiful area' with her husband within the fortnight.

Truss certainly was an active candidate: moments after her selection, she was swept off to visit protesters opposed to a new waste-processing site. The *Halifax Evening Courier* regaled its readers over the coming months with various campaigns, such as demands for more CCTV cameras in the town centre or opposing a controversial mental hospital on a former residential care-home site. One resident told *The Times*: 'I think of myself as a Labour supporter in the mould of the Fabians but I've been impressed by the campaign of our Tory candidate.' That campaign focused on local issues and sought to link unpopular local decisions to the Labour government.

But it wasn't just Truss's electioneering efforts that set tongues wagging in her bellwether seat. In early 2004 Truss was assigned a new mentor by party HQ as part of a bid to get candidates into shape for the election. Mark Field, a married high-flying Tory frontbencher who sat for the Cities of London constituency, cut a dashing figure back then. The two began an 18-month affair that continued throughout the 2005 General Election and ended shortly thereafter. During the campaign, Truss was joined by her then-lover as she canvassed for votes, according to a member of the local Tory executive. Paul Rogan, the treasurer of Calder Valley Conservatives at the time, later said that: 'After she had been selected, alarms started to ring because she brought Mark Field to the constituency and I started to realise there was more to their relationship than met the eye. Had the affair been known, she would not have been selected. After all our trouble over Sue Catling, we wanted someone who was beyond reproach in their political and private life.'[18] At the home Truss rented in Calder Valley, neighbours noted a number of gentleman callers at the address, including Field.

One 'senior Conservative' was later quoted as saying: 'The Tories have a system of established MPs acting as mentors to young activists. Liz was sent to "shadow" Mark, but it seems Mark took his mentoring duties more seriously than intended.'[19]

Some weeks after the affair ended, Truss told the politician she was pregnant. Her baby, Frances, was born on 18 March the following year. Truss told friends that the baby was her husband's, and Hugh O'Leary is named as the father on the birth certificate.

But while eyebrows were raised in private, in public there was only praise for Truss's campaigning skills. So impressive were her efforts that the *Yorkshire Post* wrote three days before polling day that her well-funded campaign 'Blitzkrieg' was giving 'the blues an edge'.[20] Of Calder Valley, its political editor Simon McGee wrote: 'the constituency and its predecessor saw five shifts of allegiance in just 30 years. And it looks very likely to make another this week.' Truss, he declared, was 'mounting a blitzkrieg campaign', helped by the 'considerable resources' and 'megabucks at her disposal'. The local Conservatives despatched 'very well-produced glossy newsletters, tailor-made for each of the towns and villages' while almost 'every bill poster from the Rochdale border to Huddersfield is a Tory one … it's the same story with road-side boards'. McGee would subsequently be appointed by Truss as Director of Communications in her government. The candidate herself seemed 'very confident' of beating the Labour incumbent Christine McCafferty, saying, 'People just don't like Blair. I'm just not sure where they think their vote is going to come from.'

Yet when the results were finally announced at 3:40 in the morning of Friday 6 May, it was Blair and McCafferty who were celebrating, with the latter pulling off one of Labour's best results of the night to save her seat. The result, after a nail-biting recount, saw the Labour MP defy the national Tory swing, although her majority was almost halved to just 1,367. Truss was crushed by the defeat, having thought she was going to win right up until the election night count.

There were some silver linings in the defeat. Calder Valley provided Truss with her first introduction to two men who would prove to be of immense importance to her future. The first was election guru Lynton Crosby, who arrived to assess whether Truss ought to be given access to the marginal seats fund. And the second was David Cameron, then a fresh-faced frontbencher under Michael Howard. Truss later recalled: 'He was education spokesman then and I remember thinking, "Who is this guy? Couldn't we get someone more well-known?"'[21] She had only previously spoken to him on the phone, calling him for advice when she was bidding for the Wantage constituency in 2002. Cameron represented the nearby Witney seat and happily gave her his insights, even though his best friend Ed Vaizey was going for the same selection, with Vaizey ultimately triumphing.

That brief meeting was apparently enough to convince Truss to back Cameron in the leadership contest that followed the 2005 Election defeat. Shadow Home Secretary David Davis was the early favourite to succeed Howard but Truss, a former Portillista, backed another moderniser to end eight long years of opposition. This was despite the efforts of Andrew Mitchell, Davis's campaign manager, who personally phoned her to try to get her to join an initiative for all defeated candidates to back Davis as the best election winner. Ignoring Mitchell's warning that she would regret it if she did not back Davis, Truss instead signed up to the Cameron campaign as a volunteer. She played little role in Cameron's surprise triumph, though she pitched up at campaign headquarters several times. The new leadership shared Truss's social liberalism and ruthless electoral pragmatism. Finally, she had a leader under whom she could flourish. Vindicated, she boasted that the party had moved closer to her than she had moved closer to it.

After eight years of fruitless opposition, finally the modernisers had control of the party machine. Change was the watchword and the chosen battleground on which the modernisers picked their first fight was the touchstone issue of candidate selections. Cameron wanted a 'priority list' of diverse high-flyers drawn up for the party's most winnable seats at the next election, with more female, disabled and ethnic minority candidates. At the time there were just 17 female Tory MPs in Parliament; in 2005 women were selected in just six of the top 50 winnable seats. By April 2006, of the 500 aspiring politicians on the party's approved parliamentary candidates list, around 100 had been included on an 'A-list' of priority candidates. Francis Maude was a key driver of these changes, as Tory chairman and mastermind of the modernising gang. After spearheading Michael Portillo's failed leadership bid in 2001, Maude went off to found Policy Exchange and Conservatives for Change. The former promoted policy ideas; the latter was an overtly political group to champion the modernisation of the Conservative Party. Maude later boasted that Conservatives for Change 'made themselves redundant when after the 2005 election I became Party Chairman and six months later David Cameron became Leader'. Truss was automatically put on Maude's A-list without even applying, in spring 2006.

Such an endorsement by the party hierarchy was exploited to the full by Truss, who had no hesitation in firing off applications to every such constituency available, regardless of local connection: it was 'shamelessness with a smile' said one rival candidate. At that time, Truss was very much a conventional mainstream Cameron supporter, enthusiastically supporting his mission to 'decontaminate the brand' as she told *Newsweek*. Speaking to the *Observer*, 'sipping an espresso in high heels like an exercise in metropolitan cool', she dismissed questions about the past, saying: 'Margaret Thatcher was quite a long time ago. We have new battles to fight.' Being cleared by party bosses to take part in the profile on Cameron's A-list, dubbed 'the rise of the new Tory woman', was another sign that Truss was clearly marked out before she had even entered Parliament.

In March 2006, Frances O'Leary Truss was born. Two months later, Liz Truss was victorious in her third attempt at local elections, after standing for the leafier ward of Eltham South, south-east London. Again, Alex Grant recalls her playing no role in the ensuing battle for her former Blackheath ward. A row had broken out over the selection of former journalist Peter Whittle for the Tories. Whittle had claimed Greenwich was being 'carved up by immigrant groups'; Labour's subsequent accusations of racism prompted him to issue a libel writ. Yet Truss did not get involved, despite her later reputation as being something of a culture warrior. Grant adds: 'I have no memory of any maiden speech, any hard-fought campaigns to expose Labour incompetence, or for that matter any gaffes or scandals.'[22] Finally, at the fifth attempt, Truss had won her first election for public office, proudly taking up her seat on her local council.

But a fortnight after that triumph came a revelation that threatened Truss's entire career. The *Daily Mail* broke the news of her affair with Mark Field, just days after she was publicly named as a member of the 'A-list'. The paper's reporting focused on Field's looming divorce; Truss was cited by Field's wife, Michele, in her case. Michele Field learnt of her partner's infidelity in autumn 2005, some months after he and Truss stopped seeing each other. Mark Field reportedly told one friend: 'These things happen and of course it was a bit of a risk. But then these things always are a bit of a mess.' Meanwhile the new mum Truss found herself at the centre of a full on tabloid storm.

Walking along with her new-born baby one morning, Truss was jumped by a grizzled *Mail* hack, waiting to probe her about the affair. Her husband Hugh was ambushed too outside their Greenwich home. 'I don't want to talk,' was his only public comment. One acquaintance in Greenwich said: 'when the tabloid furore was roaring' her 'friends locally rallied around. From my impression, they have always been a really strong couple and I have never seen any real sign that it's had much of an impact.'[23]

One friend of the couple said that period had been 'extremely tough', adding: 'There was a point where she couldn't leave the house with the baby without getting papped. Grim at the best of times but very hard for a brand-new mother.' All involved in the affair have subsequently avoided any public reference to it. However Field – who left the Commons in 2019 – did raise eyebrows in 2022, shortly after Truss became Prime Minister. In his new capacity as an Isle of Man banker, he praised her as 'an instinctive risk taker ... highly intelligent, immensely energetic and pragmatic' in an article evaluating her government's prospects.

While the affair appeared to have very little immediate impact on Field's career, Truss's ambitions temporarily stalled in 2006. She had been strongly tipped to inherit the rock-solid Bromley and Chislehurst seat in Kent after the death of maverick right-winger Eric Forth. News of the affair killed her chances, at a time when the local party was already simmering about attempts to impose a more diverse range of candidates. One elderly Bromley party member fumed to the *Sunday Telegraph* that 'We need a traditional man who has good values.' The paper sniffed that 'more than half of those on the A-list are women, many are from ethnic backgrounds and several are openly gay'. Bob Neill, the leader of the Conservative group on the London Assembly, who had a strong local following but was not on the priority list, was selected instead. He nearly lost the resulting by-election to the Liberal Democrats, with UKIP's Nigel Farage coming third. As the *Independent*'s Andy McSmith noted: 'the bombshell was perfectly timed for those in Bromley who did not want to be told by David Cameron who their candidate should be'.[24] A bid to be selected as the Tory nominee for East Hampshire in February 2007 came to nought too.

Truss tried to put the scandal behind her by focusing on her work on Greenwich Council and at her PR group. Council records show she sat on no fewer than seven committees during her first three years. Few of her speeches appear to have made an impact, though one fellow councillor recalls one on childcare – a long-time passion – and some pointed remarks about changing nappies. Fellow councillor Gary Parker said Truss had a 'limited input' in the council, as the Conservatives were in opposition at the time, adding that he believed the role was a 'stepping stone' to her becoming an MP.[25] One Conservative suggests that was unfair: Truss had spent nearly a decade trying to win a seat in the Labour hotbed of Greenwich. By the time she was elected, she had already been added to the A-list of candidates; her attention was naturally focused elsewhere.

On the council, Truss did not foster many cross-party friendships but neither was she a noted partisan. Parker says: 'I never thought of her as particularly right-wing. In fact I always thought of her as what she was for some time, which is a more liberal Cameron Conservative type.' Grant says that while 'some Labour councillors felt that Truss was entitled and petulant ... I always found her friendly and polite', adding that she would always text if running late for planning committee meetings. Truss herself has complained about those meetings – 'Hours of my life I will never get back' – but contemporaries recall often raucous council proceedings. Greenwich is and was a one-party state for Labour, with the handful of Tory councillors in permanent opposition jeering loudly to compensate for their small size. Truss had the misfortune of being elected as part of a team of three in her ward, alongside two fellow Tory councillors, Eileen Glover and Peter King, who – according to a fellow councillor – practised long-running 'internecine warfare' against one another.

But while success came at a local level, Truss's ambitions demanded national recognition. Fed up with rejection from successive Tory associations, Truss opted to make the professional jump from communications to policy in a bid to burnish her credentials. She took up the post of full-time deputy director at the think tank Reform in January 2008. The office, then located within earshot of the chimes of Big Ben, was the next street over from a string of other think tanks and pressure groups that comprised the resurgent free-market movement of this time. Situated on Great Peter Street, Reform gave her easy access to the Institute of Economic Affairs on Lord North Street, the TaxPayers' Alliance and Centre for Policy Studies on Tufton Street and the Adam Smith Institute down on Great Smith Street. It was the perfect place to network, set in the shadow of the Palace of Westminster.

Truss's work at Reform embodied the late noughties vision of much conventional Tory thinking: private companies involved in public sector reform, greater accountability, localism and higher standards. Her former boss Andrew Haldenby later said he never had another colleague at Reform quite as enthusiastic as Truss. She advocated more rigorous academic standards in schools, a greater focus on tackling serious and organised crime, and urgent action to deal with Britain's falling competitiveness. Among publications she co-authored 'The Value of Mathematics', 'A New Level' and 'Back to Black'. The latter was to cause her some minor difficulties in the 2022 leadership race after it resurfaced alongside an article she wrote in the *Spectator* calling for patients to be charged for GP appointments and doctors' pay to be slashed by 10 per cent.[26] At the time, David Cameron was campaigning to 'cut the deficit, not the NHS'. Truss's manoeuvrings did not go unnoticed, with one newspaper diary noting of her appointment: 'Glamorous Tory Liz Truss, who shot to minor fame for having an affair with swarthy former frontbencher Mark Field, is reinventing herself as a boring policy wonk, taking a post at the think tank Reform. Ambitious Liz hopes it will boost her chances of becoming an MP at the next election.'[27]

She became a frequent figure in the media, appearing and writing for a range of publications, peppering her views with pithy quotes. Her thoughts on Barack Obama's economic stimulus package? 'An audacious gamble at best, foolhardy at worst … the best thing Gordon Brown can do is to try to curb the American desire for protectionist measures.'[28] Or on the decline of kids at schools doing maths? 'We need a cultural revolution to transform maths from geek to chic' and 'a "new Alexander" … to cut the Gordian knot of political control that has made government rather than pupils and teachers responsible for results'.[29] 'White elephant' transport projects should be scrapped, with high-speed rail links dropped in favour of introducing longer trains with greater capacity.[30] As for modern policing, it had gone 'from *Dixon of Dock Green* to *RoboCop*' with a 'one-size-fits-all system' where 'bureaucratic process' had replaced 'human judgement'.[31] And even before the financial crash, 'the Pavlovian reflex of committing more public money wherever there is a problem must be discarded'.[32] Truss also became a regular contributor to the *Telegraph*'s fledgling stable of blogs. Here she called for the election of 'local justice commissioners, responsible for policing, prosecution, legal aid and correctional services within a local authority area'. She also wrote favourably of Montessori schools, which emphasise physical activity, in place of the new foundation stage for under-fives.

The exhausting blizzard of policy and personal PR eventually paid off and helped with selection meetings too. The MPs' expenses scandal broke in May 2009: the revelations by the *Daily Telegraph* forced more than half a dozen Tories in safe seats to quit. One of them was Christopher Fraser. He had only sat for South West Norfolk since 2001, but faced allegations that he had claimed a second home allowance on his property in Norfolk. His £1,800 claim to buy 200 trees for his garden was also highlighted by the paper. Though Fraser insisted that his decision to quit had nothing to do with the story – citing his wife's health concerns – his departure created a vacancy for another thrusting young Tory to fill. Not for the last time, Truss was the beneficiary of others' misfortune, with the extra seats up for grabs boosting her chances of being selected.

That August, she was named as one of 'Twenty people who would make excellent Conservative MPs' by the ConservativeHome website, alongside future stars like Sajid Javid, Nadhim Zahawi and Matt Hancock. Editor Tim Montgomerie wrote admiringly that 'Truss's Back to Black report advocating £30bn of public spending cuts [proves] that she has exactly the sort of insight that the next government will require.[33] She has also set up Educators for Reform to promote academic rigour in education.' Montgomerie's endorsement came in September 2009: within a month, she was selected to be Christopher Fraser's successor for South West Norfolk. But it was there that Truss's troubles truly began ...

2009

THE TURNIP
TALIBAN

Saturday 24 October 2009 should have been the proudest moment of Liz Truss's career so far. And it was until she accepted a telephone call from the *Mail on Sunday* while celebrating her selection in South West Norfolk that afternoon. A 'disgusted' tipster had told the newspaper that she and other members had not been made aware of Truss's affair with Conservative MP Mark Field at the selection. 'Everyone is entitled to a private life, but she should have mentioned this,' the mystery caller claimed. 'She should do the decent thing and step down.'[1] 'We received an anonymous call from a woman late on that Saturday afternoon,' the paper's now Political Editor Glen Owen recalled years later. 'She certainly sounded the part – a bit horsey, and very angry. After speaking to Liz and Mark we knew it was genuine.' Just hours earlier, the South West Norfolk Conservative Association had backed Truss resoundingly against a star-studded line-up of rival candidates, including a former British ambassador to Russia and future Cabinet member Thérèse Coffey. Truss won decisively, polling more than 50 per cent of the vote on the first ballot from 100 assembled members. But the constituency – in which the sitcoms *'Allo 'Allo, You Rang, M'Lord?* and *Dad's Army* were all filmed – was about to play host to another farce.

'Cameron Cutie who had affair with top Tory wins plum seat' roared the headline on page 11 of that week's *Mail on Sunday*. Truss herself told the paper that 'It's all been in the press, and I'm not commenting any further. That is something which is very much in the past.' Asked whether she would find it awkward encountering Field in the Commons if elected, Truss replied coldly: 'I don't have any particular dealings with him now.' Her former lover enthused: 'She'll make a dedicated Member of Parliament', adding: 'I do see her from time to time in her work for Reform.'

The story was three years old but evidently had not percolated to the quiet market town of Swaffham, where the local Conservatives convened. Furious activists claimed they had been deceived over this 'skeleton in the cupboard' and complained of a 'stitch-up'. Truss's supporters pointed out that a cursory internet search would have revealed all necessary details of the liaison. But outraged members filled the newspapers, fuming that Truss's affair had not been declared at the selection meeting. John Mortimer, a member of the Swaffham Conservative club in the constituency for 20 years, harrumphed: 'How does somebody from London understand the Norfolk way of life? They make out we're stupid, saying details of her affair were on Google, but no one in Norfolk knows how to use Google.'[2] Ironically, Truss had won the selection pledging to improve rural broadband connectivity.

The fuse was lit and the second editions that evening were all over the story. The *Sunday Mirror* brutally reported: 'The Tories have chosen a woman branded a "homewrecker" to stand in the safe seat of South-West Norfolk.' A war of words broke out, with Truss serving as a proxy for the tensions in the Tory Party between Central Office and the party grassroots. 'We are sick of being told by glitzy grandees what is good for us', thundered the local paper. 'We insist on Norfolk MPs who put Norfolk first.'[3]

Truss's selection drama quickly acquired national significance, coming at a time of intense ill feeling between Tory high command and local associations. Some excited commentators even suggested the clash between 'modernisers' and 'traditionalists' would be Cameron's 'Clause IV' moment in which he took on his party's outdated attitudes. A party grandee recalls: 'At the time there were endless battles with local associations about selections. We had the A-list and that had quite a lot of battles with what you might call the less reformed parts of the party.' A week before the Truss story broke, Cameron had even pledged to use all-women shortlists to pressure traditionalist Conservatives into accepting more female candidates. With the introduction of the A-list, local associations for 140 winnable seats were now required to choose from a selection of approved candidates, enraging grassroots bigwigs who jealously guarded their independence from Central Office. The party was a powder keg waiting for a row like this.

Matters were made worse after claims that party chiefs had referred to locals as the 'Turnip Taliban', a sobriquet Truss's allies credit to the *Mail on Sunday*'s provocateur-in-chief Simon Walters. 'We're used to carrot-crunchers,' grumbled one local, 'but Turnip Taliban is offensive.'[4] Critics argued that Truss was a 'Cameron cutie', parachuted in from Notting Hill; a woman whose knowledge of farming was limited to the organic yoghurt she bought at her local Waitrose. 'She's a bright girl,' said one, 'but doesn't know one end of a cow from another.'[5] Truss, by her own admission, had no previous links with Norfolk; her best-known party initiative 'Conservatives for Cities' had an obvious metropolitan bent.

Her affair with Field was not the only source of controversy: Truss's youthful republicanism also came under scrutiny. Such views found little favour in one of the country's most staunchly monarchist counties, home to the Sandringham estate. Among the grandees who would decide on Truss's fate was the president of South West Norfolk Conservative Association, Hugh van Cutsem, an old and close personal friend of the then-Prince of Wales. A devout Roman Catholic, he was reportedly expected to take a firm stance against Truss's extra-marital shenanigans.[6]

Two days after the *Mail on Sunday* article appeared, Truss was summoned to an emergency meeting to explain herself. Ahead of the inquisition she told the local paper that she had never tried to hide the affair: 'When you go onto the approved Conservative candidates list they ask about any issues that might arise and I disclosed it at that point. I know the regional officer knew about it and those who check out the CVs.'[7] She said she would have expected that if an issue was of concern it would have been raised when officials went through the candidates' details with the local association. She added: 'I put my case forward on Saturday about what I could offer the constituency and what I want to do. I have been upfront about this issue and it's been in the public domain for more than three years.'

That evening, Truss delivered a 'dramatic and emotional speech', in the words of one attendee. A female member of the executive committee archly described it to the *Daily Mail* as a 'BAFTA-worthy performance' that melted the resolve of some of the men, and hardened that of the women: 'She sat there with tears brimming in her eyes, telling us how much she wanted to represent South West Norfolk. She's a very clever political animal, and by the end of it she had the men, in particular, moving over to her camp.'

Her performance was to no avail: the executive voted 19 to 14 in favour of deselecting Truss – with van Cutsem reportedly among those who voted against her. A crunch meeting was then set for 16 November, at which her fate would be decided by the 350 local party members.

Reacting to the executive result, a Tory Party spokesman was quick to confirm that Truss continued to have David Cameron's backing. 'She has the full support of the national party. She was selected at the first ballot with more than 50 per cent of the vote, and is clearly an outstanding candidate. We stand by her.' Tory

HQ sent a 'hit squad' to the seat to give Truss support, with varying degrees of success. Having already had the Field romance ruin her chances once, Truss was determined to not let it do so a second time. In the weeks after the news broke in Norfolk, she spent her time in the constituency, fighting to retain the nomination and building her local support base. She moved into a rented cottage in Swaffham, held face-to-face meetings with farmers and went to the town Rotary Club's art exhibition. Along with her family, Truss attended a coffee morning at Swaffham's medieval church and made constant overtures to the 'blue rinse brigade' of the ladies of the local Conservatives. She went on 'meet the voters' outings with county councillor minders, though not all were impressed with her 'condescending manner', according to local press reports.

Having initially refused to comment and insisting 'it's an old story', Truss caved after a fortnight of silence, agreeing to an interview with the *Eastern Daily Press*: 'I am sorry about the affair – it was a mistake. The main person I am sorry to is my husband. We have now made that up and moved on from that.' She said they were, as a couple, 'a lot stronger' for all that she had 'learnt'. Truss repeated that she had been 'open and transparent' in declaring her affair on her CV and declared: 'my understanding was that [this] would be part of the CV discussion when the six CVs were selected to go forward'. She even tried to laugh it off, saying: 'With hindsight I would have taken out a billboard!' The paper's interviewer Simon Lowthorpe concluded: 'I've seen enough to believe she deserves the chance to be an MP. But what I really wonder is, given what she has gone through, do the Tories of South-West Norfolk deserve her?'[8]

A fortnight after reviving news of the Field affair, however, the *Mail on Sunday* were back. The paper made the connection that she had only secured the last-minute selection of Calder Valley in 2005 after the first candidate had been deselected for having an affair. The paper noted she 'failed to mention the relationship to the local Conservative association, which is exactly the same charge being levelled at her in Norfolk'.

Ahead of the showdown membership meeting on 16 November, the briefing wars between the two camps went nuclear, with mutinous locals even threatening to field an independent candidate at the general election to 'give 'em a bit of a shock'.[9] The local association had an unfortunate history with candidates. In 1987 it chose Gillian Shephard in a rerun after the initial choice of a male barrister from Oxfordshire caused a revolt in its ranks. In 2004 the favourite to succeed Shephard, Nick Hurd, was beaten by Christopher Fraser, who stepped down after becoming embroiled in the expenses scandal. 'We were looking for a clean, new, fresh candidate,' complained one.[10] 'She is the wrong kind of woman.' Another protested: 'I don't care what passes for decency in the Notting Hill set, but people in this part of the country believe in proper standards.'[11] But threats of a plan to print hundreds of T-shirts bearing the logo 'ET Go Home' appear to have come to nought.[12]

Local chairman David Hills was accused of orchestrating the anti-Truss campaign from a luxury cruise ship off Hong Kong, as part of his three-week honeymoon. He kept in touch with his local allies via email, sending one despatch that 'in essence, said "get rid of her"'.[13] Another troublesome 'Turnip' was Councillor Cliff Jordan, who called Truss 'damaged goods' and demanded a new candidate. Her supporters retaliated that he was 'hardly squeaky clean' – pointing out that three years earlier he was ordered to repay £17,000 of falsely claimed invalidity benefits. Jordan countered by claiming he did not 'give a fuck about gossip about him' and cited 'hundreds of letters of support'. One pro-Truss-camp source was quoted as saying: 'Some of the Turnips are far from paragons of virtue themselves and so perhaps should be a little less strident in their attacks.'[14]

Chief Turnip was Sir Jeremy Bagge, the 64-year-old former High Sheriff of Norfolk and 7th Baronet of the 1,200-acre

Stradsett Hall. A colourful local character, he had previously performed the role of guardian to Prince Nirajan of Nepal when the latter was at Eton, arranging an emotional reunion with his mother in the Ministry of Sound nightclub after the teen ran away one night.[15] Sir Jeremy said he felt 'totally betrayed' by Conservative Central Office because 'they never told us there was a skeleton in the cupboard'. He said he was irritated by suggestions he could have 'checked up' on Truss on Google, where the details of her affair are easily obtainable. 'If we've got people from Central Office who are paid to do the job, why am I expected, when I receive her CV, to go and google someone's name?'

It fell to the *Western Morning News* to point out that far from being 'another victim of Google deprivation' Sir Jeremy 'trained as a chartered accountant with Touche Ross and even has his own website'.[16] Bagge added: 'My family have lived here in Norfolk since 800 AD. I don't bring morals into it. We're not as pure as the driven snow. It's the fact they parachuted someone in on us.'[17] He rejected claims he was simply 'anti-women', telling the *Telegraph*: 'I have got absolutely nothing against women. Who cooks my lunch? Who cooks my dinner?' A member of the Truss camp hit back that Sir Jeremy had a 'vested interest' in toppling Truss because 'he wanted his brother to get the seat'.

The then-Cameron opposition had an awkward relationship with the national press. Even as Gordon Brown's administration imploded it still enjoyed air cover from unusual places on Fleet Street. While the *Sun* had declared 'Labour's lost it' in terms of the paper's support in late September, it was still some way off backing Cameron. Senior party strategists at the time were also infuriated that broadsheets like the *FT* and *Times* were still giving Labour more than the benefit of the doubt. While the traditionally Tory *Telegraph* and *Mail* had been 'very against David being picked as leader', according to a senior Tory, they had begun to soften by the time the Norfolk row erupted.

That week the right-leaning papers were erring on the side of the Turnips. One typical *Mail* editorial suggested it cast 'grave doubt on his much-vaunted commitment to "localism"' and mocked his 'eagerness to impose his A-listers (that's A for Affirmative action, not Adultery!)'. Columnist Jan Moir sneered that Truss was a 'typical New Tory' and a 'metropolitan career politician of the type that became depressingly familiar in the early days of New Labour ... shimmering with ambition and loaded with baggage, including a dislike of the Royal Family, Norfolk's most famous part-time residents'. Moir added: 'there is much about her crisp, just-minted aspiration that suggests the kind of woman who would date Lembit Öpik if he had the right kind of political profile'.[18]

Trenchant support at least came from the blossoming Tory blogosphere. Janet Daley declared for the *Telegraph* website: 'she is an extremely able and quite exceptionally intelligent political thinker'. The Eurosceptic MEP Daniel Hannan, Truss's old Oxford rival, agreed, as did Tim Montgomerie, the editor of ConservativeHome. He wrote: 'Liz is exactly the kind of MP who will enrich the Commons: intelligent, an independent thinker, she doesn't come from a conventional Tory background but is nonetheless a champion of grassroots Conservatives.'[19] Then blogger, now broadcaster, Iain Dale declared, 'Good luck to Liz Truss', while ConservativeHome published a poll that showed more than 80 per cent of supporters believed the party would be damaged if Truss was dropped.[20] She also received support from a number of Tory MPs such as David Davis: 'It's no way to treat anybody, least of all when you have been so careless as to conduct a selection without looking them up on Google.'[21] Others bloggers joked that the burghers of south-west Norfolk still stopped to point at planes that flew overhead.

Cameron himself was determined to not sit back as Truss struggled for survival. Days before the vote he intervened, phoning the rebels, including Sir Jeremy, to urge them to change their minds. Cameron's warnings to his fellow Old Etonian were duly reported in the *Daily Telegraph*, with the Tory leader fearing: 'if we really stirred things up in South West Norfolk, it could have a ripple effect across the country'.[22] 'There were a number of crisis meetings that week,' said one Cameron ally. 'We were putting through the modernisation and this was just not going to be allowed to happen. We regarded it as sexist to deselect this person – and it was made clear that the entire association would be suspended and put into special measures if they carried this threat out.' Another veteran of the era added: 'It was absurd, frankly; I don't remember anyone threatening to deselect Field and he was just as married at the time.' And the leadership backed up words with action. Then-Party Chairman Eric Pickles put veteran spinner Henry Macrory to work. As the former editor of the *Daily Express*'s infamous William Hickey gossip column, and a Lobby poacher-turned-gamekeeper, there was little that would make him blush.

The screws were duly put on the local association. It was suggested publicly at the time that the Norfolk Tories had been given an unprecedented ultimatum: if they dumped Truss then a new shortlist of centrally approved candidates would be imposed on them. Party insiders moaned to the *Mail* that the Norfolk Tories had even been 'threatened with being made guinea-pigs for the Tories' first ever forced all-women short-list'.[23] Activists were told they risked inflicting serious damage on the Tories' general election campaign and reminded that Central Office had sweeping powers to suspend a constituency association and effectively take it over. There were mutterings about incentives and OBEs being offered too. But the final ulti-matum came from Cameron himself, who made it clear the association would be placed in special measures and its execu-tive suspended if the vote did not go Truss's way.

And it worked. In a surprise move, David Hills, the associa-tion chairman, who had previously called for Truss to stand down, threw his weight behind her. Returning from his honeymoon, he observed that 'the world had gone a bit strange' in his absence. Two days before the vote, he released a joint statement with the outgoing MP Christopher Fraser, agent Ian Sherwood and other officers who all supported Truss continuing as the candidate: 'Any move otherwise will not have my backing.' She 'must not be blamed for any discrepancy between the association and the centre about information that she declared when she became a candidate'. Shocked local supporters who had been supporting the motion to deselect Truss fumed that Hills had only backed down after the pressure from Cameron. This switch meant the local party no longer had to choose between its candidate and its chairman. A week earlier 'Truss seemed to be swimming against the tide to avoid being deselected'; now her path seemed clear. 'How quickly things change in politics,' remarked the local paper.[24]

Still, Macrory and the rest of the Conservative Campaign Headquarters (CCHQ) would have their work cut out, as some of Fleet Street's finest political troublemakers were despatched to Swaffham for the great showdown. Chief mischief-maker Christopher Hope, a colourfully clad hack of the old school variety, had been sniffing around the seat for days for the *Telegraph*. And the poison-penned Sam Coates of *The Times* was not far behind. Once Michael Crick, the fearsome *Newsnight* hound, set up camp in the car park, the CCHQ spin-doctors turned white. While the hacks waited for the bloodbath, Crick went so far as to file copy to the BBC website literally from the downstairs lavatory of Sir Jeremy Bagge's vast pile: 'I can reveal – exclusively, I hope – that the walls of Sir Jeremy's loo are covered with wood-carvings of couples having sex in all sorts of different positions. So I think we can take Sir Jeremy at his word when he says his opposition to Ms Truss is nothing to do with her sexual behaviour.'

A CCHQ veteran recalls: 'You could tell it was going to be an absolute disaster because all the Lobby awkward squad were there. It was a very sporting field.' As part of the 'crack team' despatched to the frontline, 28-year-old press officer Paul Stephenson was on the ground, but he would have his work cut out that evening herding these wild beasts of the Lobby. Stephenson would later go on to lead the victorious spin team of Vote Leave and play a key role in the 2019 General Election. But back then he was green, shaggy-haired and battling against the tide once Westminster's travelling press pack arrived en masse to try to create havoc. Even the locals friendly to Truss were deeply suspicious of this young man from London sent to tell them what to do. A plan was concocted to have Truss bundled into a car regardless of the result and sped round the corner to the local Conservative Club to do one pooled interview. Yet, as so often in Truss's life, things were not as straightforward as they should have been.

On the evening of Monday 16 November some 169 members of the local party gathered to vote in the Swaffham Assembly Rooms. Party bosses had pulled out all the stops to help Truss. Lord Taylor of Holbeach, a member of David Cameron's frontbench team, was drafted in to 'independently' chair the evening. The party's deputy chairman, John Maples, sent a letter admitting that mistakes had been made in its handling of the selection process but urging members to stick with Truss. And another ambush came in the form of Baroness Shephard, the former MP still highly respected in the area. Her surprise appearance and impassioned speech in favour of Truss was credited with changing 'many' minds. Shephard said of the affair in 2022: 'It had been very publicly voiced in the press. I simply did not understand the objection that the information had been withheld from them.'

James Bagge, the brother of Sir Jeremy, put the motion to deselect Truss to attendees. On trial for her political career, the candidate herself stepped forth to make an impassioned 20-minute speech. After a tense hour-and-a-half wait, a 50-strong media scrum swarmed the steps outside the Swaffham Assembly Rooms to hear chairman David Hills announce the result.

Newsnight cut live to it, with Jeremy Paxman suggesting it was 'the most momentous thing to have happened in Swaffham since a cardboard box blew down the high street'. Standing beside Hills on the steps under the glare of the travelling media circus spotlights was a relieved-looking Truss, wearing the trace of a satisfied smirk. Sir Jeremy stormed out in a fury, face redder than ever, raging about 'betrayal' and 'deception' and the Machiavellian tendencies of Conservative Central Office. The motion had been defeated by more than three votes to one: 132 to 37.

The victorious candidate herself said: 'It has been at times challenging, at times very interesting; of course, there is an element of hurt. What the people here really want is somebody who is going to live locally and address the issues. That is what I am going to do and they are not interested in the kind of flimflam there has been in the Press.' 'This is her proudest moment,' Shephard and Hills insisted, as the CCHQ team tried to get Truss into a car. 'She shouldn't be hidden away, we shall walk to the association.' And so began a long bunfight with questions shouted at Truss by the Lobby's finest the whole length of Swaffham high street. Once at the Tory club, the plan to do a single interview was also jettisoned by the locals-know-best busybodies. 'She was fine in the first interview, but by the time it was onto every regional TV and radio outfit and paper she started to flag. They just had a deep distrust of the advice from anyone not from Norfolk,' noted one London Tory.

A defeated Sir Jeremy meanwhile declared: 'I am not proud to be a Conservative just at this moment. Conservative Central Office has deceived and betrayed us.' He reflected in 2022: 'I was very badly let down by the constituency because they were the ones who said, "Jeremy, you're the man to sort this one out", then nobody spoke in my support, except one or two. I don't really think I can say anymore.'[25] Robert Childerhouse, a member of the constituency executive that had opposed Truss's candidacy, pointed out: 'It was not so long ago that David

Cameron was making lots of noise about putting politics back into the hands of local people. That doesn't seem to be the message now.'[26] Mutterings of a High Court challenge to her selection did not come to fruition.

The divided media reaction was perhaps best shown by the *Telegraph*, which ran two contradictory pieces berating 'Cast-Iron Dave's Vichy Tories' and another declaring that 'Truss deserved her victory' within hours of each other. The BBC's Laura Kuenssberg described the result as 'a relief for Conservative Central Office'; the Taliban had been 'mashed', noted the bruised *Mail*. *The Times* suggested that the result indicated 'that a majority of grassroots Conservatives are prepared to back the leader's modernising project to return to power'. But Simon Heffer puffed that it was 'another poisonous example of alienating the core vote'.[27] Stephen Glover prophetically warned: 'If Mr Cameron continues to alienate the grassroots of his party, he will wake up one day in two, three or four years' time to find out that they are not there when he needs them.'[28] The tensions that the episode exposed were to be revived four years later during the Coalition's battle to legalise same-sex marriage, and ultimately led to Mr Cameron's downfall over Brexit. But at the time, Cameron was relaxed, even risking a joke at the Turnips' expense shortly after the deselection meeting. At an after-dinner speech to the Lord's Taverners, Dave quipped: 'A Norfolk farmer asked a nice chap to a party and said, "There'll be heavy drinking, violence and rough sex – all right, my boy?" The chap nervously agreed, asking, "So what's the dress code?!" "Oh don't worry about the dress code," the farmer grinned. "It's just you and me."'

Truss's troubles kicked off something of a trend of associations rebelling against Cameron's A-list stars: the next three months would see rows about the imposition of candidates Joanne Cash in Westminster North; Sam Gyimah, who would later defect to the Lib Dems, in East Surrey; and future Chancellor Nadhim Zahawi in Stratford-upon-Avon.[29] Nadine

Dorries, a future supporter of Truss but then a mere back-bencher, wrote in the *Guardian*: 'South West Norfolk is in no way representative of the majority of associations. They treated Truss badly and cast a shadow over associations across the country ... The result last night was the right one – for the party, for SW Norfolk and for Truss, who will have been under unbearable pressure over the last few weeks. There is an uncanny synergy between Conservative Central Office and the grassroots membership. The uncomfortable reality is that one simply cannot exist without the other. The last few weeks have been a reminder of this – for both.'

As for Truss herself, she told friends that the furore had been a character-building experience that helped toughen her up. 'At no point was she blaming anyone else,' said her brother Francis. 'She was quite good at getting on with it.' Her then-boss at Reform, Andrew Haldenby, told the BBC in 2017: 'I've no doubt that she was shaken by it ... In a funny way it's not a bad thing to have happened because I think it's a good experience, it probably toughens that person up and she was able to rise above it.'

Her selection meant she withdrew from the Esher constituency, clearing the path for Dominic Raab. It also brought her into contact with Thérèse Coffey, to whom Truss would give some helpful tips ahead of her successful selection for the nearby Suffolk Coastal constituency. But in the wake of the scandal, the newly selected candidate was forced to quit Reform. The think tank told the *Telegraph* it was to preserve their independence, even though Truss had been a serving party councillor throughout her entire tenure there. 'It was a bit too much media focus for policy wonks,' a friend of Truss would admit.

With her election to the Commons all but guaranteed by her selection, Truss spent much of her time cultivating the constituency. Not all the family-friendly photo opportunities went well though. Just a month after surviving the attempts to deselect her, Truss sparked yet another local row, of a less salacious variety, taking the place of the incumbent MP at a community bulb-planting event; no such invitation had been extended to rival candidates.[30] She also backed the full dualling of the A11, having been a vociferous opponent of the M11 in the early 1990s.

In the new year Truss and her husband did as she had promised at the selection meeting: they purchased a three-bed constituency house in the market town of Thetford, Norfolk, for £180,000. But Greenwich remained their family home: the couple kept their property there and in due course sent their two girls to local schools. But the family's life in south-east London was always kept quiet whenever Truss mentioned her backstory, preferring to speak of 'my part of the country in Norfolk' rather than the place she actually lived.

The general election campaign for Truss passed largely without event: in a sly jibe at critics, she named *ET* as her favourite film, and a blue-rosette-wearing dog attacking some chickens passed for drama on the stump.[31] Three days before polling day she went canvassing with the local newspaper. 'The decision to put me in the seat was a local decision,' Truss said. 'The vote was by local members and the selection was by local members so at no point was I imposed. I was selected all the way through the process. I've earned it twice, dare I say it. The Press will always put a label on things but you have to have a thick skin in politics. Now I want to move on.' Her pitch was simple: road upgrades, high-speed rural broadband and 'honest labelling so people know they are buying British and Norfolk produce'.[32]

Truss stood down from Greenwich Council on 6 May 2010 – the same day she entered Parliament. In the early hours of the previous morning, she was elected with a thumping 13,140 majority. Just before 7 a.m. the count was returned, with Truss delivering her victory speech as local Tories cheered her. She thanked her mother and husband, who were both present at the count and promised to work for all voters, regardless of whether they had supported her: 'The work is now to come and that's what we need to get on with. There are so many changes needed

… I see my role as getting rid of a lot of government red tape to allow people to do more.'[33]

It had been a rocky start locally, but Truss put the 'Turnip Taliban' episode behind her. Sir Jeremy and his followers admitted defeat, though it took some time for scars to heal. In one bizarre encounter shortly after she became an MP, the pair bumped into each other on a train down from Downham Market to London. To Truss's astonishment, Sir Jeremy greeted her by grabbing the scarf around his neck and twisting it up into a Taliban headdress. A peace offering of sorts?

2010

LIZ TRUSS, MP

Within 24 hours of being elected, Liz Truss had already penned a *Guardian* piece, heralding a new dawn. With 'a large number of new MPs entering Parliament', she wrote, 'I believe that change is underway.' Elected with a majority of more than 13,000, Truss was already earmarked as one of the stars of an intake that contained more than two dozen future ministers who would one day sit around the Cabinet table. David Cameron had, however, fallen short of an overall majority, with a formal coalition with the Liberal Democrats putting a damper on the Tories' return to power. Nick Clegg was the Deputy Prime Minister and the uneasy alliance of blue and yellow would soon begin to fray.

Some 38 of the original 100 A-listers had made it to the Commons, with others like Shaun Bailey and Joanne Cash falling short. A further 13 would eventually enter Parliament via future elections or the House of Lords. Of Truss's success, Michael Gove said: 'She came to great prominence because of the Turnip Taliban. So she was earmarked in the 2010 generation as something of a rising star.' Truss was one of those name-checked by the *Independent* for actually making it into the Commons alongside other highly fancied names such as Louise Mensch, Sam Gyimah and Nick Boles. She would outlast all of them on the green benches.

One ex-Cabinet minister said: 'Right from the beginning she just stood out, she had ideas, she had thoughts and she was not shy ... she was someone that made an impression very early on.' But fellow 2010 intake member Nicky Morgan would reflect: 'I suspect in 2010 we didn't think actually it's going to be Liz that's going to be the most likely person of the intake to be the leader of the Conservative Party and Prime Minister.' The huge 2010 intake, swept in on the back of the clear-out of the expenses scandal but found to be sharing power with an opposition party, wasted little time in making their mark on Westminster.

Viewed through the prism of her later career, her maiden speech was classic Truss: addressing a debate on economic affairs, she demanded more skills, better infrastructure and moving maths and science from 'geek to chic'. Innovative businesses, she complained, were being smothered by too many government agencies and too much red tape. Focused on Norfolk, it invoked two early anti-establishment heroes from the local area: Thomas Paine, an anti-monarchist champion of the Enlightenment, and Boudicca, the ancient British queen who led an uprising against a European empire. Afterwards she described the experience as 'very nerve wracking'.[1] While the speech had gone well, Truss suffered an early embarrassment after a member of her office accidentally emailed a sacked constituent in August 2010 to call him 'unhinged' after he asked for help with his case.

That same month, she gave her first interview to ConservativeHome, and was already talking about climbing the ladder. She said the 'Treasury or Cabinet Office' would be her dream Whitehall appointments as 'I want to get to grips with the government machine', and she named Ronald Reagan as her political hero, because 'he was an optimist about what could be achieved'.[2] Elected to the Justice Select Committee, she spent the summer resisting the closure of her magistrates' court in Norfolk, declaring 'it is important justice is done and seen to be done as locally as possible'. And she lobbied ministers to base in her constituency up to 150 new F-35 Joint Strike Fighters at RAF Marham to replace the existing Tornado GR4 fleet.[3] Truss argued her case in meetings with Defence Secretary Liam Fox; David Cameron publicly praised her 'hard lobbying'.[4] She won local plaudits for her efforts in the 'Make it Marham' campaign, though one complainant to the *Eastern Daily Press* sneered: 'Is there anything more nauseating than witnessing Elizabeth Truss hawking herself around the county collecting signatures to save RAF Marham from HER government's cuts?'[5] Truss was credited by her local paper for leading from the front, with 37,000 names for the petition collected in just 18 days. The base survived the threat of cuts and remains open to this day.[6]

As a new boss Liz Truss MP had an unnerving habit of grilling potential staff with mental arithmetic questions, a job interview test she would use throughout her career. Laurence Chacksfield worked in Truss's Commons office as a researcher from 2013 to 2014. On interviewing for the post, he recalls being curtly informed that Baroness Thatcher had just died before Truss moved on to more pressing matters: what was one-seventh plus one-eighth? He got the job and recalls how 'her attention to the local stuff was just superb'. 'She managed to single-handedly double the train frequency in her constituency. So many rural MPs say, "We'd like more trains in the town" and they just lobby for it and say, "Oh I want this" and that's about it. So, with Liz Truss, she said, "I would like to double the number of trains going from Downham Market. How do I do that?" And somebody said, "Well, you've got to upgrade Ely Junction", so she's like, "Alright, fine. What do I need?" And they said, "It's £7 million", so she would just badger transport ministers and she was like "Ely, Ely, you've got to do Ely." And she'd work from first principles, so instead of just shouting "I want this" she would be like the person under the car bonnet trying to fix it. So within a few years you now have half-hourly services to Downham Market.'

Chacksfield adds that Truss stood out from other politicians for the unique way she handled constituency meetings. It was not her 'fantastic' attention to detail in being able to summarise a matter concisely that set her apart but rather her refusal to 'pander' to those who came in to lobby her. One incident in particular stood out: 'Someone came in from Cancer Research where they wanted plain packaging of tobacco. They came in and said, "What we want you to do is support this" and Liz does not smoke but she is a personal freedom advocate and she looked at it and said, "I've got to be honest with you, when it comes to things like this, I take a more libertarian approach" – the woman flinched when she said the word libertarian – "and I just don't know if it's the government's role to regulate this. In all probability I will actively vote against it." She was very nice about it but firm. Some people might have been weak or pandered, but she was like no, no, no.' Truss duly became one of just two Cabinet ministers to vote against the measure in a free vote in March 2015.

Commenting on Truss's assiduous attendance at local events, the *Independent* remarked drily in June 2012 that 'here in the Great Eastern Land, Ms Truss is practically ubiquitous. Not a Red Cross garden fete opens its doors or a charity hog-roast unveils its provender anywhere between Swaffham and Downham Market without her being on hand to snip the ribbon, wield the carving-knife and get her picture in the local paper.'[7] She quickly became famed among Norfolk MPs for having 'sharp elbows' because of her habit of forcing her way to the front of any photo opportunity. Fellow Tory Keith Simpson represented the neighbouring constituency to Truss in Norfolk. 'She was always very good at publicity,' he told *The Times*. 'She employed a lady within the constituency who was her personal photographer.' Her predecessor and mentor Gillian Shephard was impressed too: 'I have never heard complaints that people haven't heard back from Elizabeth. It might not be a visit in person but I've never, ever heard anyone say that they've had no response from her or those working for her. What I liked was she was enthusiastic and prepared to put the work in. She kept it up.'

On one occasion, a group of Norfolk MPs marked the dualling of the A11 with a photoshoot organised with Patrick McLoughlin, the transport secretary. Truss arrived with her own snapper. After smiling and posing with the Cabinet minister, McLoughlin left for a separate photoshoot with Matt Hancock, whose neighbouring constituency further down the road was receiving extra infrastructure spending. Truss declared that she wanted to come along. Simpson told her, 'Liz, you can't do that!' 'Why not?' she asked. 'It's Matt Hancock's constituency,' came the reply. 'This is a photo op for him, not for you!'[8] Despite her sharp elbows, Truss was liked well enough by her fellow Tory MPs, though after a dozen years in Parliament she remains something of an enigma. 'I don't think anyone ever really gets to know Liz,' reflected one in 2022. But everyone knew of her.

Kwasi Kwarteng recalls: 'Liz Truss was someone who was just always in the news. You had the Turnip Taliban, all of that business. And I just remember thinking that she's gone through a lot to get here, that she's got a lot of grit, a lot of force, a lot of focus. When I met her, she was immediately just one of the stars of the intake. She was very disciplined, very focused, very ambitious. And I just thought this is someone to watch.'

A senior Cabinet minister at the time noted: 'She was the classic small state, low tax conservative, certainly from that end of the family anyway, and right from the beginning she impressed.' Kwarteng adds: 'I remember saying to her in our first year in Parliament, you're gonna get to the top because you're going to stick around longer than anyone else. She was just someone who was going to be a politician.' Kwarteng would go on to be one of Truss's closest allies; another would be Thérèse Coffey, who entered Parliament on the same day as Truss for the nearby seat of Suffolk Coastal. The pair quickly became firm friends.

Truss's early interventions in Parliament concerned education
– no surprise in light of her work on public sector reform.
Raising university tuition fees to £9,000 per annum was one of
the major causes during her first year in Parliament. Truss took
to the battlefield with relish, penning her first piece on the topic
in December 2010. Declaring that 'Tuition fees are the best way
to help the poor' she wrote in *The Times* that 'when the cost of
education is borne by the State, places are rationed' with universities having no incentive to 'to recruit students from all
backgrounds'. She drew on her own background to make the
point, railing against the '"magic circle" admissions process
which I witnessed the effect of at my comprehensive'.[9]

And the hyperactive backbencher did not stop there. Two
months later she was back in *The Times*, insisting that 'fair
access' must not come at the expense of intellectual rigour.
Again, she referenced her upbringing. 'When I was at Oxford,'
Truss sniffed, 'much time was put into the "target schools"
scheme to tell state school pupils how "normal" and "fun" the
university is. It would have been much more useful if pupils
from low-income families had been told which subjects they
needed to study to get to the top.' Railing against a 'poverty of
expectation' and a 'UCAS system that gives media studies the
same value as further maths', she complained: 'in the Leeds
comprehensive I attended, teachers were reluctant to "condemn"
any A-level subject as too soft'.[10] The core beliefs of her philosophy – competitiveness, meritocracy, a love of maths, and a
disdain for the state and what she called 'anti-excellence culture'
– were already on display. At an early meeting with Michael
Gove she demanded the abolition of exams watchdog Ofqual;
a demand that was met with a polite but firm no.

The former General Studies student said it was 'soft' subjects
that were responsible for state school children missing out on
top universities, with students being 'mis-sold' on educational
opportunities. Pupils should be required to sit GCSEs in five
traditional academic subjects, she suggested in August 2011.

After teenagers were told which extracts of Shakespeare plays would appear on their GCSE exam papers, Truss again popped up in the *Daily Mail* in December that year. 'It further exposes the truth behind their propaganda of ever-improving exam results,' she said; 'This is not just a case of a few rotten apples – the whole system is broken.'[11] Attacking 'grade inflation' in the *Guardian* that week, she praised the Swedish system, in which universities set exams after bidding for a franchise tendered by government.[12] She also led a parliamentary debate that same month on the use of calculators in schools, in which she regaled MPs with her love of computer club as a teenager but warned of the dangers of producing 'a satnav generation of students overly reliant on technology'. Subsequently, in June 2012, she called for all pupils to study maths up to the age of 18.

Childcare was another passion for Truss. In June 2011 she was badgering ministers about the idea of a 'baby bonus', a flexible, flat-rate payment of £5,000 per child to replace what she considered to be the current regressive and costly system of statutory maternity pay. 'We need a modern, positive narrative for women about how we are delivering freedom and choice to working families,' she told the *Sunday Times*.[13] The following year, in May 2012, she wrote a report for the liberal think tank CentreForum, arguing that the number of children allowed per childminder should be increased from three to five to make childcare more affordable. With two young daughters herself, Truss also rallied against the unfriendly family hours of the House of Commons, recalling a 'very unprofessional, very emotional' environment. 'I'd come in from working in corporates and think tanks and this is the way MPs operate … It was very family unfriendly but I did a lot to change the hours because it was ridiculous. Why do we turn up at 2:30 in the afternoon and leave at 10pm?'

But by the end of her first year in Parliament, there were signs that Truss and other ambitious backbenchers were already getting restless. Matt Kilcoyne of the Adam Smith Institute notes how quickly Truss became a favourite of the ASI and other free-market think tanks. She addressed a meeting of their Next Generation group of under-thirties within a year of being elected: 'We like to spot them early. She was really interesting, she had bold ideas, she was fresh. She didn't mince her words in any shape or form. She seemed to genuinely believe the things that we believed and therefore it was fascinating to have that.'

In August 2011, a report appeared in the *Observer* suggesting that in Downing Street there was 'suspicion about what the young guns are up to'.[14] Amid much excited talk in the Commons tea rooms, Truss had banded together with four future high-flyers – Kwarteng, Dominic Raab, Priti Patel and Chris Skidmore – to write a book dubbed a 'reassertion of Tory policy updated for the twenty-first century'. It was called *After the Coalition* and quickly branded the 'true Tory' manifesto. Policies proposed include cutting the top rate of tax to 40p, building three new south-east runways, allowing for profit-free schools and introducing a carbon tax to cut emissions. As the title suggests, it looked to a day when the hated Lib Dems would be banished from government, leaving the Tories unencumbered by compromise. All the authors except Kwarteng had worked in SW1 prior to their elections to Parliament, but it was Truss, who had worked barely 50 metres away at Reform, who coordinated her co-authors' efforts in 2 Lord North Street. Kwarteng says: 'I remember thinking the 1950 intake of Tory MPs wrote this incredibly dull book called *One Nation*. And it had lots of different essays. And they attributed all the essays to different MPs. And some of them were like Enoch Powell, Reginald Maudling was one of them, Ted Heath. And I remember thinking we've got 147 [new] MPs? We should do something like this. So the first book we wrote was *After the Coalition*, which was interesting. And Liz was a key member of that and she loved ideas, she loved debate. She had a very strong sense of what she believed in. And she wanted to back that up.'

The release was timed ahead of the Conservatives' annual conference in October and caused a bigger splash than rival books by fellow rising stars Nadhim Zahawi and Matt Hancock. Truss marked the occasion with a piece for the *Daily Telegraph* railing against doomsters who 'seem content to watch our economic standing decline'. Concluding that 'Britain can become great again, but only when we are masters of our own destiny', it focused 'on the restoration of personal responsibility and initiative' and suggested 'breaking up excessive market power to create a genuine free market for all'. The piece did not reference Europe but did contain a couple of classic Truss side-swipes, taking aim at an anti-elitist educational culture where 'hard-working children were dismissed as geeks, and celebrities extolled'.[15]

Kwarteng claims the Tory leadership were nonplussed at their agitating of the Liberal Democrats: 'The whips were kind of like "we'll let them do their crazy thing"; they weren't that bothered. I remember we had a picture of David Cameron waving goodbye on the front of *After the Coalition*. I sort of sheepishly told Desmond Swayne [the PM's Parliamentary Private Secretary], and I mean he could not have cared less; we're like we are writing this book and its "bye bye" to the Lib Dems – and he was like "whatever".'

Many Tories despaired at the constraints that the Coalition placed on their party. Not Liz Truss, who took full advantage of the fact it gave MPs the rare freedom to criticise government policy and suggest alternatives. In October 2011, Truss co-founded the Free Enterprise Group of 39 Conservative MPs. According to one source involved closely in the group, 'Cameron wasn't that interested but Osborne thought it was super useful. There's always a sense when you're in government that you're so focused on running the country that people look to think tanks instead for ideas. So having a group of MPs championing new policies was useful. It was almost an internal Conservative Party think tank, pushing the boundaries of what was politically possible.'

'We were hungry for a more robust conservatism,' Truss says. 'I think there were some areas where we could have been bolder, even with the Lib Dems. Basically, lower taxes, growth, planning reform, all that stuff and that's why we set up the Free Enterprise Group. We thought that the case wasn't being made for enterprise and there was too much trimming towards the Blairite narrative which is slightly grudging of business and things like bankers' bonuses, wanting to triangulate, rather than saying that enterprise is a good thing, this is what's driving our country and making the case for conservative ideas.'

Kwarteng explains: 'So there were three things that we did. We had had the books, and I was involved with that: I had contacts in publishing and knew a bit about that world. Not masses but I knew how a book got put together. The Free Enterprise Group was very much her idea, and I was involved in that. And then we used to have dinners, 2010 dinners with mates [held in the House of Commons dining rooms]. It was very much a movement, and we had these things we were concerned about.'

Working in conjunction with the Institute of Economic Affairs, the Free Enterprise Group aimed to champion more free-market policies and serve as an 'outrider' for austerity measures. Mark Littlewood, who has run the think tank during Truss's time in Parliament, says: 'I think Liz has been to more IEA events than Margaret Thatcher. She has been one of the most involved MPs in think tanks, in terms of the fundamental ideas of public policy, of any side in the last 50 years. I cannot think of anyone who has been as embedded in think tanks as her – not just the IEA, she's intellectually curious.'

Traditionally, newly elected members have served as 'lobby fodder', with opinions dictated to them by Whips, not intellectual gurus. But the combination of coalition and economic crisis allowed Truss and her colleagues to go further than the 'official' line. Just weeks before the 2012 Budget, they held their own public meeting demanding nothing less than the 'fundamental structural reform of the British economy: an act of defiance that would have previously been seen as a monstrous act of vanity'.[16]

But Kwarteng suggests their lobbying work had an effect: 'We started talking about global competition. And literally [during] that conference Osborne started talking about the global race. I'm not saying that we put that idea into his head. But it was strange to me that as soon as the book came out, he started talking about the global race.' Truss says: 'Osborne adopted some of our ideas, but we just thought there was an opportunity to be bolder. And I think one of the issues with the Cameron government is they talked a good game about reforming things.'

Truss was the key driving force behind the group, setting up funding via the IEA, and piggy-backing on the well-established institutes structures. A source then at the think tank said: 'Although the IEA claims all the credit, she was the driving force. She came to us on what felt like the day after the election. And she was very clear, she just said, "We are going to set up a free market caucus for Conservative MPs." There wasn't any kind of suggestion – more of an instruction that "we are now going to do this". She told us: "I will be very good at getting lots of MPs to do it, it is going to produce pamphlets, hold events, soirees, dinners." She was very good at presenting things "fait accompli". And we had already agreed when she pointed out we were going to have to pay for it.'

Truss told early supporters of the group, including Kwarteng, not to waste their time preaching to the converted, or those to the left of the party. Instead, they should focus on people who could be brought onboard to the free-market cause. One colleague recalls: 'She said we need to find people who are seven-out-of-ten "sound" and make them nine-out-of-ten "sound". Don't bother with the fours and probably don't bother with the nine and a halfs.'

While the group lacked an official leader, Truss was the key coordinator from the start: it was her office that sent out invitations to the group's conference drinks that year. The initiative helped Truss stand out among 'the class of 2010', which made up just under half of the parliamentary party and was viewed as the most impressive intake since 1983. As well as burnishing Truss's credentials, the group renewed her links to the free-market movement in Westminster. She would subsequently hire the IEA's communications director Ruth Porter to be her first special adviser upon reaching the Cabinet in 2014, reuniting again eight years later for her leadership campaign. When asked to sum up the group's philosophy, Truss's reply was simple: 'Decline is not inevitable.'

Truss also found time for lighter topics, writing the following letter to the *Evening Standard* in January 2012: 'When Mrs Thatcher was ousted in 1990, I can't say that she had influenced my wardrobe. In the grungy style of the time I wore baggy trousers and desert boots. For me, Thatcher was a fascinating but distant figure. But I think it seeped into my subconscious because I find myself drawn to royal blue and silk blouses. Politics is a visual business. She was the definitive power dresser, whose clothes reflected her personal strength. What my generation has learnt from her is that a convincing politician wears clothes that project their own style and personality.'[17]

Truss also briefly topped the women's list for the popular 'Sexy MPs' website. Amid their new-found political alliance, the Westminster gossip mill began to speculate about a relationship between Truss and Kwarteng. The rumour would persist in political circles for years thereafter, but sources close to both deny they were anything more than friends and only ever political bedfellows.

The hard work did, however, begin to pay off. The press were soon noticing the new generation of pamphleteers. By January 2012, the *Mail on Sunday* was tipping Truss as one of 'Dave's five favourite females' who would receive advancement later that year.[18] Truss's advancement would reportedly 'please the right of the party'. In a cohort that was 'Youngish, more female and less white than the Conservative parliamentary party as a whole', Truss was described as a 'policy expert' and one of its 'leading lights' alongside future Chancellors Kwarteng and Sajid Javid.[19] The group had good links to No. 11 and the Tory talent pipeline, with Chancellor George Osborne viewing them as his 'favourites' and the future of the party. 'Not since the late 1970s has there been a group of Tories thinking so hard, with such freedom, about the future of the country', wrote James Forsyth in the *Spectator*.

In April, Tim Montgomerie touted Truss's credentials in the *Guardian* as one of a group of rising Tory women 'on the right of the party' who challenge the 'perception of what it means to be a Conservative'. In June, she secured her first national profile that didn't centre on her extra-marital affair – a glowing 1,500 words in *The Times* headed 'The lady's for turning, right from CND to Conservative'. She was described as a 'leading back-bench voice on policy, from childcare to maths education to the economy'. She, diplomatically, said she preferred David Cameron to Margaret Thatcher and warned that Britain was facing an 'existential threat', citing poor productivity and a skills deficit.[20]

By late summer 2012, Truss was a strong contender for promotion. Kwarteng recalls: 'She was definitely somebody very focused on becoming a minister.' The *Daily Mail* described her as a 'prolific pamphleteer' and predicted she would be 'the first Cameron Cutie to be elevated to ministerial office'.[21] However, in August, a minor media storm threatened to derail her chances. Truss and Kwarteng regathered the quintet behind *After the Coalition* to write another screed, this time arguing the case for a radically new approach to business or risk 'an inevitable slide into mediocrity'. *Britannia Unchained* hit the headlines for the chapter that claimed 'the British are among the worst idlers in the world'. It was certainly a punchy intervention: 'We work among the lowest hours, we retire early and our productivity is poor. Whereas Indian children aspire to be doctors or business-men, the British are more interested in football and pop music.'

Dominic Raab was the author of that particular section, though the MPs had agreed to take a vow of silence on who exactly wrote each part. That was publicly thrown out of the window in 2022 when, confronted with the quotes, Truss said: 'Each author wrote a different chapter. Dominic Raab wrote that chapter – he's backing Rishi Sunak.' Raab hit back that they had all agreed 'collective responsibility' for the book, adding: 'It's up to Liz to explain why she's changed her view.' Nevertheless, the debate strongly echoed critiques Truss had made before and after the book about productivity, regional inequality and a loss of global competitiveness. The *Evening Standard*'s splash declared: 'Tories attack "Lazy Britain"'; Labour's business spokesman Chuka Umunna called on David Cameron to 'immediately distance himself from this attack on hard-working British families'.[22]

Cameron though did the opposite, promoting Truss just four weeks later to Minister for Childcare. Her new boss Michael Gove told the authors in 2022: 'Liz in effect campaigned herself into a job. She was a very good campaigner on childcare reform. Before 2010, there had been various attempts to ensure we had a "childcare offer" and George and the Treasury team hadn't come up with anything particularly striking or ground-breaking. George was particularly impressed that she had something that was distinctive.' Reflecting on how Truss had used her network of allies and books to argue her way into a job, Kwarteng reflected years later: 'I mean, [it] clearly helped her profile. But also she believed in this stuff, there was fundamental sincerity in what [she] believed. It's not a game plan, she's not a Machiavellian. It's very straight and you could work with her and you could trust her. In the Coalition there were lots of ambitious capable backbenchers coming up with ideas and I'm very proud of that. I think it was something that made a splash, people still talk about it. It had an impact.' Asked if the Free Enterprise Group was about the policy or the promotion, Truss was candid: 'They're both connected. I really care about the policy, I care about cutting taxes and of course I also want to progress and am ambitious. I'm not ashamed of being ambitious, but I didn't want to be ambitious and not be anything so it's like my approach in this job. I've not come into this job to be Prime Minister. I've come into this job because there's a whole bunch of things that I want to do to make this country better and I wanted the Coalition government to be successful. I wanted it to be more bold, I wanted to beat the case and I wanted to beat the Labour Party. That's what the Free Enterprise Group was about, it was a group of colleagues that believed that stuff.'

2012

THE LOWEST RUNG

The autumn reshuffle of 2012 was the biggest shake-up in the Coalition ranks since the election of 2010. Predictably, the *Guardian* claimed that Cameron had 'shifted his government firmly to the right', but in a sign of her increasing prominence, Truss was singled out as 'one of the most influential thinkers of the new intake'. The patronage of Osborne in particular led to Truss's first step onto the ministerial ladder. A leading Cameron-era figure explains: 'David's approach to reshuffles was you always want to be thinking about the reshuffle after next. You've got to think: "Can I get my pawns on the chessboard and into position in the next two or three years?"' The party grandee added: 'Right from the beginning of 2010 when we got into power, there was a plan to accelerate some of the new kind of Cameron MPs as quickly as we could, so that they could be in the Cabinet for the 2015 General Election. But to do that you have to really push them on every level. They have to go MP to bag carrier to junior minister. You have to push, push, push, push, push. And then people fall by the wayside, not everyone makes it. So she was part of a group that was always identified or very early on identified as cabinet material.'

Having impressed the Chancellor with her ability to ask helpful questions and stick it to Labour – and, when needed, the

Liberal Democrats too – Truss was high up on Osborne's list. One Osbornite said: 'She impressed George very early on. She had ideas, she had thoughts, she was not shy. But she was loyal.' And on 4 September 2012, Truss became that pawn on his chessboard; appointed a Parliamentary Under Secretary of State at the Department of Education. The lowliest of junior ministerial ranks, but on the up nonetheless. She stepped down from running the Free Enterprise Group, with Kwasi Kwarteng taking over its running.

Despite the success of the London Olympics, the government was in trouble that autumn as the pain of cuts to the public sector began to bite – a mood summed up perfectly by the booing of Osborne at a Paralympic medal ceremony. Keen to freshen up his team, Cameron fired his controversial Health Secretary, and old pal, Andrew Lansley, a move that was meant to buy some respite. Yet it was the sacking or demotion of three senior female cabinet ministers that dominated the headlines. On day two of the reshuffle, however, even the left-wing *Independent* newspaper hailed 'the rapid rise of Cameron's new girls' with jobs for 2010 A-listers Anna Soubry, Helen Grant and Truss. The appointments were clinically designed to neuter claims Downing Street had a 'women problem'.

Truss's promotion was hailed in the press, with James Forsyth branding it in the *Spectator* as the 'most intriguing economic appointment' of the whole reshuffle: 'Liz Truss comes in as a junior minister with a ready-made agenda for deregulating childcare that just needs to be placed in the coalition's policy microwave. Her ideas could make it profitable for many more women to go back to work. It is a great example of what Tory modernisation should be about: applying right-wing thinking to traditionally left-wing areas. It would also boost the Tories' chances of wooing women at the next election.'

Cameron's blue-sky reformer Steve Hilton also pushed for Truss's promotion. The self-styled modernising guru would walk out of government in May 2012 frustrated at the slow pace of reform in Whitehall. But friends recall that Truss 'really liked Steve Hilton in No. 10. He was a good influence.'

Within days of her promotion the new minister was setting out in the *Telegraph* her goal of making childcare 'a truly attractive profession', bemoaning the fact that many mothers want to go to work but cannot afford childcare and pointing to figures that showed how much more the British government spent on childcare than France or Germany.[1] Six weeks after her being appointed, that same paper was citing Truss as the driving force behind plans for league tables to mark out schools with the highest proportion of 'Russell Group ready' teenagers.[2] Delighted with her new post, Truss pledged fealty to her Secretary of State Michael Gove. In an interview with the *Spectator* she described him as an 'incredibly talented politician with a very strong sense of conviction'. She added that he would be a good Prime Minister; when asked if she too fancied the role, her response was unconvincing: 'No, not particularly.'

Speaking ten years later, Michael Gove insists he was delighted with the appointment of Truss to his team: 'She was a firecracker, someone who right from the off knew what she wanted from specific policy areas.' And on his new minister's abrupt management style, Gove said: 'It wasn't that she was dismissive but she was very clear at every point about what her priorities were and brooked very little opposition.' While a keen favourite of David Cameron and crucially Osborne, Truss was not greeted with universal acclaim when she arrived at the Department for Education. Her ambitions were subject to the whims of both the Liberal Democrats and Whitehall officialdom.

The frontline in the Coalition's battle against the education establishment, Michael Gove's team were the self-styled 'toughest gang on Whitehall'. And his fiefdom didn't suffer fools gladly. 'We were where the action was in government at the time and we flew the Jolly Roger,' recalls one Tory veteran of the era. 'It was buccaneering to say the least.' While critics say Gove's failure to take the teachers with him on his reforms led directly to his demotion on the eve of the 2015 Election, his allies say there was no other way to bring the so-called 'blob' of public sector critics and their supporters to heel. The term was bestowed on the educational establishment by Gove and his allies; inspired by the 1950s film about an amoeba-like alien mass that nothing has been able to stop. While never formally Chief of Staff, Gove's enforcer Dominic Cummings was head pirate. 'Mercurial' to his fans, or 'a fucking lunatic' to his many critics, there was very little velvet glove to Cummings' iron fist.

'It was like we're going to do this. It's going to be great. Shut the fuck up,' recalls an Education veteran of the era. 'That was Dom's style, and that was Gove's style, which is how we managed to do all the reforms that we did at Education. We could either do the reforms or we could "take people with us". There was no way to do both.' Despite her background in think-tank wonkery and work on Education policy at Reform, Truss was to be disappointed by her orders when she arrived on board. 'She was kept away from the important stuff basically,' a source says. 'She kind of did a bit of maths and things like that, but she was not involved in school reform in any meaningful way at all. Deliberately so.'

'Cummings took against her from day one,' claims one adviser. 'He was horrified by the appointment.' He would later describe Truss as 'truly useless', 'mad as a box of snakes' and 'about as close to properly crackers as anybody I've met in Parliament'. It was in the DfE that Cummings' nickname for Truss as the 'human hand grenade' was born. An ally of Cummings explains: 'Dom's view was that she was an absolute menace and should be kept away as much as possible from absolutely anything because the meaning of human hand grenade was not only that she would explode but everyone else would be hit by collateral damage.' Expanding on the moniker ten years later, Cummings says she 'caused chaos instead of getting things done'. For good measure he accused her of 'fragging herself inside her own blast radius' after she U-turned on public sector pay in the Tory leadership race.

Asked about the name in an awkward interview after winning the *Spectator*'s Minister to Watch award in 2012, Truss blamed the civil service for the jibe, clearly unaware it was the political team's handiwork: '"Well, there are two civil servants in this meeting," she told the *Spectator*, turning to the press officers beside her. "Maybe they can elucidate?" One uncomfortable apparatchik protested to his minister: "I'm not being inter-viewed!" "That's a Jeremy Paxman-style answer," replied Truss. "Maybe," she said, "it's because I put civil servants on the spot."' Others in the department at the time backed the idea that the nickname was not always an insult, instead suggesting it was born of Truss's low tolerance for waffle and ability to cut through the bureaucracy of meetings. Friends of Truss joke Cummings has form in rewriting history, 'like when he edited his blog' after Covid to make it seem like he had predicted the pandemic.

One special adviser from another department recalls Truss revelling in controversy from her earliest days at the DfE: 'She has this weird manner, where she has a glint in her eye and she thinks she's being edgy or naughty.' He recalls how she told him that 'I call those who are against what I'm doing the "enemies of enterprise".' Flirtatious attempts to be edgy had been part of Truss's character for years, but the wider public saw it for the first time when she was handed the *Spectator* award at a boozy ceremony at the Savoy. With a joke that someone called Truss had succeeded Sarah Teather at Education, she said of Michael Gove, 'he hasn't gagged me, he hasn't tethered me in the depart-ment'. Bondage jokes at lunchtime appear to have been a bold move given the slightly baffled response from the crowd.

Truss describes her own style of office management as 'bull-dozery', suggesting in 2022: 'maybe I've become more subtle'. Recalling her arrival at the department, she said: 'I was like a massive bulldozer in Education. I remember in my first week some civil servant hadn't met a deadline and I called them directly and said, "Why is this not on my desk?" and apparently that's not what you do, you have to go through your Private Office. I was like, "Why is this document not here?" They hated it but over time you learn to find the civil servants that are good. That was advice I got from Cummings actually, which was basically, choose the best deputy directors and task them with it.'

Ironically it was Truss's old soulmates the Liberal Democrats who were most warm about her appointment within the department. Lib Dem Minister of State David Laws wrote in his diary on 11 September: 'After Cabinet I met with the irrepressible Liz Truss, the new Parliamentary Under Secretary for Childcare. Liz is mind-bogglingly ambitious and has Duracell-like reserves of energy. I will need to keep an eye on her!' Laws would later tone down that praise, warning in his 2016 memoirs: 'Liz was not, however, someone with great self-doubt. She had strong views and little time for dissent – there was something of the young Margaret Thatcher in her, I once told her, to her obvious pleasure. Civil servants found her tricky to work with.' According to Laws, on one occasion Truss instructed officials to omit data from a consultation paper that would undermine her central argument about teachers being restricted to care for fewer children because of red tape. He said in 2022: 'Apparently, she told them to delete all the countries that were on the wrong side of the UK and publish a chart that showed us as an outlier to reinforce her argument. She is quite ideological and has a reasonably clear philosophy around competition, free markets and low taxes. The downside of that is she is not always as interested at looking at the evidence.'[3]

The 2012 reshuffle also pitted Truss directly against a new 'frenemy' – neighbouring MP Matt Hancock, who was also promoted to a junior role in the department as Skills Minister. Their intense rivalry amused Gove, who used weekly ministerial meetings to pit them against each other. A friend of Gove recalls: 'It was like an Oxford tutorial where you've got two very bright ambitious students trying to catch each other out at a supervision in front of a don who they massively wanted to impress. Michael found this quite funny, I think, and was quite donnish to them. He realised exactly what was going on – they were trying to impress him, while both wanting to do the other one over.' Their duet at the departmental Christmas party is still the stuff of Whitehall legend. 'Liz cannot sing,' was the majority verdict.

While battling for relevance inside the department, Truss had picked her first big fight as a minister. It would be one that would define her entire first foray into Whitehall. A former colleague recalls: 'She was given something that she had campaigned on as a backbencher, which was childcare reform as a project and as a way of keeping her busy – giving her something to do in effect. Now, the problem with that was that she wanted to do this crunchy supply side reform that was very difficult and she had no political cover for it. It was pure "Trussy" type politics but she had no resources to do it.'

Having written a think-tank report in May 2012 called 'Affordable Quality: New Approaches to Childcare', reform of the seven-billion-pound sector had become a hobby horse for the new minister. Plans to decrease the 27 per cent of average family income spent on looking after kids was Truss's first big pull of a political lever, but one that would end in humiliating defeat. The fledgling minister made a fatal early mistake in the job. Seeing the gung-ho way Gove's team operated, she decided to follow their tough-guy playbook. 'She did it Gonzo style and she got whacked' was the succinct verdict of one observer. 'There was very little pitch rolling on something so controversial,' another Education insider admits.

The first hurdle was the machine itself. Senior officials 'went slow' on the policy and tried to strangle it at birth on a number of occasions – making Truss if anything more determined to plough on with it. Her January 2013 White Paper 'More Great Childcare', while grammatically hideous in its title, was uncompromising on the plan to tear up red tape for childminders and allow them to expand the number of kids being supervised by each adult. But it was widely panned. Even the Tory-supporting *Telegraph* warned that the plan in no way guaranteed prices for childcare would fall, while the noises off from the sector reached fever pitch. The Tories' yellow partners in government were lukewarm too, though the ratio changes that would see childminders looking after up to six kids were eventually signed off by Nick Clegg. The changes were due to come into effect in September 2013, despite the results of a consultation in the spring showing how deeply unpopular the move was within the childcare sector.

Michael Gove recalls: 'Liz relished it because from her point of a view it was a "win win win": (a) she thought she was doing the right thing; (b) a win in terms of reducing costs but also a win in terms of an offer for families and women in particular; and (c) a win in terms of driving the Lib Dems up the wall which meant she became very popular with our team as well, on the basis that "anything that enrages Clegg, must be good".'

The press did not take kindly to the plans either. 'Plans to cut childcare costs horrify the industry', screamed *The Times*: 'Childminders and nurseries are seeking urgent talks with Liz Truss, the new Early Years Minister, amid fears that her appointment signals radical deregulation of the sector. Before her appointment, Ms Truss called for all Ofsted inspections of childminders to be axed and for childminders to be allowed to look after five children at any one time instead of three. She believes that reducing red tape will encourage more people into the role and drive down prices.' 'Show us, oh super-minister, exactly how you manage – all on your own – to care for two babies alongside four toddlers,' sneered the *Guardian*'s Polly Toynbee. 'We would all enjoy watching you try it on a reality TV show, where you illustrate your new cost-cutting plan.'

Amid widespread hostility to the policy, Truss was forced to tell *The Times* she would be happy to send her own children to a childminder with five other kids. Of course, the papers were quick to point out she enjoyed the luxury of a private nanny to look after her daughters, now in primary school. It was clear the minister was swimming against the tide. One senior Tory recalls: 'The whole thing was just sort of announced. There was no strategic comms plan; it was just here's what we are doing one day in a speech. There had been zero pitch rolling; there were no outriders. And frankly it showed. If Liz had the full support of the department, the secretary of state or even her own MPs it might have been easier, but it was all done on the hoof.'

Yet Truss kept coming out swinging for her policy, telling the *Daily Mail* in April 2013 the nation's pre-schools were crammed with toddlers 'running around with no sense of purpose'. 'What you notice in French nurseries is just how calm they are. All of their classes are structured and led by teachers. It's a require-ment. Children get into the habit of waiting their turn, of saying hello to the teacher when they come into the room. They learn to socialise with each other, pay attention to the teacher and develop good manners, which is not the case in too many nurs-eries in Britain.'

After a backlash at the comments she told the Commons: 'It is a very sad fact that 33 per cent of children arrive at school without the requisite communication and language skills that they need to take part in school education.' The *Daily Mail* branded the comments 'ill judged'. But left-wing academic John Wadsworth's criticism summarised the tone of the wider debate: 'Truss appears hell-bent on pursuing her own agenda without any apparent regard for the needs, rights and safety of either the adults or the children who will be most affected, rather like the "uncontrolled toddler" of whom she has been so dismissive.'

In a bid to soften up the public on the policy, later that month Truss took *Newsnight* journalist Allegra Stratton with her on a fact-finding mission to a Paris nursery, to show how the well-behaved *tout-petites* were perfectly looked after on a ratio of one minder to eight children in nurseries and one to four at home. 'My colleague Jacob Rees-Mogg has four under-fives,' Truss enthused, 'and they're capable of looking after them, and I think we should allow that flexibility to childminders as well.'

Truss's second problem was a lack of 'heft' from No. 10. Even Gove, one former aide claims, could see the policy was 'radio-active' and he wanted 'very little to do with it'. Gove himself disputes this, insisting: 'There was air cover and I was very enthusiastic about the work that she was doing on maths and physics overall. The thing is that she was very, very keen to get the absolute maximum media coverage for everything that she was doing, which is not a crime, and a precursor of later activity. She was very, very keen ... to get a higher profile in order to win these battles. And in fairness she probably thought, "Why are the Spads spending so much time on Gove, he's just the Secretary of State, they should be helping me as well." I suggest that would have been her feeling at the time.'

On their relationship, Gove adds: 'She might have thought that I was wet in some areas but we seemed to get on pretty well. I thought we got on pretty well. I was doing my best. In comparison to other junior ministers with whom I've worked, she was on it and a self-starter and I hope I was giving her all the air cover I could at the time.'

As childminders, unions and charities started banging their drums, the Labour Party smelt blood, but it was the internal opposition that would ultimately swing the axe. On Tuesday 7 May 2013 tensions came to a head – with Truss summoned to see Nick Clegg at the Cabinet Office. He told her: 'Liz, some of this is fine, but some just goes much too far – particularly the change in ratios for really young children. I'd like you to look at these bits again, and come back to me with some new propos-als.' Laws recorded that day in his diary: 'Liz apparently looked downcast, and her face fell and she simply stared at the desk and said nothing for a period of time.'

But, 'egged on by Gove', within hours she had written to the Home Affairs Cabinet sub-committee to seek clearance for the full policy, totally ignoring the orders of the Deputy PM to revise it. Clegg was apoplectic, not least because he chaired the Home Affairs sub-committee and saw this open subordination from the most junior of junior ministers. His anger only grew when *Newsnight* was briefed about the row in time for that Wednesday evening's show. It did not go unnoticed that the journalist with the scoop was the same Allegra Stratton who had less than three weeks previously been in Paris with Truss on her French nursery fact-finder. Well informed, Stratton told the show: 'Process wise this was a policy that was done, it was finished, it was due to come in September.' And Stratton referenced a veiled threat from her sources too, suggesting: 'In terms of what that means for other Coalition policies – the Tories are wondering what is now fair game to go around and start unpicking?' Laws was despatched to have a word, secretly suspecting that the 'pretty relaxed' Truss was 'rather enjoying all the publicity over her clash with Nick', according to his memoirs.

Dismissing the prying ears of civil servants, Laws confronted her on the Thursday afternoon over what he called the 'bad faith' letter ignoring Clegg. He claims he told her that she had discussed the Clegg meetings with both Cameron and Gove, who both told her to ignore him and proceed. A complaint was made to David Cameron about the leaks and briefings around the row. But things were only just warming up.

The way the Coalition was wired meant unpopular policies were rejected by the Lib Dems as a way to claw back popularity. Which is exactly what happened with the Truss childcare ratio reforms. Clegg publicly pulled the plug on the proposals, despite having previously signed them off during tortured and protracted negotiations earlier in the year. Amid the fall-out of the *Newsnight* leak, he said: 'I cannot ask parents to accept such a controversial change with no real guarantee it will save them money – in fact it could cost them more.' 'He has caved in to an alliance of nursery workers and the ferocious army of

Mumsnetters,' said Truss's old friends at the IEA. 'In a sign of how coalition policy making has descended into hand-to-hand combat between the Tories and the Liberal Democrats, Downing Street appeared to be caught off guard by the Clegg announcement', reported the *Guardian*'s Nick Watt.

Only after the row had gone nuclear did Michael Gove break cover to protect Truss publicly. On Sunday 12 May, he took to Andrew Marr's sofa and lobbed one straight between Nick Clegg's eyes. Gove accused the Lib Dem boss of blocking the plan due to fears of an imminent leadership challenge from Vince Cable, telling the BBC: 'I don't think that we can understand Nick Clegg's position without also appreciating the position that he's in because of internal Lib Dem politics. Nick, understandably, needs to show Lib Dems that he's fighting hard.' Not content, he went for another bite: 'You know it's understandable that within the Lib Dems these things go on. Nick has to show a bit of leg as it were on these issues. But we've seen these situations arise in the past and we've managed to resolve them in the national interest, and I think it's only appropriate that we have an opportunity over the next week or two to ensure that the logic behind Liz's position and any concerns that have been raised can be reconciled.'

Laws fired off a furious email to his boss, accusing him of a 'low-blow'. Gove would reply: 'I have to defend my ministers – all my ministers – when their positions are under attack.' The sly suggestion that Laws was also under the cosh, from Cable, did little to smooth feathers. But Gove's defence was too little too late. On the following Monday morning Nick Clegg let it be known in Downing Street that the ratios policy was dead.

Seasoned Tory politicos are more sanguine about the row these days: 'The DPM came out and whacked it because it was unpopular. Whacking it was the easy way for the Libs to chalk up a win and position themselves as "we're going to stop the Tories doing crazy stuff".' Truss herself told the authors in 2022: 'The objection was people like Mumsnet actually, it wasn't about the trade unions or the lobbying, it was about Mumsnet. It was the right thing to do. It's still the right thing to do. We've got the most childcare in Europe and we've got the lowest ratio. If we adopted the French system, it'd be much better. I think David Cameron wasn't prepared to have the fight and the Liberal Democrats wanted to use it for political advantage.'

It was a painful blow to Truss, who then 'really had fuck all to do in the department', claims one colleague. In her first big political fight, Truss had been comprehensively thumped by the Lib Dems while her own side did little to help. She has told friends it was a defining moment of her early career but mostly because it 'made her name', though some Tories reckon the incident scarred her confidence more than she lets on. One recounts: 'She was really chastened by that childcare experience. She wound her neck in and became much more cautious as a result.' Truss disputes this now, insisting that she relished the fight, but there is no getting away from the fact that her first big reform project had ended in failure.

Michael Gove says that the experience for Truss wasn't necessarily 'scarring, but it was a maturing process'. He told the authors: 'You can always underestimate people who are feisty on the outside; they can be more sensitive on the inside.' He suggests that Clegg cared much more about the policy than his Coalition partner Cameron. 'She may therefore have felt that "the posh boys didn't back me up when they needed to" and in the end they relented to Clegg. That may have made her feel that she would need to fight and win those battles for herself.'

It fell to one of only four working mothers in the government to make the announcement of a climbdown in the Commons in June. Truss did though manage to relax the minimum ratio for after-school clubs so that one teacher could look after up to 30 children, a decision criticised by childcare organisations. Undeterred, she ploughed on with alternative schemes, announcing an extra £1,800 a year to work in nurseries under plans to raise the 'status of the child care profession'.[4] She also pushed through changes to the A-Level system, in the teeth of opposition from Labour and from the unions. And she played a central role in the reform of GCSEs, toughening up the exams and overseeing the replacement of the A–E grade scheme with 1 to 9 rankings. Removing the reliance on calculators among junior-school maths pupils was another win from her early campaigning as an MP.

While the childcare ratio policy had crashed and burned, David Cameron was conscious he had let one of his leading lights down. He called her to No. 10 in late 2013, to 'semi-apologise' for pulling the plug on the policy. Friends say he told Truss: 'Look, you know, you're a great minister, I loved what you did, but we really couldn't go ahead with this one. You're one of the first ministers I've appointed to do something and you've just done it. Normally they get side-tracked by Whitehall.' It was clear that despite her setback she was still on the fast-track for promotion.

Truss's obvious ambition for a bigger role became more widely noted in public too. In August 2013, Truss was reported by the *Telegraph* to be fighting a 'private duel' with Matt Hancock for attention and advancement, having supposedly told 'fellow MPs she is expecting to be in Cabinet before the general election'.[5] The *Mail on Sunday* suggested she was competing with Andrea Leadsom in the 'race to be the new Maggie'.[6] But in October she failed to gain further advancement in the autumn reshuffle, despite being tipped for a more senior role. The likes of Sajid Javid and Hancock were preferred instead. Some in the education department detected what one colleague describes as 'the whiff of disloyalty' in the frank way Truss would talk publicly about her 'disappointment' over Gove not acting on her suggestions.[7] Laws recalled: 'At the Department for Education … we had been relatively unscathed in the Cabinet reshuffle, with both Michael Gove and I keeping our existing jobs and Liz Truss also staying where she was – to her obvious disappointment.'[8]

With a setback at home, Truss spent her last year at Education focusing more and more on the international front. But this period also saw her adopt several stances from which she would subsequently distance herself in later years. The Conservative Party in the mid-2010s was much more receptive to Chinese investment and leadership than it became just half a decade later. In 2015 George Osborne declared a new 'golden era' of partnership between the two nations. Truss was no exception to this Sinophilia. In January 2014 she declared that 'we need to copy Asian tigers' and that 'our ambition must be to out-educate the rest of the world. In the future we don't want students to choose whether to do maths at 16, but which maths they are going to take.' The following month she led a delegation of head teachers and education experts to Shanghai, arguing that British teachers needed to adopt the 'teaching practices and positive philosophy' that characterised schools in the Far East. She smiled beamingly as local students performed equations on chalkboards and oversaw the signing of a 'memorandum of understanding' between UCL's Institute of Education and the deputy Director-General of Hanban. The agency is affiliated to the Chinese Ministry of Education and funded Confucius Institutes in Britain and across the world to run educational and cultural promotion programmes.

Truss enthused on her return that Shanghai's 'skyscrapers, and its ambitions, are all built on maths. That respect for the subject, matched with that belief in every single child, is what should really inspire us.'[9] In June 2014 she announced that 'tens of thousands of pupils' would be given lessons in Mandarin under a government-backed drive to introduce 'the language of the future' into state schools. She declared that Mandarin was 'vital' to enable Britain to take advantage of China's booming economy, ahead of the opening of a Confucius Institute in London that was then the biggest teacher training centre for Mandarin outside China.[10] Nearly a third of the UK's Confucius Institutes were founded on Truss's watch, with nine of the overall 31 operating in 2022 opening their doors between September 2012 and July 2014. Within a decade of these institutes opening, Tory MPs in the China Research Group were calling for them to be banned, amid fears they were disseminating Beijing propaganda. The Golden Era had by then been dubbed in Whitehall the 'Golden error'. But in 2014 Truss was wishing 'all of the Confucius classrooms the very best of luck for the future'. In a speech, she quoted the eponymous philosopher approvingly: 'It does not matter how slowly you go, so long as you do not stop.' She added: 'I think there's a lot we can learn from China: the belief in the power of education, that everyone can master both their subject and their own destiny, that we all have it in us to improve.' Explaining her rebirth later in her career as one of the most hardline anti-China voices in the government, she told the authors in 2022: 'I'm not anti China historically, I don't like the communist government. When I was in Education, I was more interested in teaching technique. I think the penny dropped for me on China when President Xi declared himself life president [in 2018]. I think we all thought in the 1990s China was moving in the right direction and that can lead to political reform.'

After the childcare row, relations between Gove and Truss appear to have become more strained, partly due to her latest proposed Education policies. In his diaries, David Laws recalls how, in November 2013: 'Liz Truss made a strong argument for reversing £100 million planned cuts to early years. She also made a slightly odd point proposing cutting grants for voluntary groups but expanding the budget for the Communications Department in the run-up to the general election. Michael said in his usual amusing way, "Oh that's an interesting idea, Liz. So your proposition is that we should cut some of the charitable grants for vulnerable young people, and use this money to buy more DfE press officers?"' Cut out of the decision-making process and lacking support from special advisers, Truss instead focused on her passion for improving maths and science skills.

Despite her marginalisation in the DfE, Truss was still regarded in Westminster as an exciting high-flyer with a skill for self-promotion. The Coalition government was desperately short of women: after Culture Secretary Maria Miller's resignation in an expenses row in early 2014, there were just three female full members of the Cabinet. Having pledged to make a third of his ministerial list female, David Cameron had the lowest number of women at the top table since 1997. It was no surprise then that the ambitious 38-year-old again began to figure in reshuffle speculation. In April 2014, the *Guardian* reported that 'greater bets were being placed on Esther McVey and Elizabeth Truss as the next women to join the cabinet'. Colleagues recall her bitterness at being overtaken by Sajid Javid that month when he became the first member of the 2010 intake to achieve that accolade. She reportedly remarked bitterly that she had 'never wanted the role of culture secretary anyway'.[11]

Still, Truss retained her supporters in the press. Bemoaning the narrowness of David Cameron's government, Sonia Purnell, Boris Johnson's biographer, wrote in the *Sunday Times* that 'many others in the 2010 intake have caught the eye and hail from outside Cameron's social caste – the state-educated Liz Truss, junior education minister, is one. Some are expected to be promoted in a larger reshuffle slated for after next month's European elections.' That did not materialise in May, but the drumbeat to Truss's imminent elevation continued. The *Daily Mail* suggested in June that ongoing tensions between Michael Gove and Home Secretary Theresa May over a report of Islamic extremism in a Birmingham school could result in Truss's promotion: 'If Mr Gove is shifted from Education Secretary, possibly to become Tory chairman, schools minister Elizabeth Truss is tipped as his successor.' The reshuffle became the talking point of Westminster lunches and parlour games.

Laurence Chacksfield, Truss's former parliamentary aide, recalls playing fantasy reshuffle that summer and the revealing justification that Truss gave when asked for her department of choice. 'She said, "I wouldn't mind Transport" and I said, "Well you have to deal with HS2" and she said, "Well I'd quite like to get behind that." "Who in their right mind would? Everyone will hate you for it" and she just looked me straight in the eye and said, "Listen to me Laurence, if you listened to people, the M1 would never have got built. Sometimes you just need to get on and do these things and if that's me I can get on and deliver that. I don't care what people think."'

The long-awaited reshuffle finally occurred in mid-July. The day before the changes, the *Evening Standard* reported that Truss 'the forensic schools minister' was 'earmarked for a major role, possibly replacing Communities Secretary Eric Pickles'. The shake-up was tipped to see the promotion of half a dozen high-flying Tory women, ahead of the general election the following year. For the first time, the *Daily Mail* mentioned Truss as a contender for the top job, writing that the 'ice-cool schools minister ... has emerged as [a] potential future leadership candidate through her attention to detail and unflappable manner'. The paper added: 'Observers have pointed out that Margaret Thatcher got to the top of the party after a stint at Education.' Despite the uncertainty as to where she might be heading, what was clear was that Truss was on the move.

Reflecting on her first foray into government, Kwasi Kwarteng would later defend her legacy at Education, insisting the childcare row 'was not her fault': 'She was an Under Secretary. I can't think of a single Under Secretary in the last 50 years that has made an impact on anything. But as an Under Secretary she was making waves. She was already making her name, and her mark felt on policy. She was driving that in a way that Under Secretaries don't.' He insisted the mistakes made as a minister, and the fights lost, hardened her for her rise. Right on the cusp of Truss winning the Tory crown almost a decade after the childcare row, Kwarteng said: 'She's somebody who learns from experience, you know, she develops, she learns lessons, she has the humility to listen to people and learn from people. And that develops her as a politician.'

David Laws was less sure: 'I like Liz but she doesn't listen very much, and when people try to make points, she just talks straight over them in a slightly irritating and rather "deaf" way. Once she's made up her mind, she switches into full auto drive-mode. While Liz was in the middle of one of her long descriptions of how her policy should work and why it was better than all other options, I happened to glance up onto the wall behind her, and there looking down on us was a portrait of Margaret Thatcher. Liz Truss is, in fact, like a young Margaret Thatcher on speed, and either she's going to shoot straight to the top of Cabinet or she's going to overdo it and blow up entirely. I think it will be the former but we'll have to see ...'

2014

'THAT IS A DISGRACE'

Right up until the morning of 15 July 2014, Liz Truss was not going to be a Cabinet minister in David Cameron's second major reshuffle. On the whiteboard set up in the PM's den was the new-look team he prayed would sweep him to victory in the following year's election. The plan to add more women around the table had already been briefed far and wide, with polling day then just 10 months away. Although Liz Truss had been endlessly tipped for promotion, her name was not on the board as Secretary of State. Cameron later told one Tory MP it was 'gut instinct' that made him swap her little sticker to a full member of Cabinet as the Secretary of State at the backwater Department for the Environment, Food and Rural Affairs.

Until that point Truss had been earmarked as a mere Minister of State at Business, with only the right to attend Cabinet rather than officially join it. One source recalls: '[Cameron] came downstairs the next day and said he was switching Liz. And then simply said: "Right, let's crack on with this then." That was it. No other explanation was given.' Michael Gove says Truss had been tipped for the post for some time, however: 'I think I suggested that Liz should be Education Secretary, but I remember Dave saying: "No, Liz will be perfect for Defra, she represents

Gillian Shephard's seat", a sense that if she's Norfolk, she is farmer friendly.' Be it divine intervention, or a twist of fate, or the recommendation of Gove, Liz Truss walked up the famous street and into the history books as the youngest-ever female Cabinet minister at just 38.

But that historical footnote barely made the *Daily Mail*'s retro double-page spread hailing the 'Downing Street catwalk' the next day. Nine women who were promoted were given the full *Mail* treatment: 'The new Environment Secretary is very patriotic in a red, white and blue ensemble consisting of a snakeskin navy dress and red jacket oddly finished with black patent shoes. Truss, 38, MP for South West Norfolk and the former junior Education minister, looked bright and sensible but a little bit too eighties air hostess.'

Unsurprisingly, Twitter and much of the media were burning hot that night with righteous indignation at the sexist coverage. But behind the scenes there was a proper Tory shouting match brewing too. As the *Mail* noted, almost as an aside: 'The ice-cool mother-of-two, increasingly tipped as a potential future Tory leader, replaced Owen Paterson, who clashed angrily with the Prime Minister as he was sacked.'

An archetypal shire-Tory, Paterson was popular with the farmers and membership but a pantomime villain to the anti-countryside movement. The near religious zeal with which he approached a badger cull to combat TB infuriated the left, the Twitter mob and – most dangerously for him – No. 10's pollsters. And when he told reporters the reason a controversial culling pilot scheme had flopped was because those pesky omnivores had 'moved the goalposts', his fate was sealed. A Downing Street figure from the time recalls: 'David had always been very loyal to him and friendly with him, which was somewhat surprising because they were not obvious bedfellows. But there had been a long feeling that we can't keep this guy. He had been put in there because he was a good sort, a huntsman and from Shropshire. But you actually needed some brains on the flooding issues, which were important, and it was felt he was just not up to it intellectually.'

But Paterson did not take his firing well, raising his voice on the walk of shame from the PM's wood-panelled Commons lair, ranting 'You're making a huge mistake.' Cameron would remember Paterson 'storming out'. According to the respected No. 10 historian Sir Anthony Seldon, Paterson even called up Liz Truss on hearing she was to replace him.[1] He told her: 'I think it is bloody disgraceful what the Prime Minister has done to you. You've been in Parliament for three nano-seconds. You know about Education, you wanted to go to Education. But here you find yourself dummied into Defra, where you have no background at all. This is my phone number. Ring me anytime you want help.'

'I have absolutely no idea why she ended up at Defra,' recalls another influential figure involved in the reshuffle. 'I suppose the logic went that she had a rural seat and needed an entry-level job.' Paterson's defenders in the rural lobby were not much kinder. Regional papers branded the reshuffle a 'cull of the middle-aged white men', with Nigel Miller, president of the National Farmers Union for Scotland, lamenting the third Secretary of State in the department in just four years. 'For a long-term industry like farming, the revolving door at Defra makes building relationships and driving consistent policy challenging,' he warned – as a taste of things to come.[2] One leading countryside campaigner told Melissa Kite of the *Spectator*: 'We don't care. It doesn't actually matter, because she's obviously been put there to do absolutely nothing until the next election. The animal rights lot wanted Owen Paterson's head on a platter and Cameron has given it to them. In his place, he's put Mrs Nicey Nice to keep everyone happy. She'll just do whatever Cameron tells her to.'

Truss's anonymous defenders were quick to hit back, with one, not entirely helpful, friend telling the *Western Morning News*: 'She is ferociously intelligent and will pick it up very quickly, even though I observe scant interest in agriculture and rural affairs beyond what she absolutely needs as an MP with an agricultural constituency.' Truss's old stalwart Baroness Shephard stood up for her mentee, telling the *Eastern Daily Press* it was an 'absurd déjà-vu' that Truss had got the job exactly '21 years after she herself' was made Secretary of State for Agriculture, Fisheries and Food. 'She will be a great success in the job as she is so obviously hard working. I am just so thrilled,' she gushed. David Cameron himself told *Farmers Weekly* she would be 'absolutely excellent' as the pair posed for photos looking at a Welsh cow later that week. 'She's at a farming constituency herself in Norfolk. She has shown great interest in this industry. And I think she will work extremely hard. Owen did a good job, but you know, you do have to move talent through your ranks and that's what I've done.'

Truss, meanwhile, was proving a hit on Fleet Street. Already the *Sun* was tipping her to reach the very top rank, dubbing her 'Thatcher 2.0' in her first major interview in the job. She delicately sidestepped whether she wanted one day to be the PM four times. But it was her comments about Cameron's lifelong rival and a barb at soundbite-driven lines-to-take politics that risked infuriating No. 10: 'I try to be as clear and straight as I can in what I am putting forward. I think people are fed up with politicians where there are lots of bland lines to take. People want an honest exposition of views. Boris Johnson, for example, is very effective in the way he puts opinions across.' As interviewer Tom Newton Dunn wryly noted: 'Just like the Iron Lady, neither is she afraid to be outspoken.' On the other side of the coin even hard-left environmentalists Greenpeace were warm, noting her vocal support for the 'importance of science to education and the economy'. They added: 'If she can bring that respect for evidence and rigour into her new role, then we should see a more coherent approach to the environment than the embarrassing shambles of the last few years. Common sense and the laws of probability dictate that Liz Truss will be better than Owen Paterson. She starts with a clean slate and we wish her well.'

Within 36 hours of being appointed, Truss was due at the Despatch Box of the House of Commons for her department's regular oral questions session. The monthly hour-long Prime Minister's Questions-style grilling can be hard work for even the most seasoned of Cabinet ministers. So for it to fall so close to being appointed was supreme bad luck – and there were only so many friendly questions planted by the Whips to ease the pain of the bearpit.

Armed with a massive red folder stuffed with briefing notes on every possible policy row, the new minister was quick to point out 'in the 48 hours since my appointment, I have not quite been able to speak to everyone or look at every issue, but I know from my work in Norfolk how vital this Department is'. But it was clear the nerves got to her, with a strange use of 'let us be clear' as the start of multiple answers pricking the attention of the sketch writers and the green benches alike.

'Let us be clear, air quality is very important,' she told MPs. But the main topic of the day was whether she would continue with her predecessor Paterson's hated badger cull. And she claimed to be clear on that too:

'*Let's be absolutely clear*, the reality is that bovine TB represents a massive threat to our dairy and beef industries, and we are looking at a potential of a loss of over £1 billion of economic growth in our country and we need to look at the best scientific evidence ... *Let's be absolutely clear*, we are asking Natural England – a proper expert body – to assess the way that the culls are going and to look at what we can do in the future ... But I am *absolutely clear* that we must use every tool in our toolbox to address this threat to our beef and dairy industries.'

Her Labour Shadow Maria Eagle was brutal in her response: 'That's a disappointing reply – I'm afraid you've just flunked your first test and missed a golden opportunity to put scientific evidence back where it ought to be in Defra, at the very centre of the decision making.' John Crace's assessment in the *Guardian* the next day was equally scathing: '"Let's be absolutely clear," she said as a prefix to almost every answer she attempted. It sounded slightly better than "you know what, I haven't a clue, so I'll just read out what's in front of me," if not as honest.'

As if the crash course in departmental matters was not enough of an unwelcome introduction to the job, 'a squeal suddenly reverberated around the chamber'. Oral questions mean topics are peppered willy-nilly across the department's brief with junior ministers opting to answer some of the more technical questions on their patch. A strange musical chairs game is needed with three or four ministers shuffling along to allow whoever is up next quick access to the Despatch Box. Though Truss was a seasoned frontbencher from her time at Education, she was perhaps unused to being the boss. Either way, junior minister George Eustice went to sit down, only to plonk himself firmly in her lap. 'MPs, startled out of their daydreams, had to stifle guffaws, as the inevitable jokes about the junior minister ingratiating himself with his new boss were made', reported the *Eastern Daily Press*. All in all, a tough first outing.

It was all glamour from there. Former colleagues at the Department for Education were amused by her first write-round proposal to reach their desks a few weeks into the job seeking permission to tweak the regulatory system 'for the control of small sewage discharges'. David Laws recalled in his memoirs: 'Although being Secretary of State is a very nice thing this really is the last department I would ever want to go to. Liz must wonder whether the promotion was really worthwhile.' The Thames Tideway Tunnel, a major new infrastructure project to modernise London's antiquated sewerage system, was given the go-ahead in September as one of Truss's first major actions at Defra. As was a 30-strong food crime unit to protect against organised criminals infiltrating the food industry in the wake of the horse meat scandal.

In her first appearance before the Defra select committee Truss sought to strike a friendlier tone than her predecessor, a long-standing critic of the 'Green blob': 'I fundamentally don't think we have to choose between economic progress and environmental progress.' Like Gove being replaced by the far less aggressive Nicky Morgan at Education in the same reshuffle, it was openly suggested her appointment was an effort to tone down the government's previously hostile rhetoric, ahead of the forthcoming election.[3] But her support for the badger cull and repeal of the fox-hunting ban won her few fans in the animal rights' lobby.

While Truss's promotion came as a surprise to many, one place that knew her name well was the ministerial private offices of the Department itself. Since she was elected in 2010, Truss had been a vociferous letter writer to her predecessors as Secretary of State. In less than four years she had written 29 letters, covering a range of subjects from fields to fly-tipping, droughts, floods, litter from cars, septic tanks, fly-grazing of horses, sugar subsidies, bird flu, red tape and of course repeated lobbying against cuts to farm subsidies from the EU.

And one particular cause célèbre – perhaps due to the fact that Britain's largest legal cannabis farm sits in her constituency – was relaxing regulation of hemp. While she campaigned to legalise weed in her Lib Dem days, Truss was aiming a little lower 15 years later: 'I strongly support further deregulation in this area', she wrote in November 2010, criticising the 'administrative burden' of Home Office rules because of 'the impact this has on the competitiveness and livelihoods of British hemp growers'. But it was the EU's controversial Common Agriculture Policy that kept Truss most busy, regularly updating testy Defra meetings of her 'Farming Forum' held in pubs across her seat. Brussels reforms of the European-wide farming subsidy scheme saw Britain at the sharp end of a reduction in Pillar 1 funding – cash that went directly to farms – due to an increase in Pillar 2 funding – which is money diverted to deprived rural areas for wider development instead. The letters released under Freedom of Information show that Truss tore into these 'overly compli- cated' schemes that 'do not sufficiently incentivise UK competitiveness'. But tellingly, by February 2013 she was already demanding answers to what would replace CAP 'if there is a referendum and we come out of Europe'. A reply, came there none.

But now it would be Truss replying to the deluge of letters. Despite howls of protest the second stage of the four-year badger culls in Somerset and Gloucestershire ran from September until October 2014. A tussle in the courts did not stop it, nor could the best campaign efforts of Queen's Brian May and campaigner Dominic Dyer. Sore from defeat, Dyer would later brand Truss 'one of the least confident and charismatic politicians I have ever met … unlike a number of her predecessors at Defra she had no close links to the farming or food industry, and seem- ingly little interest in environmental issues'.[4]

Her new job also brought Truss into the orbit of the future King for the first time. With a reputation for 'meddling' on envi- ronmental issues, the summoning of Truss for private talks with the then-Prince of Wales at Clarence House was noted with some interest in the royal press in September 2014. But far from the meeting being a dressing-down for Truss, sources say that it was a discussion about the Prince of Wales-backed Coronation Meadows, a scheme launched in 2013 to plant 60 wildflower meadows across Britain to mark Queen Elizabeth's 60 years since the coronation.

With her feet under the desk, what did the new Secretary of State hope to achieve in the job? 'Liz was sent there not to fuck up,' a former senior official succinctly put it. 'Defra is basically a department where bad things happen.' Truss recalls: 'Defra secretaries got sacked for things like BSE, bad response to foot and mouth, bad response to floods. So I just thought I'm going to make sure that it was totally copper-bottomed. It was all about grip and I did weekly meetings on risk, all the bad stuff that could happen.' Following Cummings' advice at Education to seek out the officials she rated, Truss cleared out a number of senior mandarins in her early weeks. And in the initial few months of her appointment the department seemed happy with a new-found 'grip'.

While flooding had blighted the government for two years, Truss quickly got the Flood Re scheme up and running. The joint programme between the government and the insurance industry was designed to ensure affordable cover for households most at risk. Another major issue was the blighted IT system around rural farming payments. While the early years of the Coalition government were dominated by rows over the bungled rolling out of the new Universal Credit payments system, the Rural Payments Agency – the second largest Whitehall IT project at the time – was equally wobbly. 'She identified the red lights on the dashboard, and was very methodical about stopping the blinking,' one Defra official said. 'She approached the whole thing as a giant risk assessment.' Some wondered whether that caution came down to protecting her own cherished Cabinet job more than anything.

Officials recall Truss badgering Cabinet Secretary Jeremy Heywood to demand more staff. 'She would be endlessly saying: "I need this person, or that person. I read about them in Civil Service World. Can they come work for me? I need this skillset, this person has it, why can't I have them?"' And Heywood, for his part, often responded positively 'because she had a good reason for it'. Another veteran of the era put it: 'Her famous zeal for reform was replaced in those early days with a zeal for stopping things going wrong, and it was a full-time job.' While there was no great reforming legacy for Truss at Defra, internally she 'tore the place up' says a former aide. Truss was also determined to approach Defra as an 'economic department', giving short shrift to those who said it needed more funds to function. In the run-up to the 2015 Spending Review, she maintained that the latest round of George Osborne's cuts to their so-called 'unprotected department' could be swallowed, insisting: 'There are ways that we can make savings as a department.' The litany of bloated quangos that the department had oversight over also came under review, with Truss highlighting that the Environment Agency and Natural England still had their own HR, finance and IT systems. She told *Farmers Weekly*: 'There is a big opportunity for us to put those back offices together and work more closely together so we are actually delivering things better on the ground.'

Truss also had her eye on the media game. 'She was always asking the question, what actually could we be doing better, what's the positive story?' says one department worker. 'She landed very early on the fact that food manufacturing is actually the largest manufacturing sector in the country and that was something she really tried to push.' With a view to cementing Defra as an economic department, her attention turned away from political journalists to the financial press. One official recalls: 'I remember sitting in on endless lunches with these economics editors and she would say to them "When you do the ONS monthly update on the economy, why are you not using food manufacturing images?"' Some suggest her support for the 'Britain is GREAT' export campaign at Defra was a forerunner for her post-Brexit drum-banging for trade deals. 'That sense of positioning Britain out in the world, it's something she's always been motivated by,' an ally claimed.

While inevitably some noses were put out of joint at the parts of the department the new broom did not think were up to scratch, a number of officials who had worked for both Paterson and Truss were pleased with the new impetus. One recalls: 'There were about four of five things then that could have gone spectacularly wrong that did not. Truss came in and set out three or four things she wanted to happen before the election and the rest was out on the backburner. The thing about civil servants is they like clear direction. The problems come when they aren't told what to do.'

Then junior Defra Minister Rory Stewart – later deselected by the Tories by text message in 2019 for voting against Brexit – tells a different story: 'She obviously thinks about departments very much in terms of budgets, cuts, and I think that's very much part of her style. It's much less about focusing on the particular nature of the department. I never felt in Defra she had a deep affection for rural affairs or landscape. She sees it very much in [terms of] IBM business management of the 1980s.' He described his experience of working under Truss for a year as 'traumatic'. 'I always felt that I was rushing from pillar to post. She would stop me in the lift and say "where's my 25-year environment plan?" And rush off and then I would try to write the 25-year environment plan. And then it would turn out that she'd asked three other people in the department to write it as well. So we were writing these plans in parallel. One of my great moments – again she was sitting with the 25-year environment plan and she'd rejected the fourth draft of it and said "this is not at all what I want, go and rewrite it". Finally I plucked up the courage to say, "what is it that you don't like about it? Is it 'A'? Is it 'B'? Is it 'C'?," to help us redraft it. She said, "Rory, I think everyone around this table knows what I don't like about the plan." And all the other civil servants kind of nod and when she leaves the room I turn to them and go, "what is it?" They said, "oh I'm really sorry, I was really scared there, sorry not to back you up".'[5]

Others try to counter this. One former aide says: 'She doesn't look at things emotionally, she just doesn't have an emotional kind of response. She looks at everything as a logical problem. We can solve it with maths and logic. So she will work through things, but in a very dispassionate, very calm way. And then when she's made her mind up, she's taken a decision. She would bring in the civil servants and she would pursue all sorts of lines and ideas. And you could see the panic in their eyes and them thinking "does she really want to do this? This is nuts, why would she want to do that?" More often or not, no, she didn't want to do it, but she just wanted to know what the options were. So I think one of those great misconceptions about her intelligence or that classic kind of sneer you get from some, I wonder whether some of that is because she processes everything and you can see people thinking: "Why is she asking that? She can't possibly want that" and she doesn't; it's just how she works.'

That summer Truss was reunited with Ruth Porter, who spearheaded the PR offensive for the Free Enterprise Group when she was at the IEA. Porter was appointed Truss's first special adviser and would follow her to Justice and eventually No. 10. Throughout Truss's career, she either brought out intense loyalty or extreme scepticism in staff. Nearly all note that Truss worked them hard however, often calling at odd hours of the night, but never forgetting birthdays and often socialising with those members of her team in favour.

Though usually in bed by 10 or 11 p.m., Truss is an early riser, often waking at 5 a.m. and rarely in bed after 7 a.m. One former adviser recalls missed calls before 7 o'clock on a Saturday morning, often repeated to multiple Spads until one of them picked up: 'There were three Spads and she would call each of them over again until someone answered. If you missed a call and then rang back, she would seem baffled if she had already spoken to someone else about the problem,' the ex-adviser said. 'I think she thought we were constantly in communication with each other even at dawn on a weekend without realising people do have a life outside Planet Truss.' Another Tory who worked for her said: 'As much as she can sometimes be a bit tough on people who work with her, she is fundamentally protective of them. She can give them a hard time but at the end of the day she's going to back them.' Her Defra special adviser, Guy Robertson, came from farming stock and thus received a giant pork pie on his birthday; when going on maternity leave Porter received a copy of *Lean In*, the bible of women in the workplace, co-written by Facebook's chief operating officer Sheryl Sandberg. Friends detected an undertone of 'make sure you come back' to the gift. Another former adviser who once admitted to Truss that she struggled helping the children with their maths homework saw the Secretary of State clear time in her diary for an algebra lesson with their son. At the same time some who have worked for Truss have vowed never to speak of the experience again.

While Truss was becoming more astute in Whitehall management, there is no escaping that her early days at Defra will be remembered for one thing only: the speech about apples, pork markets and cheese. The 2014 Conservative Party Conference in Birmingham was the last chance for the faithful to gather before the widely expected election the following year. With the polls pointing to a hung Parliament, and fears of years more of Coalition, it was red meat galore. George Osborne put the £100 million weekly benefits bill on notice, while David Cameron basked in some rare warmth from the membership after seeing off Salmond and co. in September's Scottish referendum. Liz Truss that week picked a fight on two fronts. First, she declared war on the Hunting Act, and then she turned fire on her least favourite pudding: Angel Delight.

Campaigners were certainly upset by a *Sunday Express* interview in which she wished the Tories could reverse Tony Blair's ban on fox hunting. But it was the 1970s dessert that drew the minister's ire in a bizarre pre-conference intervention, most notably in *The Times* where she blamed the 'new-fangled' instant pudding for the decline of Britain's orchards. 'Apples are a symbol of a wider failure to take pride in and cultivate our own food', she wrote. Citing the fact that two-thirds of UK orchards had been 'ripped up in the past 60 years' and that Britain was now importing '65 per cent of the apples we eat', Truss was on the warpath: 'Consumers reach for easily made, new-fangled products such as Angel Delight or Instant Whip rather than make an apple crumble.'

She continued the crusade from the podium in Birmingham, in her first speech to a conference as a Cabinet minister: 'At the moment, we import two-thirds of all of our apples. We import nine-tenths of all of our pears. We import two-thirds of our cheese. That is a disgrace. From the apples that dropped on Isaac Newton's head to the orchards of nursery rhymes, this fruit has always been part of Britain, it's been part of our country. I want our children to grow up knowing the taste of a British apple, of Cornish sardines, of Herefordshire pears, of Norfolk turkey, of Melton Mowbray pork pies and, of course, of black pudding ... I will not rest until the British apple is back at the top of the tree.'

Counter to history, at the time the speech landed fairly well with important rural regional papers, and barely made a ripple in the nationals as anything other than a boilerplate, if a little quirky, speech by a lower-tier Cabinet minister. The row over Angel Delight received far more column inches in the days running up to the gathering of the party faithful than the short 12-minute love letter to pork pies, Wensleydale, and, of course ... black pudding. The *Eastern Daily Press* certainly gave it a warm reception: 'A woman on a mission, a stateswoman in waiting, she told the Tory massive she would be off to Paris to "big up" British produce. The big question is, will the party faithful remember this fruity speech in years to come when they are looking for a leader? The applause suggested she impressed.' The *Telegraph* leader column gave it a thumbs-up and while it amused some at the conference it hardly made a dent on the day. Michael Gove recalls: 'I went along to the first conference speech she gave, the cheese and pork markets speech where we were enthusiastic applauders and led the standing ovation, which probably won't be remembered by many.' It's worth noting too that Truss's speech was scheduled on the same morning as those of her rivals Sajid Javid and Matt Hancock; all three were trying to outdo each other to grab media attention. 'It was one of George Osborne's little jokes,' says one Westminster insider. And Osborne himself had seen the speech before it went out, along with Michael Gove, who Truss had sent a draft to for advice.

All smiles one moment, and furious the next, Truss's delivery of the 'pork markets' speech is what gave it a place in the history books. Her stilted and cringeworthy pauses for applause may have worked in the room but looked painful on camera, as demonstrated when *Have I Got News For You* picked it up four days later. Comedian Jennifer Saunders, the programme's host, mocked the Environment Secretary's facial gestures; responding to Truss's promise that 'In December I'll be in Beijing, opening up new pork markets', captain Paul Merton quipped, 'She likes to enjoy herself on holiday, doesn't she?' Truss's least radical conference speech would become her most famous as a meme, gif and 'that is a disgrace' punchline of political jokes for years to come.

'I was amazed and I think I was one of the first memes but it didn't even come out straight away,' Truss told the *Spectator* some years later. 'I thought the speech had gone quite well but I think a lot of people were quite two-faced. They told me it was brilliant but then probably behind my back were saying something quite different. But then it got on *Have I Got News For You* and after that that's what sort of made it a viral thing.' More recently she said: 'To be honest I didn't think it would get that much attention. So basically I hammed it up a bit too much.' Truss's friends would later confess she had been on a crash course for 'corporate management presentational training' shortly before the speech. Reflecting on it eight years later, close ally Kirsty Buchanan would tell the BBC such training 'plays into the worst elements of Liz's communication because it makes her more stilted – over pronunciation and pausing is not her problem, it's the exact opposite. You need to loosen her up in speeches and get her to relax. In private when she's relaxed, she's articulate, sharp, witty, funny, engaging. Put her in front of a camera, until recently when she's grown in terms of confidence, she kind of clams up.' According to Matt Kilcoyne of the Adam Smith Institute: 'At the time in CCHQ and No. 10, they were doing training for ministers, trying to train them in a certain way. You saw that with the weird stance that they all took: legs akimbo, standing.' A leading Tory sympathetic to Truss notes the difficulty in delivering a modern conference speech: 'addressing a conference hall while being told to address a headshot camera and speak to viewers at home. It's a difficult balancing act to get right, with speakers attempting to build a rapport with delegates while trying to deliver carefully crafted lines more suited to a party political broadcast or social media clip.' George Osborne told the radio station LBC that the bad press Liz Truss gets is 'frankly quite sexist', with senior Tories believing a man giving the same speech would not have taken the same amount of flak. A party grandee added: 'So she gives the kind of leaden conference speeches as Defra Secretary, well I can give you any number of different Defra secretaries who have given very boring, very wooden conference speeches, right? Why is hers picked upon? Her presentation isn't totally Oxbridge slick, but I think in a man that wouldn't be noticed as much. Yet she gets unfairly labelled for some of that stuff, and I think that is because she's a prominent woman.' Still, the reference to 'pork markets' nevertheless raised eyebrows. One then-special adviser to another department says: 'I think she was trying to be suggestive, it's all part of the whole naughty and weird act. I think because I've seen her be suggestive so many times, I assumed it was deliberate but it might just have been accidental.'

Following the speech, allies admit Truss undertook additional training to avoid a repeat of the mockery. Buchanan says: 'There has clearly been a lot more work done on bringing the voice down and slowing down the pace of delivery.' Kwarteng adds: 'She worked on her presentation. What I find so incredible about Liz, a lot of lesser people would just never make a speech again, or would be terrified of the media. But she just bounced back. And that is what makes her a really formidable politician.' Still, Kwarteng accepts it was a low moment for Truss: 'I think it was a bit unfair ... it was weird, the delivery people thought was a bit strange. The point she made was a fair point. But again she bounced back. She's totally resilient, totally focused and she learnt from Defra, she learnt from that experience.'

One Cabinet colleague notes that Truss can at least laugh about the speech: 'The number of times that I've been in meetings with her and she's gone "That is a disgrace" and everyone chuckles because we all know what the reference is and she laughs along with us like "what the fuck was I doing?"' Truss says: 'My daughter loves it though, she plays it all the time.' And what is noticeable eight years on is how many of the themes that Truss stressed in her 2022 leadership campaign were evident in that speech even then: her left-wing upbringing, meritocracy, the example of Margaret Thatcher and being 'a practical Yorkshire girl'.

Undaunted, Truss picked herself up and threw herself back into her departmental work. An aide recalls: 'There's a sort of delightfully Terminator quality to her: she just keeps going. And you know if you combine that with a very thick skin this will lead to this almost relentless optimism. It's quite a powerful force in politics.' And while Defra might not have been the natural home for a Greenwich-dwelling espresso addict, it did school her in the ways of Whitehall. 'She learnt how to negotiate with officials, she learnt how a department works,' says Kwarteng.

By late 2014 speculation about an EU referendum was taking up most of the government's bandwidth. Truss was not one of those Tories who doubted David Cameron's ability to win next year's general election, telling lobbyist Iain Anderson over breakfast at the Cinnamon Club that 'We are going to get a majority all on our own next year.'[6] Throughout late 2014 and early 2015, Truss was regularly despatched by CCHQ to the Lib Dem stronghold of south-west England as the Tories tried to cannibalise their Coalition partners. An aide recalls: 'Lynton Crosby basically told her to get her arse down there and decapitate Clegg's lot. The message was basically farming and flooding, farming and flooding, and don't let Labour fuck it all up. And it worked.' Truss returned from the South West confident of victory, telling friends: 'You knew, you could feel it on the ground.' Such trips worked wonders, as the Tory machine evicted Nick Clegg's Coalition partners from their South West strongholds for the first time in living memory. Cameron was triumphant, with a slim majority of 12. In the reshuffle that followed, Truss remained in post; a decision that came as no surprise, though she was soon hoping for further advancement.

In the run-up to the 2015 General Election, Truss broadly achieved her goal of keeping Defra out of the news, and therefore her seat in Cabinet secure. But her record at the department would come under fresh security during her tilt for the top job. One such decision was Truss's policy of trimming official rules and inspections, which campaigners claim meant farmers were able to dump waste in their local watercourses without much fear of being caught and fined.[7] Between 2016 and 2022 raw sewage discharge in England and Wales more than doubled: Labour charged that Truss's cuts to the Environmental Agency were partly to blame. But the lack of disasters between 2014 and 2016 was regarded as a huge success by Truss, despite no obvious legacy at the department for someone so proud of her reformist credentials. 'Liz, to be fair, was a pre-Brexit Defra secretary,' says Michael Gove, who ran the same department between 2017 and 2019. 'So there was much less that she could do, she was much more constrained in terms of policy terms. Her vision of Defra was: this is an economic department. It is her job to increase exports, improve productivity. It is the "f" in Defra that ended up being the most important whereas for me it ended up being the "e". She was very much the farmers' champion, the marketeer in every way.'

And it was in that enterprising spirit that Truss approached the EU referendum. The 2015 Tory manifesto had promised that if the Conservatives won power, they would hold the first vote on the question of European membership since 1975. In the misguided comfort of a media mogul's garden party shortly before the 2016 plebiscite, Liz Truss was in a candid mood; 'In my heart I am Leave, but Remain are going to win. So what's the point of pissing off the Prime Minister?' In the biggest political judgement call in her career to date, Truss ended up on the wrong side of history.

Even as a backbencher, 'Brussels-bashing' never held much appeal for Truss; her most lacerating criticisms in both public and private were reserved for the Whitehall blob. Just when she was co-founding the Free Enterprise Group in October 2011, a rival set of ambitious 2010 MPs were launching a different initiative: the Fresh Start Project, to envisage a new, looser form of EU–UK relations. Yet Truss, even when on the backbenches, did not join the group or sign up to its aims; she wasn't one of the 81 Tories who voted for a referendum in October 2011. Thereafter, she was in government and bound by collective responsibility. But Europe does not seem to have enthused her, either way, as it did other Tories of her vintage. A friend recalled: 'It just wasn't very high on her political priority list. Liz cared deeply about reforming the economy, cutting taxes and being a successful country. She cared about education reform and worried that Europe was taking up a lot of time. She believed the EU was neither the cause of our problems nor the solution, but she was never some EU fanatic.'

Still, as the referendum approached, Truss did give the situation serious thought. One long-standing political ally recalls going for a long agonised walk around Greenwich Park discussing her decision. 'She did spend a long time trying to work out what to do and I think she felt very torn about it … I think her feeling was that there were a lot of things that needed changing in the UK, which is why she had got involved in think tanks and then politics in things like the education system, the tax system, infrastructure, things within the UK.' Truss says in 2022: 'When I left the Lib Dems there were two motivating factors, one was the tax stuff and the other was them wanting to join the Euro. I was very against joining the Euro and becoming further integrated.' On Brexit one friend says, 'she just didn't believe it would happen'.

Mark Littlewood, Truss's confidant since Oxford, was one of many who went from being pro-Europe in the mid-1990s to staunchly Eurosceptic by the mid-2010s. He recalls how different 'Europe' was viewed to a young free marketeer in the 1990s: 'On the face of it, the European project was on an exciting, liberalising trajectory' he wrote in the *Telegraph* 'It was about removing barriers erected by nation states in order to facilitate trade and free exchange. Over many years – and only incrementally – did the EU's obsession with regulatory conformity oblige free-market liberals to seriously question whether the European Union was now more of a socialist than a liberal enterprise.' Truss shares much of the same analysis about the EU's shortcomings, though stopped short of joining Littlewood in backing Leave. He says 'her view on Brexit was basically that the juice wasn't worth the squeeze'.

Kwarteng agrees that Truss was concerned about the opportunity cost of Brexit: 'I think her main focus was on getting productivity and incentivising investment and growth in the UK … Now the referendum is seen as this great big either/or, black or white decision. I think a lot of people at the time thought it was a finely balanced decision. It has taken on this mantle of this great defining issue of our time where you were either in one corner or the other. But I remember thinking this is actually quite finely balanced, but on balance I think we should go out. She was never a massive Europhile. But I think she thought on balance maybe we should stay. I think she came out for what she was: a soft remainer.'

The fear of endless negotiations and compromises was certainly used by David Cameron and his team to try to convince Truss to back Remain in early 2016. In his account of the referendum *Unleashing Demons*, Cameron's press chief Craig Oliver recalls the Prime Minister deploying his formidable charm on the younger members of his Cabinet: 'DC moves on to the argument he's used with Priti Patel and Liz Truss: "You're going to be a big figure in the Conservative Party. Do you really want to spend the next ten years dealing with the fall-out of this?" It's a powerful argument and one that's integral to our comms strategy: who the hell knows where we'll land if we take the Brexit leap.' David Cameron's own memoir *For the Record*, recalls Truss as 'wavering'. A Cameron-era figure says: 'We divided the cabinet up a bit and David took the most difficult cases, he was meant to land Gove and Johnson. And Osborne did the rest of the Cabinet. Liz was not a particularly difficult sell.' Osborne told her: 'If you believe in lower taxes and the free market you should vote remain.'

The strategy worked. Oliver recalls seeing the Environment Secretary just before the extraordinary Saturday Cabinet meeting at which each minister made their views known about Cameron's last-ditch renegotiation with Brussels on immigration reforms ahead of the June vote. 'I see Liz Truss and chat with her about her decision to be In. She is concerned by Michael Gove being Out, but says she is persuaded that she doesn't want to spend the next decade of her life wrestling with Europe.' Gove had tried to convert Truss, but to no avail: 'I remember when I was trying to persuade Liz to back leave, as I tried to persuade Saj unsuccessfully, I remember her saying to me: "Michael I don't think there is anything that we need to achieve that we can't achieve inside the EU."'

The Cabinet showdown was held on 20 February 2016. Every minister spoke in strict order of Cabinet seniority, with Michael Gove being the first person to make the case for Out. Truss was reported to have argued for In on the 'grounds that the Tories have a golden chance to reform Britain over the next few years and that they didn't want to instead spend that time negotiating Britain's exit from the European Union'.[8] 'She was quite low down in the pecking order,' one attendee recalls of the meeting. 'But she gave a clear statement. She said that she had listened to all the things Iain [Duncan Smith], Michael [Gove] and Theresa [Villiers] said were impossible to do in the EU. But she said she didn't agree with any of them. She said we could do all of those things in the EU.'[9] Ironically, as one parliamentary observer remarks: 'Her argument about the cost opportunity of Brexit has been proved right: it took years to do, at the expense of other things.' The day after the Saturday Cabinet, Boris Johnson backed Leave.

Despite claims she had been wavering, once the 'official' campaign actually began in mid-April, Truss played a regular role as a low-ranking Cabinet member. Press attention preferred to focus on bigger personalities and the psycho-drama of Cameron versus Boris and Gove. Green issues were largely overshadowed by the focus on immigration and the economy, though the Defra secretary gamely played her part, making the case for an 'In' vote in a prominent *Guardian* interview. She also appeared alongside George Osborne at the infamous press conference at which the Chancellor declared that a Brexit vote would leave every family £4,300 worse off. Truss also made headlines after being bested in a BBC *Question Time* appearance by an immigration-sceptic teenager. Truss was left temporarily speechless, with fellow panellist Diane Abbott being forced to ride to her rescue. Explaining Truss's role, a Cabinet colleague said: 'It's not like she led the campaign; she was a fairly junior Cabinet minister but she had a walk-on part.' Explaining her devotion, Truss blamed her competitive nature: 'I'm a team player; when I agree to do something, I go and do it and get on with it. When you've joined a side in a campaign, you want that side to win don't you?'

In May, appearing to speak from the heart without notes, Truss addressed the British food and drink industry at a dinner: 'I have great faith in the British people. I think the British people are sensible people. They understand fundamentally that economically Britain will be better off staying in a reformed EU.' One Westminster veteran who met with her at this time recalls Truss confiding her fear that 'If we leave the EU, we'll become more European – a high-tax, high-spend state along the lines of France'. Her argument was that responsibility for all the problems facing Britain – too much taxation, too much regulation, too much spending – lay with London not Brussels. Europe, in Truss's mind, was not responsible for any one of the 'top twenty' issues confronting the UK. She used her free-market credo to publicly justify her 'In' vote. Writing in the *Sun on Sunday* on the cusp of the historic poll she said anyone who thought leaving the EU would lead to deregulation was 'living in cloud cuckoo land'. Truss also raised eyebrows with the claim that Leavers were 'extreme and outdated' in a joint attack with Ed Miliband and the Greens. Five days before the vote in June, she tweeted derisively: 'Leave cannot name one country we would get a better trade deal with if we left the EU.' Words she would come to regret when appointed Trade Secretary three years later.

On 22 June 2016, the day before the referendum, Truss hosted Osborne in her seat, posing for a pint of the Adnams brew and hailing the fact 'they are clear that being in the EU is good for their business and jobs'. The following evening after casting her vote she pitched up at the Stronger in Victory party shortly before midnight. Minutes after the polls closed, Nigel Farage had conceded defeat; a triumphant atmosphere reigned supreme. But by the time Truss arrived, the atmosphere had already soured, as it became clear that postal votes had returned a big lead for Leave. Truss left within minutes, sensing the defeat and not wanting to be caught on camera as the mood darkened; one attendee recalls 'Liz has a very keen political antenna.'[10] Was she disappointed by the result? No, says a friend: 'It was quite exciting that Britain had voted for it. It's a bit like the 1997 Election, even if you didn't want Labour to win. It was a weird night.'

Hours later Truss was back on Twitter to declare: 'The British people have spoken. We must now put our shoulder to the wheel and ensure we leave the EU in the best way for Britain.' Kwarteng says, 'When the vote happened she was a democrat. She said "right we have to move on".' When pressed by Andrew Neil in 2017, Truss explained her decision thus: 'All of us had to make a judgement based on what we thought the future would look like. And I made a judgement thinking it would be bad for the economy. Since we have left it's been more positive. So the facts have changed and I have changed my mind.'

2016
ENEMIES OF THE PEOPLE

David Cameron had barely resigned on the morning of Friday 24 June 2016, when Liz Truss picked up the phone. 'Michael, you should run,' she told her old boss. 'Oh no, I couldn't possibly,' came Gove's reply. 'Why don't you back Boris? We all are.' After a call to Boris Johnson, Truss was quickly signed up to the so-called Vote Leave Johnson/Gove 'dream team'. She made her views public in the pages of the *Telegraph* the following Tuesday: 'I am backing Boris Johnson to be the next leader of the Conservative Party and our next Prime Minister. Though I took a different view during the campaign, Boris argued his case with passion and conviction. Our exit from the EU will require careful, detailed and tenacious negotiating and I am particularly delighted Michael Gove and Boris will be working together on this task.' Truss would be an early supporter of Johnson's leadership campaign, which nearly a hundred of her colleagues would join in the coming days.

Two days after her *Telegraph* article it would be Gove that called Truss early in the morning of Thursday 30 June: 'I've changed my mind Liz, and I am running myself. Are you in?' That conversation would be the last time Truss would allow her old boss to let her down. 'What? Absolutely not,' came the immediate reply. 'You've led me up the garden path here frankly.' Livid Truss decided to vacate Westminster that afternoon to attend her daughter Liberty's school play, rather than watch the amateur dramatics unfold out in SW1. By the afternoon King Boris was torpedoed, withdrawing from the race after Gove's betrayal, and Theresa May had picked up the phone to her Cabinet sister. While some Johnson supporters like Dominic Raab and Rishi Sunak did switch to Gove, Truss told May that same day she would have her support. 'I thought it was appalling behaviour by Michael,' a seething Truss would tell friends. Up until that point, she would have described herself as 'a Gove fan' but now she could never trust him again. 'It was a massive betrayal of trust.'

The Tory Party has a long history of punishing perceived backstabbers, but the brutality with which Theresa May despatched Michael Gove to the backbenches to reflect on the 'value of loyalty' surprised even seasoned Westminster-watchers. After living in his shadow as a junior minister, it was Truss who benefited the most from Gove's defenestration from the Cabinet. 'I want to make you the first female Lord Chancellor,' May told Truss two weeks later after seizing the keys to 10 Downing Street.

Foreign-facing departments were given to Leavers; domestic departments were given to those considered reformers, with a number reserved for women. According to one aide closely involved in the changes, May 'always thought Liz was fine, she was promising. She had done a quietly competent job at Defra, I think she thought she'd done ok at Education as a junior. You get feedback from the Whips and from the civil service and the Perm Secs and they had all reported positively.' A key May lieutenant recalls: 'Theresa was very shaped by her time in the Home Office and was determined over two things. One, the lawyers should not be run by a lawyer, and she wanted someone who was a reformer. Liz had shown a bit of that in Education, if not Environment.'

In becoming the first female Lord Chancellor and Justice Secretary, Truss smashed another glass ceiling, And, at 41, she would be the youngest holder of the office since George Jeffreys, the 'hanging judge' of the 1680s. But the falling shards cut deep; her appointment was met with howls of anguish from the legal establishment. Before her robes of office had even been fitted, her number two at the department walked out, saying she was a lightweight.

Lord Faulks QC grandly told *The Times* that Truss was a risk to the entire justice system: 'I have nothing against Ms Truss personally. But is she going to have the clout able to stand up to the Prime Minister when necessary on behalf of the judges? Is she going to be able to stand up, come the moment, to the Prime Minister, for the rule of law and for the judiciary ... without fear of damaging her career?' Truss later remarked that she had never met the man and that he had not called before going public with his criticism.[1] He later privately apologised for his behaviour, but his words were prophetic.

It was a rocky start but Truss had not helped matters when she emerged from No. 10 by replying, 'I served on the select committee', to shouts from the media asking what she knew about Justice. Her two immediate predecessors Michael Gove and Chris Grayling had not been lawyers either, but received far less vitriol from the legal world when they were appointed. While Grayling was widely seen as a book-banning hang 'em-and-flog-'em disaster, there had been grudging respect for the work done by Gove. In the 14 months after he was resurrected to the full Cabinet by David Cameron after the 2015 Election, he had set in motion major reforms to both prisons and courts. Most of Gove's work, he would later joke, was spent undoing the actions of his predecessor. He removed the 12-book limit on prison books imposed by Grayling, dropped a toxic attempt by the government to bid to run a Saudi prison and – most crowd-pleasingly – ditched cuts to legal aid. But an ally of Truss would later remark he had perhaps 'spent quite a lot of time campaigning in the referendum rather than dealing with prison safety issues'.

The legal establishment, however, was reeling from the referendum result – many of the best-paid lawyers in the land had earned their country piles on the back of the European Courts of Justice and were now itching for a fight. There were choppy waters ahead as some of the brightest judicial minds plotted to frustrate ministers' Brexit efforts. Herding this enraged pack would have tested the skills of any politician, let alone one whose own lack of legal training instantly earned her the suspicion of much of the profession. Truss entered the MoJ with a bullish attitude to vested interests and opponents of reform: But taking on the judiciary and bar would be her biggest battle yet.

While the legal world loves nothing more than introspection and their criticism could have been handled, the alarm bells rang when Truss's own Tory colleagues in the Commons were also breaking cover to slam her appointment. Enter Bob Neill, who had beaten Truss to the Bromley nomination 10 years previously. Unlike Truss, he had backed Gove's abortive leadership campaign less than three weeks earlier. And he was clearly looking for his pound of flesh.

'As chairman of the Justice Committee, I'll be writing to Liz to meet us urgently', he decreed to the *Guardian*. 'My concern is this: while it's not necessary for the Lord Chancellor to have a legal background, they have a specific role under the constitutional reform act to represent the interests of the judiciary and to represent the judiciary including its independence within government.' He went on: 'It helps if the person in charge has been a lawyer or has been a senior member of the Cabinet. I have a concern, with no disrespect to Liz, that it would be hard for someone without that history to step straight in and fulfil that role.' For good measure he added that 'he was also very concerned that there could be a loss of the impetus for prison reform. There is no reason that this should be allowed to slip. But it's important to ensure that the person in the job has enough commitment, enthusiasm and drive to take on the vested interests.' On top of Faulks's early criticism, this was shaping up to be a crisis for Truss. She had rarely played the sexism card when in tricky spots earlier in her career but she now authorised a retaliation briefing to the papers: 'This is coming from old white male judges and politicians' a source close to the Justice Secretary told the Lobby. 'Liz will of course be having a series of meetings with the relevant stakeholders. She will be doing those into summer recess. But as far as I can see, this is thinly veiled misogyny.'

A week after her appointment, and after she made a hasty trip to legal outfitters Ede and Ravenscroft, the Lord Chief Justice handed Truss a Bible as she swore to protect the rule of law, defend the independence of the judiciary and provide adequate resources for the courts. 'As the first woman Lord Chancellor,' she added, 'I am proud to be part of our constantly evolving justice system.' Hugh and the girls sat in the grand court as their wife and mother took the oath, wearing heavy gold and black robes. Like Grayling and Gove before her, Truss was conspicuously wig-less – an honour saved for only learned appointees. But in a sign of troubles to come, there was a coded dig at Truss's claim to the history books. The Lord Chief Justice Lord Thomas used his speech to point out that Eleanor of Provence, the wife of Henry III, was Lady Keeper of the Great Seal and wielded the powers of the Lord Chancellor in 1253, even though she was never sworn into the role. For her part, and with playful menace, Truss put the legal establishment on notice as a 'great supporter of reform and modernisation through the courts and tribunals'. 'It was all nicey nicey face to face,' recalled one official present that day. 'In fact they basically flirted with each other to distract from the fact neither of them were very happy.'

An unenviable task awaited Truss: as a non-ring-fenced department, the Ministry of Justice had suffered successive deep cuts to its budgets and severe restrictions on the availability of legal aid. In her in-tray was a UK Bill of Rights, long promised

by multiple holders of her office to fix the UK's testy relationship with the European Convention on Human Rights and its
meddling court in Strasbourg once and for all. The department
was also in the middle of overseeing a challenging £700 million
court modernisation to get rid of an annual paper mass equivalent to the height of London's Shard building. But within days
of Truss being sworn in, Parliament broke for recess after a
frenzied month that had seen the culmination of the referendum, the fall of Cameron, the implosion of Johnson, the rise of
May and a bloody reshuffle. Westminster was ready to put its
feet up by the pool – but this at least gave new Cabinet ministers
a much-needed August to brush up on their briefs.

Things did not improve for Truss when Parliament returned
in September, however, as she was hauled before Bob Neill's
Justice Select Committee. Four months previously, Gove's
Prisons and Courts Bill had been the cornerstone of the 2016
Queen's Speech, but an inadvertent suggestion that legislation
was now on the backburner sparked a fresh furore. For newly
appointed special adviser Kirsty Buchanan, it proved to be a
tricky first week: 'It was one of those "what is your entire role,
what are your thoughts on x y and z?" sessions and she had not
even been in the job very long.' Buchanan is a tough-as-nails
former Political Editor of the *Sunday Express*. She had worked
for Eric Pickles during the Coalition at the Communities
Department and knew her way around both Whitehall and Fleet
Street. Brought in by Ruth Porter, it was a streetwise hiring for
a Secretary of State who needed urgent reinforcements.

If Truss was ever in doubt that the committee she once sat on
would be a hostile crowd, the opening salvo set the tone. Bob
Neill took great pains to make sure every single qualified lawyer
around the table declared their interests at the top of the meeting as if to prove a point. After reading a statement of her
priorities – which included prison reform and standing by the
Human Rights Act promise of the 2015 manifesto – Truss was
quickly back to her wonkish comfort talk of 'systems', 'silos'

and 'returns'. But as with her first outing at Defra two years previously, the red folder was never far from her glance.

Buchanan recalls: 'I made the mistake of sitting behind her so the cameras were on me, but reading Twitter at the same time. The whole thing took on a kind of car-crash quality – to sum up the one tweet that almost made me burst out laughing but fortunately did not – one of the journalists said: "I don't know why you didn't just spare us a load of time, open the door, shout I DON'T KNOW, and shut the door and go off again." She had literally been in the job for a matter of months.'

When it came to Gove's Prisons and Courts Bill reforms, Bob Neill asked if she was going to go ahead, and the new minister paused for too long before saying: 'We are looking at that at the moment.' And getting out a spade, Truss went on: 'It will be in the plan ... I am not committing to any specific piece of legislation at this stage.' By the time she added 'my predecessor was specifically focused on reform prisons, which I think are an excellent idea', the damage was done. And when she said: 'I am working on a delivery plan at the moment, which we do not currently have', it became a full-blown row. Bob Neill nearly combusted: 'Are we not going to get one? It is surprising that you can't tell us whether it will happen in this session.'

According to Buchanan, Truss 'was planning to go ahead with it but wanted to recalibrate it a bit, and that is what the pause was. But it came across a bit, you know – "new justice secretary may ditch Gove's flagship reforms". So at the end of this thing, everyone is busy blowing smoke at her and telling her "that was amazing". And she looked at me and she said, "did I make a mistake with the bill?" And it was one of those moments where I thought, this is a pivotal moment for our relationship. And I looked at her, and said, "Yes you did but I can fix it." And she went, "Well what are you doing still standing here then? Go and fix it."' Soon Buchanan was at work, trying to explain Truss's misstep. A Ministry of Justice spokesperson said: 'The government remains totally committed to legislating on prison reform and will come forward with plans in due course.' 'In hindsight we had sort of under-prepared,' admits another MoJ source. But there was to be no sugar coating of the mess from her newly appointed adviser. Buchanan said: 'She is direct and honest and she values direct and honest.'

Given the turmoil of her first few months in the job there was little time for Truss to settle into the trappings of high office – quite literally the case given her bare walls on the ninth floor of the imposing Ministry of Justice headquarters. Formerly the Home Office, 102 Petty France inspired comparisons to the dystopian 'Big Brother' facades in George Orwell's *1984*. Staring at her sparse office one morning early on in her tenure, Truss turned to her aides and sighed expansively: 'I need art.' 'Excuse me Secretary of State,' came the nervous reply of an official, perhaps bracing for another of Truss's regular intellectual spot tests. 'I need art,' she repeated a little more tersely; 'I've got no art. Everyone else has art in their offices.' 'Well what sort of art would you like, Secretary of State?' 'Look, I don't have time to get into this. I don't know, just get me some art,' was Truss's only order.

An apparatchik was duly despatched to Admiralty House, home of the government's vast taxpayer-funded art collection. But it was not a successful mission. 'All the good art has gone,' they were told by the stern curator, for whom reshuffles were seemingly a busy time. Assuming countryside scenes and portraits of horses were out, a collection of modern British and pop artists were earmarked for delivery to the Department a few days later. When it arrived, the private office team gathered to look at what had been chosen. Truss was silent. 'So do you like it?' one asked. 'No' came the reply. Amid frantic offers to change it, Truss waved her hand and simply said: 'Just stick it on the wall.'

Her new-found role added pressure at home too, with Truss trying her best to balance her commitments with the demands of family life. Her two girls, Frances and Liberty, were midway through primary school and while husband Hugh looked after them most of the time, Truss made time when she could. 'She used to leave early on a Thursday for pizza Thursdays, it was sacrosanct,' recalls Buchanan. 'She doesn't gush about being a mother but she's fiercely proud of them.'[2] Early in her tenure, when addressing a room full of female barristers, she was asked what advice she would give her daughters and other young women. They likely expected a feminist platitude about fighting in a man's world; instead she replied bluntly: 'Be good at maths.'

By the summer of 2016 the Ministry of Justice had earned the internal nickname 'HMP Shitshow', and Truss entered at its lowest ebb. Cuts to the prison service were blamed for a dramatic surge of violence on the prison estate. When figures released in October 2016 showed assaults in Britain's jails were up 34 per cent in a year to 65 a day, the department was candid in its assessment: 'The rise in assaults since 2012 has coincided with major changes to the regime, operating arrangements ... For example, restructuring of the prison estate, including staff reductions, which have reduced overall running costs.' But the assessment also noted 'an increase in gang culture and illicit psychoactive drugs in prisons'.

While cuts had made things harder in prisons, an influx of powerful new drugs had compounded the problems. The then-legal, lab-made synthetic cannabinoids 'Spice' and 'Black Mamba' were bad enough on the streets, but were lethal in the boiling pot of Victorian-era prisons.

Truss herself said in September 2016: 'Their consequences are devastating and go far beyond the confines of the prison walls, spilling out into our streets and communities. As well as the dangers to both physical and mental health, trading in these illicit drugs can lead to debt, violence and intimidation. Prison reform is my top priority. I am committed to making prisons places of safety and reform, where our dedicated officers are given the support they need to help offenders turn their lives around.' An initial £14 million was earmarked for the ten worst prison estates, but it was clear that more money would be needed. That would bring just 400 extra frontline staff to jails in Leeds, Liverpool, Nottingham, Winchester, Exeter and Chelmsford. Having gone along with the cuts agenda while serving at Defra, Truss was quickly pitched into her first major battle with the Treasury. With her mentor George Osborne in the political wilderness, Truss wasted no time abandoning his legacy of austerity and was quickly demanding to his successor, Philip Hammond, that years of spending restraint be ripped up.

Rising levels of prison violence was a problem Truss would approach with 'maths rather than emotions', but there was an element of politics at play too. Chris Grayling had cut the number of guards in prisons and the blame game was in full swing. One Tory source puts it bluntly: 'Chris Grayling had cut a load of prison officers, but we needed to navigate the blame game in a way that didn't burn him.' Grayling had made a remarkable political comeback at Transport after being an early backer of Mrs May's leadership campaign; it would be much easier to blame his legacy had he not been sitting opposite Truss at the Cabinet table.

As so often, Truss turned for help to Tufton Street and the back-up of her favourite free-market think tanks. Data analyst Adam Memon had worked for her briefly at Defra after she poached him from the Centre for Police Studies, where he headed up their economic research. He was immediately put to task digging though official data to work out exactly when, where and how the violence was brewing. 'If you looked at the graph, there were the Grayling cuts and yes it went up a bit, but then you had the year that Spice started to flood into the prison state and it went off the charts,' Buchanan says – and she was not alone in her analysis. On 23 September, the independent Prisons and Probation Ombudsman broke cover with an intervention on drugs that up-ended the narrative that Tory cuts were solely to blame.

As chief of the prisons watchdog, Nigel Newcomen used a speech to a junior wardens college to call time on 'Spice', calling it a 'game-changer in terms of reducing safety in prison'. In his startling speech he directly aligned the drug to 'our rising numbers of suicides, as well as to other types of death, including deaths from drug toxicity, apparent natural causes and even homicides'. His speech continued: 'Staff and other prisoners may also be at risk from users reacting violently to the effects of NPS [new psychoactive substance]. There are also cases of prisoners being given "spiked" cigarettes by others who want to test new batches of NPS, as a way of gauging the effect before taking it themselves. In other cases, prisoners have even been used as unwitting NPS guinea pigs, sometimes just for the amusement of onlookers.' The speech was exactly the ammunition Truss needed to go into battle with the Treasury.

Through Osborne's cuts, the number of prison officers had fallen by more than a quarter – more than five thousand by headcount – since the Tories came to power in 2010. According to data from the Prison Reform Trust in 2016, the prison estate in England and Wales was holding 10,000 more inmates than it was designed for. Truss was under pressure, as the *Sun* warned in October: 'We are on our fourth Justice Secretary in just six years – which is part of the problem. It is too soon to accuse the latest of being out of her depth. But Liz Truss must immediately re-establish order.' In a coruscating leader column, the paper put Truss on notice: 'Our prisons are awash with drugs, legal highs, mobiles and other smuggled contraband often flown in by drone. Violence is soaring. Escapes are commonplace. Some prisons are ancient and squalid, others so lax lags cook illicit steak dinners and post pictures on Facebook. The system is in disarray. The problems are overcrowding, with too many non-dangerous criminals banged up, and catastrophic under-staffing after cuts.'

A hastily concocted White Paper offered measures like no-fly zones around prisons to stop contraband being smuggled over the walls by drone. While that may have generated a temporary reprieve from the tabloids, without serious cash the government risked losing control. With the help of Adam Memon, Truss ordered a simple logical answer to the problem. 'The question was obvious,' Buchanan says. 'How many extra officers would you need to create to bring stability within the system at speed and actually rehabilitate people? Liz worked through all this and came up with quite literally a mathematical equation: one officer was needed for every six inmates. So her next question was, "What does that cost?"'

The answer was 2,500 extra officers at a cost of £104 million. And with that began a furious Whitehall lobbying operation to get the cash. Letters to the Treasury included dire warnings about spice as raised by the prisons ombudsman, and amid a climate of increasingly negative headlines just months into a new government, Chancellor Philip Hammond folded. Buchanan was impressed, having only worked for Truss for a matter of weeks: 'She took it to Hammond, who never knowingly opened his purse, and made the case and won £100 million for a Cinderella service: it was hats off.' She adds that Truss had set out clearly what she wanted and did not stop until she got it: 'What I've learnt working in politics is that the most important thing you need is the ability to make a decision. There's nothing potentially more dangerous for a government than people that can't make a decision. And it was clear there Liz could make a decision.'

According to Buchanan, after four years as a minister, Truss was getting the hang of running the show, and getting the better of the mandarins. A long-running civil service joke among those who had worked with Truss was: 'What is the difference between Liz Truss and a Rottweiler? The dog will let something go eventually.'

Going public with the recruitment of 2,500 extra officers in the run-up to Philip Hammond's first Budget, Truss warned that the prison system was at a 'breaking point'. In a direct blue-on-blue jibe she echoed Tory hardman Michael Howard's insistence that 'prison works', stating, 'What is clear is that the system isn't working.' The right-wing papers lapped it up, and even the *Guardian* cheered on the 'end of austerity'. Behind the scenes the Treasury had already signed off the package as part of the Autumn Statement due at the end of November. However, with daily headlines of tumult in another prison the announcement was brought forward. As such, Wednesday 2 November 2016 produced not only Truss's best headlines, but also her most successful moment in the entire role.

But what happened at the High Court the following day nearly ended her career. As the *Mirror* reported on Thursday 3 November: 'At 10am this morning the High Court could deliver a judgement that threatens to create constitutional chaos. The judges have been asked to rule on whether Theresa May has the right to trigger Article 50 – the process which begins our leaving the EU – without parliamentary approval. The claimants, led by a fund manager Gina Miller, say MPs should have the right to decide and vote on when Article 50 is invoked.'

The result was greeted with fury by the Eurosceptic press, which interpreted the High Court's ruling in favour of the claimants as an attempt to deliberately frustrate the Brexit process. And there was no paper more furious, or more articulate in that fury, than the *Daily Mail*. It splashed images of the three offending High Court judges on its front page, above the infamous headline: 'Enemies of the people'. Its sister website *Mail Online* also initially described one of the trio – Master of the Rolls Sir Terence Etherton – as an 'openly-gay ex-Olympic fencer', a label that prompted uproar on social media.

Truss was mingling with senior members of the judiciary at a dinner at Middle Temple when the front page dropped. Despite it being discussed that evening, allies of Truss say 'nobody seemed that bothered or thought it was a big deal straight away'. But amid the running sore of the referendum, the backlash to the *Mail* splash was fierce. The following morning barristers, politicians and others queued up to demand that Truss condemn the 'serious and unjustified' attacks on the judges, while the hashtag #wheresliztruss started trending on Twitter. Former attorney general turned Euro-fanatic Dominic Grieve said, with his characteristic understatement, that the newspaper's comments were 'chilling and outrageous' and 'smacking of the fascist state'; Truss's nemesis Bob Neill was quick to suggest they were 'threatening the independence of our judiciary' and had 'no place in a civilised land'.[3] Truss recalls: 'It was one of those things where, a bit like the cheese speech, it blew up afterwards. But for me it was always an issue of free speech and the idea that you have an independent judiciary doesn't mean that it can never be criticised or scrutinised and I think that's a fundamental belief of mine.' While Truss's Spads were split on whether to respond, the order from No. 10 Chief of Staff Nick Timothy came down from on high: 'say nothing'. Truss's allies are still angry that 'she was not allowed to get out there and make her case despite the reality being a bit more complex than the row would suggest'.

'The problem with Theresa's whole operation at the time was they were basically control freaks,' one source involved in the row says; 'They would rather nothing was said than anyone actually get out there and explain the logic.' Buchanan and fellow Spad Tim Pitt, a lawyer by trade, scrambled for a middle way. While Truss had sworn an oath to protect the independence of the Judiciary, Pitt had dived into complexities of the law to try to work out what was actually expected of the Lord Chancellor in practice. Buchanan explains that while the job of the Lord Chancellor is to defend the judges, 'it doesn't say that you have to do that within 45 minutes of a disobliging headline of the *Daily Mail*'.

Sources say Truss's 'absolute instinct at the time' was to say: 'Well it's not my business to tell a free press what they can and cannot do. The two fundamental pillars of a liberal democracy are free speech and an independent judiciary and I'm not going to prize one over the other.' Buchanan adds: 'So we were caught in this kind of Scylla and Charybdis dilemma; we were damned if we did and damned if we didn't.' One aide told Truss: 'You've got two choices, and both are shit' – defy No. 10 and face the sack, or defy the public pressure to step in and lose the confidence of the sector. In the end the worst of both happened. It was only after the Bar Council passed a resolution demanding Truss condemn the 'attacks' as a 'matter of urgency' that she finally issued a terse three-line statement on Saturday 5 November, two days after the drama had begun. 'The independence of the judiciary is the foundation upon which our rule of law is built and our judiciary is rightly respected the world over for its independence and impartiality. In relation to the case heard in the High Court, the government has made it clear it will appeal to the supreme court. Legal process must be followed.'

Truss's allies claim that the form of words had been agreed with Lord Thomas in a call that weekend, but it did little to quell the row. Even then No. 10 were furious amid confusion over who had signed off the quote, despite its anodyne nature. Truss's comments spoke of the need to defend judges' independence and impartiality; but its timidity and tardiness simply fuelled critics further. Too little too late was the view from the judiciary; meanwhile, the battle had been adopted as a new front in the Brexit culture war. Fellow Tory MP Anna Soubry, still seething from the referendum result, lambasted Truss, saying she 'has a duty to condemn the vilification, including a homophobic attack, of our judiciary … she has failed in her duty to defend our judiciary. As a former barrister I'm embarrassed and appalled.' Labour's Lord Falconer demanded her dismissal as her response 'signals to the judges that they have lost their constitutional protector'.[4] Truss was becoming increasingly agitated that her career was now collateral damage in a bigger battle. A friend says: 'She was caught between stools. But there was so much nonsense around that No. 10 would not allow her to correct.' Looking back on the episode, Truss is the first to admit: 'I think I could have gone out and done a better defence, and got on the front foot. On the other hand there is no point in doing these jobs unless you stand up for what you believe in.'

It was Truss's worst weekend in politics since news of her affair rocked Norfolk seven years earlier. That Sunday, Theresa May called her at 7 a.m. to ask how she was, and to warn her that she would be doubling down on the row when she spoke to reporters on board her plane ahead of a trade trip to India. The PM told the travelling Lobby: 'I believe in and value the independence of our judiciary. I also value the freedom of our press. These both underpin our democracy.' But Truss found little support in the wider party, with Tory backbenchers criticising her at a private meeting the following day; hardly a surprise perhaps given that 119 MPs had practised or read law.[5] 'From that moment,' says an aide, 'she was fucked in the job basically.' Buchanan says: 'She is a very optimistic, very resilient person; I've only seen that falter twice and this was one of the times. The pressure on her from sections of the media to come out and the pressure from the judiciary was intense. Downing Street were, you know, "nope, hold the line" and her own gut instinct was it's not my job to tell the media what they can and cannot write.' While there might have eventually been a long-term benefit to the row – with Buchanan suggesting it 'helped cement that Brexiteer icon status'[6] – it felt like Truss was closer to the door that weekend. Some senior Tories, though, think Truss would have enjoyed the predicament more than she let on, as was the case during the childcare ratio row with the Lib Dems four years earlier. 'This one really did put her on the map,' a Cabinet colleague would claim.

Recollections vary as to whether this was a fight encouraged by No. 10. One May ally recalls: 'People have convinced themselves that "Enemies of the People" and "Crush the Saboteurs" was government rhetoric: it wasn't, it was the media.

If the independence of the judiciary is so fragile that it's damaged by what someone writes in the *Daily Mail* then I'm a bit alarmed by the independence of the judiciary in the first place.' They continue: 'Theresa had a bit of an attitude with the MoJ because the Home Office and the MoJ rub up against each other so much. Theresa thought of it as the department for lawyers, by lawyers, of lawyers, only really interested in lawyers and quite consciously wanted a non-lawyer in the job.'

The following week Truss denied she had failed to defend the judges and suggested she was seeking to balance the rule of law with the liberties of the press. 'An independent judiciary is the cornerstone of the rule of law, vital to our constitution and freedoms', she wrote in a letter to *The Times* with the permission of No. 10. 'It is my duty as Lord Chancellor to defend that independence. I swore to do so under my oath of office. I take that very seriously and I will always do so.' She also said that the independent judiciary was robust enough to withstand attacks by the *Daily Mail* and other newspapers.

The defence still did little to silence her critics. Lord Judge, who served as Lord Chief Justice from 2008 to 2013, said she had caused a 'constitutional breakdown' and may have broken the law and her oath of office by failing to defend judges.[7] He accused Truss of collaborating with Downing Street, citing her hesitation in responding and the wording of her eventual statement. 'The whole point of the Lord Chancellor's job is that he or she is there to take an independent line,' he said. Given Truss had agreed on the form of words with Lord Thomas, the Lord Chief Justice held off from public criticism that weekend but would eventually put the boot in five months later on a different matter. Lord Dyson, the former Master of the Rolls, contrasted in his memoirs the 'charming' Gove with the 'disastrous' Truss and suggested the latter was more concerned with trying to avoid upsetting the media than performing her statutory duty.[8]

Kwarteng says that Justice 'was probably the most challenging of all her jobs. I don't think it was a natural fit. But again she put her shoulder to the wheel and wanted to do a good job. I think there was a natural bias against her, [from] the legal establishment. They were a bit snooty. I think she was still quite inexperienced and it was obviously a challenging time.' The 'Enemies of the People' scandal 'undermined her in that job, but again I think she learnt from that. I think she was quite deferential to Theresa, but I think Theresa's Number 10 was a total shit show; they didn't have a clue what they wanted to do. They didn't back her, they didn't do anything.'

With her confidence knocked, Truss struggled to regain her stature in the job. In the House of Commons a few weeks after the row, one Labour backbencher asked Truss how the MoJ intended to stop contraband from being dropped into prisons. She outlined several measures before proudly telling the House that: 'Last week I was at HMP Pentonville, which now has patrol dogs whose barking helps to deter drones. We are using all sorts of solutions to deal with contraband entering our prisons.' The answer sparked mirth in the chamber: behind her, prisons minister Sam Gyimah smirked and pursed his lips; one Labour MP shouted: 'It's the minister who is barking!' Tory backbencher Victoria Prentis meanwhile stood up to ask tongue-in-cheek about the training being given to governors to ensure proper procurement process for 'the recruitment of the dogs that bark at drones'. Ridicule was instant but what followed two weeks later was even worse.

In the middle of December 2016, a 14-hour riot involving at least six hundred prisoners broke out at the G4S-run HMP Birmingham. 'Chronic staff shortages' would eventually be blamed for the mass disturbance that broke out on four wings on the morning of 16 December. The riot was sparked after two prisoners climbed on the netting in one of the wings and, along with four other inmates, were able to seize a set of keys. 'The whole prison nearly went under,' a Truss ally admits. 'We were getting reports of someone bleeding out in the yard and we couldn't get an ambulance in. There was some suggestion the prisoners might have the capacity to scale the walls and run amok in Birmingham. It was about as bad as it gets.' Relations between the Justice Secretary and Prison Service boss Michael Spurr had been 'trixy' for some time according to insiders, but given that HMP Birmingham was a privately run jail, the MoJ had to wait until invited before sending in specialist riot squads. When that finally happened after 11 hours of rioting, more than £2 million worth of damage had been inflicted in one of the worst prison riots since Strangeways in 1990. Truss responded by declaring that 'the full force of the law' would be used against the rioters; a response quickly lampooned, given their incarcerated status. But a year later the five ringleaders would be jailed for a further 36 years and the prison was brought back under MoJ control from G4S in 2018.

In spite of her prominent post and the very public setbacks, Truss was still yet to become a household name. League table rankings for ConservativeHome, compiled from Tory member preferences, show her in lower-mid-table obscurity around this time. Even Truss's old school friends struggled to recognise her at the 2016 Conservative Party Conference. At a bar an extremely inebriated delegate approached Truss, saying: 'I know you – didn't you used to go to Roundhay?' 'Yes I did,' replied Truss. 'Do you remember me?' continued her interrogator. 'It's Pete, I went to Roundhay at the same time as you! How are you doing?' 'Well, what do you do now?' he added. She replied: 'I'm the Lord Chancellor.' It would not be the only time Truss's past would rear its head that week in Birmingham. At a *Spectator* party, witnesses claim Mark Field had enjoyed the flowing Pol Roger champagne, and made a number of extremely 'ungentlemanly' comments to fellow partygoers about his affair with Truss. When word got back to Truss's team, warnings were sent to Field via an emissary that the Chief Whip would be notified if such an incident was ever to happen again.

Little improved for Truss in 2017. Lord Thomas had kept his powder dry at the height of the 'Enemies of the People' row, but would take aim in March over Truss's plans to spare rape victims the brutality of court-room interrogation. Truss told the *Sunday Times* on 19 March that video cross-examination would be introduced in adult rape trials after a pilot scheme involving child victims. The MoJ added that the new nationwide scheme 'will spare rape victims the trauma and inconvenience of attending court [and] will be rolled out across the country from September. Victims of rape and other sex crimes will have their cross-examination evidence pre-recorded and played during the trial.' Truss herself said: 'I am determined to make their path to justice swifter and less traumatic.' The plan was to include the measures as an amendment to Gove's resurrected Prisons and Courts Bill that had caused her so much grief in her first days in the department. The MoJ had even signed off the press release with a senior judge.

But enter Lord Thomas. Usually the House of Lords Constitution Committee is a sleepy hollow when it comes to Westminster fireworks. Not so on 22 March when Thomas gave a valedictory appearance before his impending retirement. Asked by fellow peers what his concerns were about the state of Justice, he warmed up with 'the first area of extreme worry for my money is Brexit'. And then he unloaded on Truss's announcement about rape trials: 'I regret to say that we had to correct a serious misapprehension that had arisen as a result of what the ministry said at the end of last week about the rollout and the way we were proceeding with pre-recorded evidence. They had misunderstood the thing completely.' Thomas claimed the policy only applied to minors, adding: 'Yesterday, I had to write to all the judges to explain that unfortunately what the ministry had said was wrong. It is very time consuming. It is fair to say that there is not sufficient depth … We have put it right now, but it is not something we should have to do.' As softly spoken drive-by shootings go, it was unprecedented. But Thomas was not content to leave it there.

Asked about the great row with the *Mail*, he hit out: 'In short, I believe that the Lord Chancellor is completely and utterly wrong in her view. I regret to have to criticise her as severely as I have, but to my mind she is completely and absolutely wrong about this, as I have said, and I am very disappointed. I understand what the pressures were in November, but she has taken a position that is constitutionally absolutely wrong. I am sorry, but there is no point mincing words.' Picked up on that, he replied: 'I do not think I have said anything controversial, at least to lawyers.'

'It certainly felt like revenge to us,' says a source close to Truss, with her policy announcement in tatters. Ironically, one of the first acts of her new government in 2022 would see the very same measures rolled out across the country for adults as well as minors.

With Thomas on the way out, relations with the senior judiciary came under fresh strain a month later in April when the Lord Chief Justice vacancy was advertised. It stipulated that the successful candidate must serve four years in the post – in effect ruling out the legal establishment's preferred contender Sir Brian Leveson because he would have to serve beyond the usual judicial retirement age of 70. Famed for his controversial media inquiry, his selection would have been an incendiary appointment. Truss instead wanted Sir Ernest Ryder, a 'low-key moderniser', as the next head of the judiciary. As senior president of tribunals, he had worked closely with Truss – a fellow northerner – on court and tribunal reforms, including introducing more online hearings. 'She likes Ernie,' a senior Conservative told *The Times*. 'He's not a chin-stroker but someone who rolls up their sleeves and gets the job done.' But her support reportedly made other senior judges 'livid'; and it was seen as revenge for her treatment over 'Enemies of the People'.[9] In the end events in Westminster would take the decision out of her hands.

On 18 April 2017, Theresa May unexpectedly called a snap general election. Like the vast majority of the Cabinet, Truss barely figured in the Tory campaign. By this point Cabinet Secretary Sir Jeremy Heywood was said to have been advising the PM that relations with the judiciary were in such dire straits that Truss would have to be moved, if as expected the Tories crushed Jeremy Corbyn and returned with a massive majority.

Reflecting on Truss's time at Justice, a friend said: 'She knows that she made mistakes there, she alienated everyone. At the end of the day that whole department is really pro judges, and really anti prisoner. And Liz was very anti judge and very pro prisoner. So she alienated everyone. But she finally learnt a hard lesson that actually, you have to be quite pragmatic and move people with you. She had no friends there.' Another adds: 'It was a grim time for Liz. There was someone dying in a prison every three days, prison riots, and constant battles every day with people who dismissed her as a ditz.' But her defenders are quick to point out that securing the cash for 2,500 extra guards was no small feat, even if it was to be eclipsed by everything else.

Truss had arrived at Justice all ears. It was a significant step up from Defra, and one that meant she leant on advice. 'She walked in there and told herself, "I'll listen to what everyone's telling me",' recalls one ally. But fast-forward 11 months, 'and her view is that it almost ended her career by being too dependent on advice and not following her own instincts'. It was not a mistake she was willing to make again.

2017

DEMOTION

Friday 9 June 2017 was the day the machine took back control of 10 Downing Street. As the sheer scale of Theresa May's humiliation dawned, senior civil servants sensed the government might fall over at any moment. Her election gamble had spectacularly backfired and her routed political team had mostly scarpered. The strong and stable PM had bet the house on securing a landslide; instead the Tories shed 13 seats and lost their majority. May's once feared Chiefs of Staff Nick Timothy and Fiona Hill were off, the markets wobbled and the 317 Tory MPs that remained were mutinous. The Prime Minister was in mortal danger.

With Chief Whip Gavin Williamson sent to Belfast to try to negotiate a deal with the DUP to prop up the Tories, No. 10 was left politically rudderless. As Cabinet Office Director of Probity and Ethics, Sue Gray was used to being the Whitehall judge and jury. Usually her role during reshuffles was limited to asking the successfully appointed ministers questions about their finances, mistresses and internet search histories. But that weekend she was playing executioner too. By Friday lunchtime Gray was holed up in May's private office, running the infamous reshuffle whiteboard in lieu of Spads and spinners ... except no one could be put to the wall with a PM too weak to actually sack anyone.

Throughout that disastrous eight-week campaign, Fleet Street had claimed there was one Cabinet minister who was clearly for the chop: Philip Hammond. Those closest to May do little to dispute that getting rid of the Chancellor was a post-election 'priority' for the team. As polling day approached, the PM had also openly discussed with her now-vanquished chiefs whether it might be time to bring back Michael Gove, having banished him to the backbenches just a year earlier. 'There was no specific plan to sack Liz,' one insider recalls, 'but she was certainly vulnerable to being moved.'

While Truss's departure from Justice looked likely, the election result meant that stability was now the order of the day. Reeling from the disaster of yet another hung Parliament, a boring reshuffle was one of the only tools left to No. 10 to try to restore order. With the markets jittery, the big three jobs were quickly reappointed that Friday afternoon: Hammond would stay at No. 11, Boris Johnson at the Foreign Office, and Amber Rudd at Home. Michael Fallon was also given the nod to continue at Defence and David Davis would carry on at the Brexit Department – where divorce negotiations in Brussels were due to commence in just 10 days' time.

'The stardust sprinkled on the reshuffle' was the return of Gove to Environment. But the PM needed friends fast and that meant promotions for senior allies with no desire for the crown themselves. Damian Green – an Oxford contemporary and family friend of the Mays – was the new Chancellor of the Duchy of Lancaster, with the added bauble of de facto Deputy Prime Minister. Had Gray been doing her ethics job with her full attention, she might well have asked Green about historic allegations that he once watched porn on a Commons computer; a revelation that led to his downfall just six months later. But it was all hands to the pump that day saving May. Green's elevation left a hole at Pensions that was filled by another Remainer in David Gauke, triggering a vacancy as Chief Secretary to the Treasury. With May building a praetorian guard around her of somewhat-over-the-hill greybeards, her 'obvious ally' David Lidington also needed to be 'higher up the Cabinet batting order', according to one involved in negotiations. With that decision Liz Truss's fate as Justice Secretary was sealed.

Truss did not take the rejection well. Friends say the erratic behaviour that followed that Sunday evening must be blamed squarely on the food poisoning she had suffered at her Norfolk count four days earlier. Others who saw her when she arrived to meet the Prime Minister suspected she may have been drowning her sorrows in the sweltering sunshine like many Tories that weekend. Michael Gove, the new Environment Secretary, had been at the cricket and looked well refreshed as he walked into No. 10 for his Lazarus-like return. An hour later Truss arrived too, looking somewhat pallid after hot-footing it straight from a 'thank you' BBQ with her local donors in Swaffham. 'It wasn't made clear the reshuffle was going to happen before Monday until suddenly it was,' an aide recalls, 'so it was a bit of a rush to even get her there.' 'Theresa had to see Truss before she could give her job to Lidders,' says a Mayite; 'the whole thing was manic.'

But it was the boiling rage that Truss was in after a notably brief chat in May's study that most witnesses remember to this day. Demoted, and stripped of a £15,000 salary, Truss was livid. 'I think this is incredibly unfair,' she told the PM after being informed she was being downgraded. After four years as a full member of the Cabinet, she was now only invited to attend its meetings. It was a relegation to the fringes of the top table and a very public blow. Truss felt the loyalty she had shown over 'Enemies of the People' was now being thrown in her face. As the new Chief Secretary to the Treasury was guided through the usual post-appointment paperwork, one witness said: 'She was incandescent. Absolutely furious.' When she reached an anteroom to be briefed on new lines to take, an official remembered 'pure fury in her eyes'. A one-sided A4 script of the government's stabilising messaging was put in her hand, but Truss simply screwed it up into a ball and threw it onto the carpet. Witnesses are split over whether she stamped on the offending document for good measure. But she walked out of the famous black door without a word to anyone – leaving No. 10 staff equally speechless.

Demoted and demoralised, Truss took up her post on the Monday morning. Licking her wounds, she was 'seething for a good couple of days' according to one ally. For the third time in a row Truss had ended up in a role almost by accident rather than by design. While she had dreamed of the Treasury for years it was as Chancellor rather than the penny-pinching, bean-counting and ultimately thankless role of Chief Secretary. Your mission is to simply keep saying no to colleagues who want more money, while the Chancellor plays good cop handing out sweeties. As ever in times of strife for Truss, it fell to Gillian Shephard to see the wood from the trees. According to a friend, Gillian told her: 'Honestly Liz, this is a dream job for you. This job will be the making of you.' Whether she believed her or not, Truss was convinced by Baroness Shephard to dust herself down. 'Gillian made the case that Liz could get herself across policy, across government and get her tentacles into all the things she liked, all over the place.'

The move also reunited Truss with old ally Kwasi Kwarteng who, still some way down the pecking order, had been appointed Parliamentary Private Secretary to the Chancellor Philip Hammond. Recalling the demotion, Kwarteng says: 'I think she showed a lot of character there, I mean a lot of people – someone like a Sajid Javid – would have just walked. He would have, but she didn't. She wanted to be a team player. She wanted to stay in government. She wanted to contribute as a minister and I think the chief secretary role really made her.' She was to part ways with Kirsty Buchanan, who headed to No. 10 after Justice, though the pair stayed in touch. Instead, Truss had to rely on the services of novice Spad Kane Daniell, a CCHQ researcher best known for trying to infiltrate a UKIP conference under a fake name. Buchanan told the BBC's *Newscast* that the move to CST shook Truss's confidence in her abilities, though 'she has a bounce back factor like Tigger'. Another friend points out the move gave her the 'bandwidth to think' about the future, adding: 'It was, in some ways, less intense than Secretary of State and she'd got a young family as well. It was good to have a role that allowed her to step back and give her a bit of space. She still talks about that as quite an emotional pivot point for her, that she decided at that point to much more lean into being herself and be who she was and not be ashamed of that.'

At Justice and Environment Truss had fronted two spending departments; now, as Hammond's deputy, she was to be poacher-turned-gamekeeper, taking an axe to profligate Whitehall spending. Early reaction to Truss's appointment was negative: the commentariat predicted her imminent demise at the next reshuffle. Yet Truss's time at the Treasury proved to be a turning point. Previously, the Tory leadership had promoted her at every turn, and she in turn was – publicly at least – a model of conformity. Now though, her fortunes had changed: her career was in the balance, with few admirers in No. 10. Colleagues in the Treasury remember Truss for the first few months as 'very, very unsure of herself'. One staffer puts it: 'Her confidence had been knocked a lot and [she] didn't really have anything to do, candidly, because Philip Hammond kind of cut her out of everything. Her advice was not welcome or sought.' Hammond's former special adviser Sonia Khan insists the pair got on at the beginning, however: 'They are both very, very forensic. I know people called him "Spreadsheet Phil" but Liz can master a spreadsheet better than anyone else I know so I think as PM people will be surprised that she will have such a keen eye on numbers. It was a good relationship and where they did disagree, it wasn't personal. It was just professional. Neither of them are people who are very emotional.'

Hammond's staff insist that he had full faith in her role as steward of spending, joking to his team: 'if there's anyone more hawkish than me on spending in the Conservative Party then it's Liz Truss'. Problems arose, however, due to a lack of formal Spending Review for her to oversee in 2017, with the 2016 settlement rolled over on a yearly basis due to the chaos of Brexit preparations. But Hammond's supporters accepted he ran a tight ship on major fiscal events and budgets – with little room for input from his number two. According to his then-PPS Kwasi Kwarteng, 'Hammond liked her, but Hammond was quite a closed, very centrally controlling Chancellor. He is a very capable guy, but I think he liked to keep things within a very tight circle. Him and the very senior officials.' Khan remembers: 'There was real nervousness around big set pieces. I don't think it was that she wasn't in a particular set or grouping but I think there was a sense that the Chancellor had to keep the fiscal events really tight. But probably out of all the Treasury ministers, Liz is the one that he liked the most and respected the most.' Truss herself would later joke to her team that if she had to choose to have a drink with either Hammond, Rishi Sunak or Keir Starmer, then it would be Hammond.

Khan insists the relationship with 'Big Phil' 'was much better than people say and report. I think he really respected the fact that she always stood her ground. She would say what she thought, she would never shy away from the causes that she was interested in. She would speak her mind even if people didn't like it. And I think they would be quite happy having a bit of a row, a bit of back and forth and then both just [leaving] it there.' A Treasury insider tells a different version of events though: 'The Spads basically just tried to manage her away from things. The Treasury didn't take her seriously. She was very unsure of herself. Hammond and the Spad team were like "what is this?" basically, and they wanted her to be a very, very loyal pliant number two who didn't do anything. That was never going to work for Liz. The Treasury civil servants basically saw her as someone to be managed. But that was always going to come back to bite them in the arse.'

While ministerial relations could be distant, there were a number of officials with whom Truss got on, including James Bowler, the then-Director General in charge of public spending, who would later join her as Permanent Secretary at Trade. Friends say other DGs and deputy DGs, including Anthony Segal-Knowles and Jean-Christophe Gray, who now works for Prince William, were fans. 'They were people who basically took her seriously and could see that, actually, she was a very kind of serious, wonkish type person,' one Treasury staffer says. However, Treasury boss Sir Tom Scholar was said to be dismissive of Truss, setting in motion his own ousting five years later.

Scrambling around for a role in the building, Truss began to commission research and advice on monetary policy, tax reforms and regulation. 'She treated the Treasury like her own personal think tank,' one insider remembers. Amid fears that some of the wilder research would leak and plunge the whole of HMT into a row, some of the advice sought was blocked. Truss fixated on certain areas, constantly badgering Hammond's advisers about free ports to the extent it became a No. 11 in-joke. A friend recalls: 'She struggled to really have anything to do, basically, to be totally honest. So she rolled into a lot of other policy areas that were not relevant to the brief. She started doing a bit on crypto, she started doing loads of stuff on maths, but she was poorly managed, so she got bored and ended up causing mischief.'

Nowhere did that mischief come into play more than on social media. All politicians have their favoured medium of communication: Winston Churchill had his wireless, Harold Wilson had the television. Liz Truss preferred Instagram. It was in December 2017 that she really began to embrace the medium, turning her account public on the advice of Jason Stein, a Treasury official with whom she rapidly forged a close political alliance after he was made her official spokesman. A wily operator, Stein was something of a gun for hire. After a brief stint as a reporter for the *Jewish Telegraph*, he cut his PR teeth in the

European Parliament spinning for the Party of European Socialists before transferring to the Department for Work and Pensions. A card-carrying Tory however, Stein would become one of Truss's closest confidants over her time in the Treasury – often to the chagrin of Hammond's team, who were suspicious of their motives.

Sonia Khan says Truss was inspired by social media influencers: 'I always wonder if she just spotted someone from another country or someone from like a popular TV show who had a really great Instagram and she just thought, "No one's doing that in politics, I'll do that." She knows what influencers are doing, what trends are coming up, what entrepreneurs are doing … It was very driven by her.' A Treasury official recalls: 'She started putting all kinds of zany photos out. And people started thinking, "Oh, actually, she's quite interesting." Guido started tweeting about her a bit more. And it just kind of grew and grew into something that it was actually never intended to be. It was supposed to be a little bit of fun. But what actually happened was it became kind of a way for her to express her views without ever having to actually say anything, staying just on the right side of the line, but making her point.'

Ministerial visits began to be shaped around photo opportunities, but quirkier than the standard 'dress up in high-viz and point at things' mantra, so loved by some politicians at the time. Khan says: 'I remember when we were looking at visits, and one of the fashion chains was on the cusp of becoming a unicorn [a startup valued at more than $1 billion] or reached a big milestone and she went to visit them. That was just really reflective of Liz, rather than doing the George Osborne uniform which was very popular at the time of let's get a hard hat on and go on a construction visit. She was always thinking about "what's the best creative visit and how can I get the best content and what's going to look good on my Instagram?" It was all driven by her, people have advisers but her Instagram was hers alone.' At the time Instagram was a little-used tool in Westminster, with a classic example being a much-mocked series of stilted images posted by CCHQ of scowling ministers allegedly enjoying the 2017 Party Conference. 'Into the middle of that comes Liz Truss with loads of funny hashtags and weird shit and she got the piss taken out of her,' says a Treasury source. 'And whereas others would recoil from that, she almost thrived on getting that flack and she got this profile where she doesn't care.'

As so often with Truss, data came into play, with the private office setting targets on the number of followers she needed to reach by certain key dates. Her posts became more frequent and sophisticated. 'I remember her asking me how to put filters on an Instagram story,' Khan says, 'and I was like, "I've got no idea", so she just worked it out herself. She was really particular with visits and photographs. I think she probably was the queen of a good photograph before Rishi Sunak – and she always said that you can't take one without getting your feet in there.' Truss quickly developed a taste for showing off her quirky side with humorous captions too. 'The barriers have been broken down between politicians and the public,' she explained. 'You just have to be what you are actually like and people can take it or leave it.'[1]

Her posts on Twitter also reflected a change in tone. Out went slavishly punting the latest CCHQ line-to-take; in came tweets about 'crypto-communist Corbyn', step-counts and hashtags like 'megabantz'. Pop culture references came in the form of quoting Calvin Harris when attacking Corbyn's policies that were #acceptableinthe80s, or affectionately referencing Destiny's Child when giving economic commentary about 'All The Honeys Making Money'. In the torturous purgatory of the 2017–19 hung Parliament there was little for Tories to cheer, so Truss's posts about vegan burger bars and vape shops as the 'modern pioneers of British freedom' provided some light relief. One sketch-writer christened her 'the part-time minister for Instagram and full-time human GIF'.[2] Truss's own mantra was: 'Post first, think later.' By 2019, when her feed was littered with celebrity selfies with Taylor Swift, Toff from *Made in Chelsea* and Andrew Lloyd Webber, the account had something of a cult following across Westminster and the picture desks of Fleet Street.

This somewhat unconventional approach divided opinion but began paying dividends in aiding Truss's political regeneration. Her public image had been of an awkward, dull careerist, best known for that speech about cheese. Those early posts played a part in knocking off the harder edges, allowing her to display more of the relentless humour that her friends know well. One former aide says of her Instagram posts: 'I don't think it was about her upping her profile actually, I think it was more about her going "there's quite a fun side of me which I try to keep to the side in politics" and actually her going "you know what, life's too short, I can be fun and I'm going to not hide that bit of me any more."' Another friend rejects any comparison with Theresa May, whose falteringly robotic performances in the 2017 Election had earned her the nickname 'the Maybot'. 'She's much more fun than Theresa and her politics have a much more decidedly libertarian bent. Her time at the Treasury helped display her personality more.' Reflecting on this period in an interview with the *Sunday Times* in 2022, Truss said: 'I thought: "I'm not just going to sit here and take the hits, I'm going to do what I think is right and what I want to do and I'm going to follow my political instincts." That experience unleashed me. Theresa May did me a favour.'

While Truss's Instagram rebrand took off, so did a personal style makeover. Gone was a signature blue dress and grey blazer, in came bold colours and power suits. Aides recall her seeking style inspiration from a very unusual place: a particularly well-dressed young civil servant that Truss took an intense shine to. The official, who worked in the Treasury digital team, was quickly befriended by the Chief Secretary and invited to go shopping one Saturday morning. Khan remembers: 'She was really junior. She can't have been much older than her early twenties. Liz really took inspiration from the young women around her and took counsel and I thought that was quite nice, because it's kind of unusual for a minister in their forties to go shopping with a 20-year-old.' Trips to New Look, Karen Millen, LK Bennett and Whistles saw an entire new wardrobe acquired over a number of months, and on the advice of her new young friend. 'That's where the bold colours started to come from and the trouser suits so moving away from some of the politician-type clothing,' Khan added. 'It reflects a willingness to always listen and learn and evolve and lean on people who have the skills or expertise that she doesn't have. There's a great deal of self-awareness with her.' The friendship, however, came to an abrupt halt. Accounts vary of exactly why, but insiders say a fall-out over a planned shopping trip cancelled at short notice due to personal issues lay at the heart of the rupture and the young civil servant refused to ever speak to Truss again.

The Instagram project was not without its problems either, and as Truss's profile rose, so did the sniping from sharp-elbowed colleagues. One snap shared by Truss from a private party fundraiser revealed controversial Russian donor Lubov Chernukhin being entertained by Theresa May after donating £135,000 to party funds, splashed the *Daily Mail*. The PM had pledged to crack down on Russian influence on British politics in the wake of the Salisbury nerve agent attack in March 2018, so was particularly aggrieved. Another selfie of the Treasury team on the frontbench breached Commons rules about photography. The former incident enraged her colleagues, with one MP claiming: 'This is why she'll have three supporters come election time.'[3]

Despite raising her profile, Truss was left languishing in the Cabinet second division throughout 2018. Multiple Cabinet ministers left office in two reshuffles that year, with no promotion granted by Mrs May. On a day of Whitehall musical chairs that January, Truss greeted the changes with a tongue-in-cheek Instagram post on a visit to a carpentry shop captioned 'learning how to put together a cabinet'.

'I think there's a danger in politics of being too risk-averse,' Truss said in an interview with the *Spectator* that year: 'I've fallen into that trap in the past and I'm not going to fall into it again. I'm now more honest about what I think.'[4] That new philosophy certainly took shape in some battles she chose to have with her own party. Her public speeches now revealed much more of her private dry sense of humour too. One address to female entrepreneurs at a No. 11 reception decried sexism in venture capitalism, which she compared to a Conservative government dominated by posh men: '90 per cent of all of the money that is coming out of venture capital is going in to all-male teams, not even mixed teams,' she hit out. 'That's a bit like the Conservative Party being entirely run by the Bullingdon Club ... Or like the pop music industry being 90 per cent boy bands – and never having Little Mix or the Spice Girls. That is what we're missing out on.' To her detractors, such speeches validated their criticisms of Truss: self-serving, not a team player. But a growing number of supporters were warming to her public embrace of free markets and her unconventional habit of quoting Beyoncé to make her case. It's clear she took the cause personally too, adding: Women are the ultimate new entrants – we have moved into places that have previously been domi-nated by men. We've had to make our voices heard, we've had to do things differently to get through and to get our message through. I've worked in the oil industry and I've worked in politics, and often you get told 'play the game, don't rock the boat, behave yourself, and just keep quiet', and that's what people do. Girls get told that at school. That is a fact – we are brought up to be compliant. To behave yourself. Well I say no to that. I think we need to be disruptive, and to face the fact that as a smaller share, whether it's in business or politics, we need to make our voices louder.'[5]

In that vein Truss began to flex her muscles more inside the Treasury. In April 2018 she flew to South America for invest-ment talks, but it was an FT interview in Brazil that raised hackles back home. The paper reported: 'There will be no further rise in public spending unless the UK economy grows faster than official projections, said Liz Truss.' She had told them explicitly: 'It would be wrong just at a time when we've got the public finances under control to put the spending cart before the growth horse.' With May and Hammond negotiating a massive increase in NHS spending, signalling the end of the austerity era back home, she was wildly off message.

But Truss was not done there. When an *FT* hack promoted the story online as 'under pressure across Whitehall, HMT barks from abroad', she sarcastically retweeted the sneer to her 600,000 followers adding 'Woof, woof …'. Hammond hit the roof. A former aide recalls: 'The tweet set off a firestorm. Hammond was immediately on the phone, complaining she had broken the collective department position. And at that point she bluntly said, "Well, tell me what the economic strategy is?" And she had a point, they would never read her into anything, so it was a self-fulfilling prophecy when she went rogue. She was never told anything so she was never bound into anything.' 'I don't think it was unusual for Liz to have her own line,' remembers Sonia Khan, but, she adds: 'People were grumpy but it wasn't the worst thing in the world. I think that's probably where most Treasury civil servants were: they liked Liz and liked a lot of what she said, it's just she probably shouldn't have said as much on the record as she wanted.'

The *FT* interview was not the only outburst that got Truss into trouble that trip. Truss lost her temper and told one aide that they 'should have been shot at birth' during an argument. Multiple sources say the official in question was signed off from work for a number of weeks after the incident, but a Treasury spokesman claimed in 2022 that was unrelated. Picking another major fight on calorie counts on menus that summer, Truss sought permission to formally object to the policy when it reached Cabinet clearance 'write round'. But the Treasury position was in favour. Frantic phone calls were made from the newly promoted Health Secretary Matt Hancock, who stepped up after the resignation of Boris Johnson over Brexit saw Jeremy Hunt promoted to Foreign Secretary. An insider recalls, 'Hancock called and said, "Look Liz, I don't want to do this. I got lumbered with this. This is all Jeremy Hunt's stuff. Theresa May's pushing this, you know, please, please, please can you not make my life hard?" And she told him, "I think this is mental. Why are you doing this stuff?"' In the end Hammond put his foot down and said, 'we can't have two Treasury positions'.

Truss was certainly getting used to rocking the boat. On the future of the party, Truss had been in close discussion with Johnson in the run-up to his resignation that July. A source said: 'She was always on at him about organising a state visit for Trump, saying she wanted to meet Ivanka.' When Johnson walked out after May showed her hand at the Chequers summit, upon hearing the news, Truss turned to aides and said: 'That's it, he's gonna be PM.'

Aware of the changing currents around her, Truss sought to build new alliances for the future. One Treasury source contrasts the behaviour of Hammond – aware that he was likely in his last big political job – with that of Truss in how the pair approached briefings with Tory MPs. Hammond did only 'a small amount' of such outreach whereas Truss did it every week, meeting with MPs on topics of interest or by region in either her Treasury office or No. 11. The source says: 'I definitely got the sense that she was just focused on a longer game. I don't mean that she had some *House of Cards* plan to become PM … but the enthusiasm and the time she put into meeting MPs demonstrated she was really trying to build not a constituency but individual relationships with people or really be on their radar.' A friend of Truss would argue, 'Philip Hammond is quite cautious and quite details focused. He's not a big-picture person.' She told friends: 'I just wanted the Conservative Party to move in the right direction, I was going to do whatever it took to make that happen. I'm a campaigner – it's just what I do.'

While Truss was branching out more and more to colleagues, suspicion was deepening about her motives internally. It would lead to the lowest point of Truss's time at the Treasury in October 2018 when she was completely and openly frozen out of the preparations for that year's Autumn Statement. Hammond and his team ensured that Truss 'was cut out of everything, she was not allowed to be in the room for anything'. Her policy suggestions were ignored; Treasury staff were forbidden to speak to Truss about the contents of Hammond's statement. Attempts were even made to have Jason Stein seconded to a different department for the duration of planning, so deep was the mistrust in Hammond's team. At the end of planning meetings, Hammond aide Poppy Trowbridge would close proceedings by saying: 'Not a word of this to Liz Truss, this Budget does not leak.'

But the day before the Statement, Truss was expected to go on the media and 'roll the pitch' on behalf of the Chancellor. She was booked on John Pienaar's 5 Live Sunday-morning radio show, but was extraordinarily still utterly clueless about what would be in the following day's announcement. It fell to one sympathetic Treasury official to smuggle a copy of the sacred Budget Scorecard – the list of all tax and spending changes coming up – out of the building, and brief Truss on its contents in a coffee shop. The move was extremely high risk, and probably illegal, but the copy of the highly secret document slipped back into the Treasury before anyone noticed it was missing.

Truss found out about a massive hike to NHS and Universal Credit spending just minutes before fielding Pienaar's questions about the measures on 5 Live. A Treasury source says: 'That was the first time that Liz Truss, the Chief Secretary to the Treasury, knew what was in the package, it was absurd.' Truss was seething at her treatment – and clearly smug at getting one over the Treasury establishment. The next day she would pick a striking red dress from Karen Millen for the famous No. 11 budget day photoshoot, completely upstaging the drab Hammond on his big day.

But another Treasury figure who was close to Hammond defended the Chancellor's behaviour, insisting: 'Specifically with Liz, she was increasingly cut out of things for the sole reason that she was a leaker. It was either her or people around her who were leaking. For that Budget and Autumn Statement in 2018, she was a lot more excluded [than she was] for the one in autumn of 2017 and that was solely to stop this leaking.' Her sense of isolation would have been increased by Hammond's preference for working from his office in No. 11 rather than the Treasury. This restricted the access for junior ministers, who would have to negotiate via their respective private offices to meet the Chancellor face to face. In the busy days of Brexit, such 'bilaterals' had a habit of getting rescheduled repeatedly, rather than meeting daily; the pair could go weeks without a one-on-one conversation. Hammond's view was 'You get on with your job and I'll get on with mine', according to a former aide. This left Truss trying to 'generate her announcements out of nothing', touring the country and posting facts about different areas on social media.

Mark Littlewood says she 'absolutely' hated aspects of the Treasury and did not hide her contempt. He recalled one meeting in which she convened a range of people from think tanks, business groups and academics when the government was going through its Comprehensive Spending Review. 'She wanted to get in the "sound" people to tell the Treasury exactly what to do and she didn't want any lily-livered people around the table. She was going to construct the agenda in such a way and she wanted me to lead the march. "Make sure you call for everything to be slashed and burned Mark; that's why I've brought you in."' Littlewood added that she 'wanted to rip up some trees, change the dynamics, change the way the system worked'.[6]

Her rhetoric changed that year at the Treasury and, consciously or not, began to echo the style of Boris Johnson. One such example came at the launch of Freer in spring 2018: the IEA-backed successor to the Free Enterprise Group that Truss had begun seven years previously. Truss's relaunch speech mocked Labour as 'humourless po-faced hat-wearing socialists'; she declared that Britain's youth of 'Uber-riding, Airbnb-ing, Deliveroo-eating freedom-fighters' were really 'Tories with attitude'. It was not just her style of speech that changed: the content did too, with Truss drawing on wider themes – a sure sign of any potential leadership candidate. With Tory discontent rising at the May administration's woes, even the ever-cynical Guido Fawkes blog was impressed: 'at a time when the government is dominated by the anti-libertarian, anti-free market, statist dogma of Theresa May and Nick Timothy, this was refreshing to hear'.

It was at the launch of Freer that Truss declared: 'As Chief Secretary to the Treasury, I aim to be the disruptor in chief; I want to challenge those who aim to block change, stop development and restrict success.' Optimism became a staple part of the Truss brand. Gone was the talk of national decline, in its place was what Andrew Marr called a 'cheerful right-winger'. Truss publicly hinted at her frustrations with the misery of the May government: 'We need to look like we're enjoying ourselves because no one wants to go to a party where everyone is looking miserable.'[7] She cultivated the Lobby more assiduously too. One veteran hack recalls lunch with her as the cheapest meal that he had ever claimed on his expenses: 'All she wanted was a burrito.'

By July 2018, Johnson was on the backbenches and trying to torpedo May's premiership. But by that point Truss had identified a rising star who she claimed would be the next big thing in Tory politics. She helped organise a dinner for the junior minister at the IEA a few months previously, where she insisted on introducing him. She hailed the first-term MP as the best hope for free-marketeers in the party, noting his qualities and impeccable Brexit credentials. His name was Rishi Sunak, and Truss said he was 'heading for great things'.

Unlike many Cabinet colleagues who ended up walking out, or even leaving politics altogether, Truss performed an impressive political balancing act as the Brexit wars waged: staying publicly loyal to the official government line while making her private feelings perfectly clear. One friend describes it as a 'slightly raised eyebrow which conveys a lot more … her social media stuff is in that vein'. The thin gruel offered by the May government was certainly not to Truss's likening and her frequent speeches extolling the virtues of unfettered capitalism were in noticeable contrast to her colleagues. She also floated ideas that weren't official party policy, such as overhauling the planning system to allow cuts to the £34 billion housing benefits bill. Mark Littlewood told the BBC: 'Even as a cabinet minister she's somehow straddled this ability of being a kind of maverick while consistently being in a range of cabinet jobs … What staggers me about Liz Truss – and I'm not quite sure how she's pulled this off – she seems to have been able to simultaneously be a party loyalist and yet speak her mind, even against prevailing government policy.' Truss's demotion certainly emboldened her in making her views perfectly clear: May and her team had shown her little loyalty, she reasoned, so why should she show much in return?

One Treasury source closer to Hammond than to Truss admits that, publicly, she stuck to the notion of collective ministerial responsibility. 'There were two taxes actually created while she was there: the digital services tax and the plastic bag tax, both of which she made very clear in private that she didn't like. But to be fair, in public she would go out there on the media round after round and sell them. So in that sense she's very professional; she'd make her views known privately.'

But her attempts to stay just about loyal were not always successful. In December 2018, lunch with a senior Lobby journalist was inadvertently broadcast to the whole of Westminster. Without realising she was sitting next to a Green Party activist in one of SW1's swankier coffee shops, Truss conveyed her candid assessment of the entire government in an off-record gossip fest. All the while at the neighbouring table Zack Polanski was live-tweeting their conversation. 'The only person worse at managing people than David Cameron,' Truss confided to her journalist pal, 'is Theresa May. She's such a pacifist whereas I embrace the chaos. I'm a thrillseeker.' On May's floundering Brexit deal, she was withering: 'Theresa should have used Michael more when making the deal. Used him to get the Brexiteers out. Mind you everyone hates him – they all blame him for not letting Boris be Boris. Then we wouldn't have had Theresa as Prime Minister – and to be fair, they're right.' Most controversially she even broke Cabinet omerta, revealing: 'At Cabinet … Jeremy said we need to get Brexiteers out. Liam and Michael suggested – someone suggested Penny and Andrea and there was silence. I found it a bit sexist really.' And after their defence-spending row, she asked: 'Have you noticed Gavin's gone quiet?' On Hunt, 'Jeremy is so charming. There's no consistency though. One minute he's all about the free market and the next … Matt Hancock is actually getting stuck into policy whereas Jeremy was all about the game playing.' It was an acutely embarrassing blunder, but one that only confirmed what No. 10 and No. 11 already believed.

Colleagues began to get rattled. One adviser noted: 'We did start to notice a real uptick of briefing against her in 2018. Matt Hancock wanted to cut funding for milk in schools and he wrote to Liz asking for permission. She wrote back basically saying, "This is mad, I'm sure you can find the money from somewhere within your budget, but go ahead." Then it got briefed to Sam Coates at *The Times*, as Liz Thatcher, milk snatcher.' Stein was swiftly deployed to kill the story, with the final report pinning the blame on Theresa May and Hancock instead.

But nothing came close to the pitched battle that Defence Secretary Gavin Williamson waged that summer. Asking for at least £20 billion more in defence spending 'and not a penny less', the renowned master of the political dark arts waged an astonishing public campaign against the Treasury over the summer of 2018. Despite being told repeatedly all year that, like all other departments, Defence would have to wait until 2019 for a multiyear settlement, Williamson waged one of the most high-profile campaigns for cash in modern Whitehall memory. Having already promised more money to the NHS, Hammond was not going to budge. And Truss backed him to the hilt. An aide recalls: 'Liz's view was basically you cannot give into blackmail. Even when it got nasty.' Give in to the bad behaviour of one, and every Cabinet minister would use the same tactic. But Williamson had opened the fight by dramatically cutting off the Chancellor's use of the RAF for official business until the Treasury settled a six-figure bill for No. 32 (The Royal) Squadron, the trio of aircraft available to ministers. He was also pushing for a 5 per cent pay rise for troops, which put him on a direct collision course with Truss.

In one of her first acts in the job in 2017, Truss had lifted the formal public sector pay freeze pursued for the better part of a decade by her mentor George Osborne. Soon every department was coming begging, not least the MoD. A friend reveals: 'Gavin cornered Liz in the Members' Lobby to warn: "I will write to every single British troop and tell them Liz Truss blocked your pay." He made crazier and crazier threats like banning her from RAF Marham in her constituency and "painting your face on the front of every F-35".' 'It was totally ridiculous behaviour, but Liz was most annoyed that the whole thing leaked, that one wasn't her,' another source claims. When sketchy reports of the exchange appeared in the papers, Theresa May was shocked and personally called Truss to apologise. 'That made Liz even angrier, she just didn't want this perception that she'd felt threatened. Her view was broadly: "Who gives a fuck what Gavin thinks?"' The pair eventually settled on a 2.9 per cent pay settlement. Williamson would achieve £800 million in the 2018 Autumn Statement for his troubles. 'He would have got more if he hadn't been such a dick,' a Hammond ally confides.

Occasionally though, the disruptor in chief did overstep the mark. A public jibe at the expense of her old rival, Michael Gove, her successor at Defra, sparked the biggest public row of her entire tenure at the Treasury. As Truss sought to assert herself as being pro-enterprise, she also began to define herself against the things that 'I was doing at Defra, like air quality and so on,' says Gove in 2022. 'She regarded that as nannying ... it was still for the most part fairly good tempered but Liz thought then that one way of succeeding was defining herself against what she saw as backward-looking or wet or compromising tendencies within the party.' Delivering a speech to the LSE, Truss complained of an excess of Whitehall regulation, pointedly joking: 'Too often we're hearing about not drinking too much, eating too many doughnuts, or enjoying the warm glow of our wood-burning Goves – I mean stoves. I can see their point: there's enough hot air and smoke at the Environment Department already.'

She told her audience, 'my role as Chief Secretary to the Treasury is to be on the side of the insurgents – I see myself as the disruptor in chief', but in a dig designed to generate headlines as an attack on Williamson, she added: 'We do have to recognise that it's not macho just to go out there and demand more money.' Her speech went on: 'The really tough skill is being able to take on the vested interest within your department, the blob, as I sometimes call them, and get better value for money. And I'm afraid to say that some of my colleagues are not clear about the tax implications of their proposed higher spending.' An earlier version of the speech accidentally uploaded on the government website also lambasted Gove's plans to ban plastic drinking straws.[8]

The speech was written in secret, with her civil service speech writers and her long-suffering special adviser Kane Daniell kept in the dark. A friend recalls: 'The funny thing is that the line that was supposed to get picked up was the one about macho Gavin. And then she threw in the "wood-burning Goves" and he went tonto.' That night Gove texted Truss: 'Liz, I've now seen the content of your speech and I'm not happy.' She called; he didn't answer. But the 'highly unusual attack' was not viewed favourably by colleagues; one Downing Street source commented acidly: 'As I understand it, several parts of that speech were intended to be humorous.'[9] One headline read: 'You know Theresa May's cabinet row has turned into an all-out war when Liz Truss gets involved.'[10]

Hammond was not amused by the outburst, opening the next meeting of Treasury ministers with an invitation: 'Perhaps Liz would like to update us on her *Weltanschauung*?' [German for worldview.] 'She laughed it off, she didn't give a fuck what Hammond thought,' says a colleague. But after months of her trouble making, Truss's allies felt No. 10 were happy for there to be a 'pile in'. Kwasi Kwarteng had been due to go on the *Today* programme the day after the Gove speech, but was blocked. Instead ultra-Govite Ed Vaizey hit the airwaves to decry the 'full frontal assault' on his friend. He went on to question Truss's motives, suggesting 'Liz Truss has achieved what she wanted to achieve, which is re-positioning herself and getting herself much more noticed than perhaps she has been in the past.' Gove's solicitous special adviser James Starkie had vowed to 'machine gun' the Treasury in revenge, but was told to stand down by Gove, who eventually took to the airwaves to call for a truce two days later. He told ITV: 'We are the best of friends, and that's why we can crack jokes. One of the things about politics is sometimes it is assumed that politicians don't have a sense of humour. One of the things about Liz is she has a fantastic sense of humour, and she was teasing me gently. And that's in the nature of our relationship.'

Meanwhile Truss's Spad Kane Daniell was unfairly called in for a dressing-down from Robbie Gibb, the Downing Street Director of Communications, despite his limited role in the drafting of the offending remarks. Daniell would shortly leave government after a tumultuous 11 months as Truss's Spad. The

Lobby were quick to write up the speech as a disaster for Truss, but her supporters playing the long game were content with the row. 'It got a little heated that week, but Liz said at the time, "I don't think this is that shit actually." She made a point about free markets, and not always reaching for the spending and banning levers. She felt it was a really important marker to put down.'

A sign of Truss's new-found confidence to speak her mind was the speech she gave at the *Spectator*'s Parliamentarian Awards in November 2018. Six years previously she had won 'Minister to Watch': now she was the star turn. One attendee recalls how she 'basically machine gunned everyone' and made jokes about half a dozen Cabinet colleagues. They included veiled swipes at the ambition of Health Secretary Matt Hancock to become Chancellor – his 'car keeps pitching up outside 11 Downing Street' – and Home Secretary Sajid Javid, who had recently sat in her seat in the Commons during a debate. 'I'm glad he and his sharp buttocks haven't turned up tonight, at least I get a seat at the table.' She also mocked Jeremy Hunt, the Foreign Secretary, for accidentally describing his Chinese wife as Japanese: 'Some ignorant people don't know the difference between China and Japan.' A disgruntled colleague subsequently complained to *The Times* that Truss's speech had 'annoyed ministers'.

Truss was able to survive such spats – and even emerge strengthened – because of the May government's enduring weakness. One former ministerial colleague suggested that Truss 'was known to be an inveterate leaker. Theresa would probably have liked to sack her, but she didn't have the authority after the 2017 election.'[11] The election result and ongoing tensions over Brexit meant open feuding became the norm, but her under-the-radar position at the Treasury in these years might well have been a blessing in disguise. By not being intimately involved in the negotiations or the inevitable rows that followed, she avoided publicly pinning her colours to the mast as the party tore itself apart.

Allies though made sure to brief her scepticism of May's deal to helpful outlets while the free-market think tanks were always on hand to provide her with a platform for regular interventions. Truss's time at the Treasury revitalised these links. Among those on the outside Truss enlisted was Sophie Jarvis, head of government affairs at the Adam Smith Institute, who was once described as putting 'the tank in think tank'.[12] She would be a key lieutenant in Truss's rise to the top.

Truss never quit the Cameron, May or Johnson administrations on a point of principle – unlike some of her 2010 contemporaries like Sajid Javid or Dominic Raab. Soul-searching was not for her: one friend suggests she sees little point in such 'gestures' or threats. A former aide recalls a train journey where Truss signed off a succession of policy papers from other departments, known as 'write rounds', while repeatedly muttering: 'Don't agree with that, don't agree, don't agree.' 'If you don't agree with them, why are you signing them off?' he asked. 'Because,' she replied, 'there are bigger battles ahead.' According to Matt Kilcoyne of the ASI: 'She's ideological but she is loyal. When you've got collective responsibility above you and you've got a boss who decided the policy above you, she's loyal to that. When she gets to set the weather, then she's more ideological.' Sonia Khan, her former special adviser, observes that Truss developed a very thick skin at the Treasury: 'She's not the kind of person who reads something about herself and gets upset. I remember when she read the interview with Elizabeth Day, it was slightly snarky and it made reference to the mice in the House of Commons scurrying. I remember just watching her as she read it and saying "So what do you think?" thinking she might say "I want to call lawyers" or "I want you to do this". But no, I think she accepts that that's part of political life … She's very thick-skinned – impressively so. I think that's probably why she was able to succeed at the Treasury. She didn't really take it too seriously when they said no.'

The closest that Truss ever did come to quitting was over Theresa May's efforts to pass her Brexit deal. One close friend says that Truss 'thought about quitting but didn't. She thought there was no benefit to her [doing so] really.' Instead she was one of a handful of ministers who met regularly in Andrea Leadsom's so-called 'Pizza Club' in late 2018 and early 2019. Over takeaway meals, Truss, Leadsom, Raab and others gathered in Leadsom's Commons office to discuss ways to stop a 'soft' exit from the EU, much to the irritation of No. 10. Naturally Truss responded by tweeting a picture of a slice of the popular Italian dish to her 54,000 Twitter followers: 'Starting recess as I mean to go on. #coldpizza #evenbetter.'

Having survived the no-confidence vote in December 2018 by 200 votes to 117, May was faced with the choice between trying to get her own party and the DUP back on board, or going for a softer Brexit to win the votes of Labour MPs. Truss was firmly in the former camp, telling Robert Peston that 'there are 118 Conservatives that we have the potential to win over, and I think that's where we should start'.[13] But in the weeks that followed, an enfeebled May was forced to appeal to the Labour leadership and bring Jeremy Corbyn to the negotiating table. Truss was disdainful of such efforts, with Labour demanding a permanent customs union with the European Union. Appearing on Sky, she refused to rule out resigning if May acceded to this demand, saying, the UK must have an 'independent trade policy'.[14] Truss teamed up with an unlikely ally in Gavin Williamson in early 2019. The pair argued in Cabinet that Britain should be prepared to leave the EU without a deal on the grounds that 'Theresa would be finished' if the Cabinet didn't pursue that option to try to pass her deal. Years later Truss remarked privately that it 'would have been better' if the May government had wholeheartedly embraced 'no deal Brexit' as a viable option.

Truss's dilemma was one shared by her colleagues, who were rapidly turning against May with every vote on her deal. The

Prime Minister pledged to resign in March 2019 if her deal was passed at the third time of asking' but it was rejected by MPs once again. The combination of a disastrous set of European parliamentary elections – in which the Conservatives polled just 9 per cent – with a revolt by donors and party members forced May to throw in the towel. She announced her resignation on 24 May, four days after Truss suggested she would 'maybe' run to replace her.[15]

Like many of her Cabinet colleagues, Truss did not stand idly by throughout the dying days of the May government. In the weeks and months before the Prime Minister's inevitable resignation, she was one of many quietly canvassing opinions among friends and allies about her chances should she stand. Yet despite endless media rounds in seven years of ministerial service, she remained something of an unknown outside Westminster. One poll in March found that just 7 per cent or one in every fourteen people would recognise her in the street. Other members of the 2010 intake such as Sajid Javid, Amber Rudd and Dominic Raab all scored much higher with 33, 25 and 11 per cent respectively.[16] And she didn't score much better among her fellow MPs. A colleague of Truss's recalls asking her how many supporters she had around this time. 'I've got one,' replied Truss – her ever-loyal friend and karaoke partner Thérèse Coffey. As the maths geek knew all too well, and told the *Spectator*: 'In politics – it's not really about what you say, it's all about the numbers.'[17]

The brutal reality of parliamentary arithmetic meant Truss would soon abandon any tilt for the leadership herself, but she made sure to exploit the attention to the full first, posing in a glossy magazine shoot with the *Mail on Sunday*. The paper spent thousands on outfits for her under the headline 'Is this Britain's next Prime Minister?'[18] 'You have to be prepared to put yourself forward,' she said, 'because nobody else is going to.' Having courted the attention of the media for weeks, Truss ruled herself out on 25 May, declaring, 'we need someone who has backed Brexit from the start, because of the situation we're in now'. The following weekend she became the first Cabinet minister to endorse Boris Johnson, using the hashtag 'freedom fighters'. In doing so she avoided the fate of several colleagues who launched fruitless and embarrassing bids for the leadership that attracted little or no support. 'You only get to run once, and that was not the time,' Truss would tell friends later.

Truss's role in the campaign was to loudly and frequently support Johnson at every turn, doing endless media rounds in which she defended him over charges of deceit and deception. She also advised him on economic policy and was credited with being the architect of his plans to cut taxes for people earning over £50,000. The plan was soon scrapped though, following an outcry over the plans. Johnson's status as the frontrunner was apparent from mid-June, with much talk of Truss being promoted to another economic brief: perhaps as first female Chancellor or as Business Secretary in a 'souped-up' ministry. A fortnight before the conclusion of the contest, she addressed a lunch of the parliamentary press gallery. Both the subject of the speech and the accompanying quips hinted that she would shortly be replacing her boss Philip Hammond. She made an unapologetic defence of tax cuts for higher earners to the assembled hacks, referencing Nigel Lawson's 1988 Budget and suggesting that 'the reason that Boris is getting flak for this is that the Conservative Party haven't been prepared to make these arguments for at least a decade'. She teased that, unlike her rival Sajid Javid, she had an A-Level in Further Maths and joked that Jacob Rees-Mogg – then tipped as her replacement as Chief Secretary – would be only just down the corridor from her in the new regime.[19]

But before the campaign had ended Johnson had privately discarded her as his Chancellor-designate, in part because of the row the tax plans caused, and because Javid was seemingly more willing to spend freely. A short-lived 'LizforBiz' campaign by her free-market admirers also fell flat. Truss privately had her hopes set on Business Secretary and told friends of her disappointment when the post went to Andrea Leadsom in a sop to the Brexiteers who had helped the new leader over the line. Still, after two long years, Truss had pulled herself back from the political abyss. Though not top league, it was clear by July 2019 that she was heading back to the Cabinet proper, and under a PM Truss would be far more aligned to – at least in style if not in spending habits. Reflecting on Truss's time at the Treasury, one friend calls 2017–19 Liz Truss's '"Rolling Stones years": You can't always get what you want. But if you try sometimes, you might find you get what you need.'

2019

TRUSS UNCHAINED

With Boris Johnson sweeping to power on Tuesday 23 July 2019, Liz Truss still thought she was in with a chance of being made Chancellor. Those hopes were dashed, however, when Dominic Cummings was spotted entering No. 10 alongside the new PM as his all-powerful enforcer. Kept secret for the final weeks of the campaign in order to avoid scaring off MP supporters, Cummings' presence was an immediate issue for Truss given their past at Education. When she was appointed Trade Secretary, friends say she was a little miffed to have missed out on a bigger department given she was first out of the blocks to back BoJo.

But any animosity was clearly soon forgotten, with Truss determined to make sure her words as Trade Secretary would land perfectly within her first few weeks. 'We were working on an op-ed for the *Sun on Sunday*,' says Sonia Khan, who briefly joined her at the new department. 'And she was still making changes until very late. I remember she called me and I could hear glasses clinking in the background. And I was like "where are you?" and she was like "Oh, I'm just at my anniversary dinner with Hugh."'

Truss took to her new role with customary bulldozing zeal, to the irritation of some in No. 10. That summer the all-powerful new Downing Street team were determined to clear the decks before a possible general election in the autumn. Johnson's Director of Communications Lee Cain and Cummings could not have been clearer in an early meeting with Truss: 'Stop pushing so hard on a US trade deal.' They feared their campaign strategy would be distracted by rows over chlorinated chicken and privatisation of the NHS that critics say would be part of any deal with the United States. Summoned to No. 10 for this point to be hammered home, Truss was ordered very firmly to shut up. When the pair had repeatedly made their point, she simply replied: 'I want to sign the biggest trade deal with the US there has ever been.'

It was clear that an election was coming, but, in the words of one aide, 'Liz felt that there was zero time to waste if she was going to make any progress in her new job'. She hired two new special advisers, as ever from the Tufton Street mould. Sophie Jarvis joined from the Adam Smith Institute after a brief stint on the *Evening Standard* diary, while Nerissa Chesterfield was imported from the Institute of Economic Affairs. Chesterfield's job interview consisted of one question from Truss: 'No maths A-Level? Pity.' But her strong reputation for making the free-market case on TV and across the press while at the IEA secured her the gig.

Desperate not to repeat the mistakes of the past, where toeing the No. 10 line had left her either on the hook or in the shadows, Truss hit the diplomatic stage with force in her first few months in the job, travelling to Washington, New Zealand, Australia, Japan and back to New York within her first eight weeks. Having honed her free-wheeling politics in the Treasury, it was time to go global. And her first tour was something of a whirlwind …

On her first visit to Washington, DC, the newly appointed Trade Secretary was given a clear brief ahead of a first meeting with her US counterpart. Robert Lighthizer had 30 years' experience on the beat, a Trump-supporting protectionist who had first served the Office of the United States Trade Representative under Reagan. Liz Truss had been in the job exactly 14 days.

'The officials kept telling her not to get her hopes up, don't get overexcited, this is just a preliminary meeting,' one aide recalls. Warned there would be little discussion of the actual details of tariffs the US government had slapped on British goods like gin, whisky and smoked salmon in retaliation for EU aerospace subsidies, Truss was dismissive.

In a cramped room at the USTR the pair sat across the table for the first time. Welcoming her to Washington, Lighthizer started with the usual diplomatic preliminaries. Truss was having none of it though, interjecting immediately: 'So what are we going to do about whisky tariffs then?' One present recalls: 'It was the perfect example of Liz's total misunderstanding of social context and social norms. Lighthizer would start saying something just being nice, and Liz would just interrupt him and just go off on like a weird tangent about shortbread.' But was there a method to the madness? 'It got to the point that it happened so many times he started looking at his officials as a bit like "what the fuck is going on here?" But she was just like a wrecking ball and didn't really care about what was actually expected, or what people thought was possible, or what the civil servants were telling her. She just got straight to the point.'

Taken aback, Lighthizer responded to her questioning with a warning there were many 'dependents' in the way of movement. One attendee recalls: 'Full credit: the wrecking ball was unusual but it was not a negative. There wouldn't have been results if it wasn't for her approach, they would have been happy to just sit there and prevaricate.'

Despite the warnings before her departure, Truss was determined to make a speech in Washington and had coordinated with conservative allies at the Heritage Foundation – the king of the right-wing think tanks in DC. Despite the speech being drafted by civil servants, Truss was clear with all staff: 'Don't tell No. 10 what's in the speech.' But her own department had tried to put the kibosh on it themselves, serving up a watery mishmash of platitudes for her to deliver. Truss was furious and stayed up 'knocking back espressos' until 3 a.m. in the bar of the hotel, rewriting the speech herself with Chesterfield and Head of News Joe Watts, 'the only civil servant in the building Liz trusted at the beginning,' according to one ally. Rewrite after rewrite hardened the speech that was eventually titled: 'Why the time is now for a US–UK free trade deal.' The final draft was incendiary, going against everything No. 10 had warned Trade not to push, ahead of an election: a sweeping Free Trade Agreement that would infuriate every vested interest group going.

Up at 6 a.m. and spotted in the hotel gym with Dominic Raab, the Foreign Secretary, who was also visiting Washington that week, Truss arrived at breakfast to a grim-faced-looking team. 'What time do you want me to send this over to No. 10?' Chesterfield asked, 'because they need to see it before you give it or there is going to be trouble.' 'Hold it as long as possible,' Truss ordered. 'You deal with them.' Ever more angry, senior staff in Downing Street, five hours ahead, were already fielding calls from journalists about a speech they had not seen. Press Secretary Rob Oxley was first to contact Truss's team, demanding answers. Next was Lee Cain, before eventually even Chief of Staff Eddie Lister was demanding to see a draft of the remarks. When eventually the speech was sent, Truss's allies say 'all hell broke loose'. 'There was a lot of unhappiness,' one Downing Street official recalls. 'Edit this out, what the fuck has gone on, why haven't you told us about this; this is all really, really unhelpful style. We said don't push the US trade deal too hard, blah, blah, blah,' was the summary of those on the receiving end. But Truss was holding firm, 'do a couple of changes to make them happy, but I am not going to change the fundamentals'. Within hours, she was on stage at Heritage hailing 'an organisation which gave so much impetus to the Reagan administration in the 1980s, unleashing enterprise and opportunity'.

Two years later an ex-British diplomat Alexandra Hall Hall, who at the time was Brexit Counsellor at the Washington embassy, would claim Truss privately told Heritage that the only people worried about a no-deal Brexit were 'farmers with a few turnips in the back of their truck'. Truss's allies claim they 'do not recognise those words' from the off-record private lunch after the main speech. It also later emerged Truss had told them she was keen to hear 'what we can learn from "Reaganomics" on things like regulation and red tape' and that she was 'committed' to that cause. But on the day, despite No. 10's paranoia, the speech flew broadly under the radar. Amid a painfully delayed flight and over chicken burgers in Ronald Reagan Washington National Airport, Truss conceded to her aides, 'I think we've got away with it.' After she'd spent a day Instagramming her way round New York, Hugh and the girls joined her for the weekend. But Truss, unchained on the global stage, was only just warming up.

As the Trade Secretary arrived at New Zealand's Wellington International Airport, the British High Commissioner Laura Clarke was there waiting to meet her incoming VIP. Only Truss was nowhere to be seen. Fired up after double espressos on the flight, she had disappeared to find the perfect spot for a landing photograph. A travelling official recalls: 'She'd had so much coffee and just wasn't interested in meeting the ambassador.' Spads and officials awkwardly greeted the High Commissioner, while Truss sought a location with better light that was not just the outside of an airport. In a breach of protocol, it was left to Joe Watts to break the ice, asking Clarke nervously: 'Would you mind coming to have a photograph with the Trade Secretary?' Photo duties fell to Chesterfield while Sophie Jarvis tried to soothe worried officials about the tight schedule of meetings ahead. 'You could tell Clarke was thinking "what the fuck?" as we held things up for like 20 minutes looking for a decent picture place.' In the end the snap was taken in front of the High Commissioners' SUV with a Union flag on the front. Only after Truss was satisfied with the picture was the convoy allowed to leave.

Relations were not any easier in the car. Keen to brief the arriving minister on her impending meetings with her Kiwi counterparts, Clarke began talking about the day and firing off trade stats. But Truss was glued to her phone, checking with her press team the draft tweets that included kiwi emojis, completely ignoring the briefing. 'She just looked up after a few minutes and told Clarke: "I'm doing my social media,"' putting an abrupt end to the conversation. When some minutes later Truss was happy enough to send the vital tweet, she put her phone down and turned back to Clarke, declaring: 'I'm ready for my briefing now.' 'They were obviously rather perplexed about the priorities there,' says one person in the car that day.

Four days later Truss landed in Sydney in a similar whirlwind. With just six hours scheduled in Australia's biggest city, the minister had her priorities and the civil service planned itinerary was swiftly shredded. On arrival Truss insisted that the convoy be diverted to a coffee shop in the suburbs she had read about that served British coffee. When this tiny café was found, it was barely big enough for two people to sit down – let alone the entourage of seven. 'We drove around the houses for ages because Liz insisted on a picture in this typical area of Sydney – insisting that it was ironic that the hipster coffee capital of the world was relying on British imports,' says a former aide. In the end the photographer had to stand outside in the rain snapping Truss, British espresso and a sausage roll in hand, through the window. Outside, aides and officials huddled under umbrellas. A mystery surrounds what happened to the pictures, as they never featured on either Truss's prolific Twitter feed or her carefully curated Instagram account; perhaps falling foul of her tough editorial standards.

The next stop in Sydney would become a defining image of Truss's boosterist style of promoting both Brexit Britain and herself. With the rain still pouring, it took many, many goes to get the final snap of Truss on a British-made Brompton bike with a Union flag umbrella in a car park under Sydney Harbour bridge, with the opera house looming large. Freedom of Information requests would later reveal a £1,483 freelance photographer was hired for the trip – but the picture went around the world. 'Get on your bike and look for exports', Truss tweeted. While it was nearly as widely mocked online as her pork markets and cheese speech, her defenders insist the picture struck exactly the right tone. One ally says: 'That picture, more than any press release, more than anything she could have done or said, just explained what her job was and that's what she got. As much as you can take the piss out of her for doing photo-shoots left right and centre, she did have a total understanding of how to make the best out of the brief and got the fact it was her job to go out there and sell, sell, sell.' Another former adviser recalls: 'Liz to her core is a retail politician. She understands what speaks to people, a bit of the Boris stuff, the positivity, but also how to shape an agenda. One of the big struggles that we did have in trade was so many people outside London just don't understand what trade is. So she was trying to communicate what it meant in a very simple way.'

But beyond the photos, staff worried Truss had a lack of patience for the more tedious elements of her diplomatic role. 'Sometimes she could be demanding and borderline rude to people' is far from an unusual complaint from former staff. After the coffee shop detour and the Sydney Harbour photo-shoot, the team were now 90 minutes late for a reception organised with British non-alcoholic gin brand Seedlip. Hundreds of expats, including one of her former teachers, and dozens of British businesses were at the event. 'She got a photo pouring a cocktail and glad-handed a few people and then was like "right we need to get our flight". But we still had hours until take-off, but she was just like "I'm done". There was no interest whatsoever so we left after about half an hour,' one official complains.

Yet when she reached Canberra for meetings with Australian PM Scott Morrison and his ministers the next morning, Truss was in full charm-offensive mode. She met almost every senior member of the Liberal government but struck up a particular rapport with Bridget McKenzie the environment minister. Noticing a black-and-white photograph on the wall showing 1920s women armed with shotguns, and captioned 'Ladies who shoot lunch', Truss was tickled pink. 'Do you shoot? You must come over and shoot in Norfolk,' she declared. 'Her eyes lit up,' recalls one present. 'She loved the whole girl power vibe.' Conversations between private offices continued for months afterwards trying, unsuccessfully, to sort the trip. Aides say that when Truss was interested in someone she would 'move heaven and earth' to be as charming as possible. But if she was bored or lost interest in a meeting or event, 'she wouldn't even try to hide it'.

While there were ups and downs in the whistlestop diplomacy, as in Washington the previous month, it was only a matter of time before a row broke out with No. 10. On this occasion the time zones and a very boozy ball played havoc. If Truss had got away with being outspoken in DC, her press conference in Canberra permanently marked her card with the comms team in Downing Street. After talks with her Australian counterpart Simon Birmingham, the pair faced questions from the press – a first for Truss on the world stage. 'We did a bit of prep on her statement at the top of the presser, but in hindsight we were woefully underprepared for the questions ... that's where it all started going wrong,' remembers one of the travelling entourage.

When asked if a future trade deal between Australia and the UK could include a loosening of visas for Aussies to come and work in Britain, Truss strayed wildly off her patch. She told reporters: 'We've been clear on the fact that we want to adopt the Australian-based points system in terms of our new immigration system as we leave the European Union. We've recently made an announcement that we're extending the work period after foreign students come to the UK for two years. But of course, our two countries have a special link and a historic relationship, and it's certainly something that we will be looking at as part of our free-trade negotiations.' When the quote hit the wires that evening in Britain, once again, 'all hell broke loose'.

Nerissa Chesterfield was on the receiving end of a full Malcolm Tucker-esque barrage from No. 10, furious that she was straying outside of her brief. 'What the fuck are you doing, why has she said that, this is going cause us mayhem, this is not what we need' was the general gist, a friend recalls. Jarvis, Watts and Chesterfield took the brunt of the fall-out that evening, 'the calls carried on literally all night as they tried to row back from the comments with little success'. Truss meanwhile was a guest of honour at Canberra's Midwinter Ball – a highlight of the Aussie political season. Out until 3 a.m. and somewhat worse for wear, Truss returned to the hotel to find her team trying to patch up the damage. A suggestion that Truss should call Eddie Lister to apologise for the comments was met with short shrift by a tired minister. 'Oh, I don't care,' Truss told them. 'She literally didn't give two monkeys. Her calculation at the time was "I'm still new to this job, the whole Cabinet is new, they're not going to start firing people for minor things like that," and in the short term she was probably right.' But on the plane to the next leg of the trip in Tokyo there was bad blood at the lack of care over the mess, with Truss preferring to regale her team with stories and gossip from the ball. 'She just doesn't care when people are angry with her,' said one official on that trip. 'But she did notice that Chesterfield had taken the barrage from London particularly badly.' 'Don't let these bullies upset you, Nerissa. Don't worry about it, you're doing a great job,' Truss said before finally getting some sleep.

While formal trade talks with Japan had begun, they were still at a very early technical level when Truss became Trade Secretary in 2019. So her first visit there was broadly ceremonial – which came as a relief after the gruelling five days Down Under. 'We had been on the plane longer than we had been on the ground by this point, so everyone was knackered,' remembers an official. Everyone that is except the minister, who used the light diplomatic schedule to convene yet another photoshoot. At Tokyo's landmark Shibuya Crossing, the busiest pedestrian crossing in the world, Truss spent more than an hour perfecting a shot of her walking. By now the *Telegraph* was in tow, so multiple cameras and videographers were there to capture the moment. 'It was so dangerous, there was traffic everywhere and she just kept bowling through it take after take, even when the traffic was still coming,' says a witness. Another ally on the trip remembers: 'She was just so focused on looking straight down the camera lens for a fantastic photo, but I really don't think it was worth 10 shots and also getting run over.' While the image did not gain the same notoriety as the one in Sydney Harbour, Truss's team defended it: 'It was a famous monument of that country and there she is, selling Britain.'

With six days on the road and only one major row triggered, the last night in Tokyo was time to party. After a reception celebrating that year's Rugby World Cup, sushi was sought, with shoes off and cushions on the floor. Protestations from the Principal Private Secretary that he didn't eat raw fish fell on deaf ears. 'Liz was just rolling her eyes as he tried to explain to a waitress that spoke very little English that he would like his salmon cooked,' one present says. At the bosses insistence, it was on to cocktails at the Park Hyatt hotel – the bar at the top of the Shinjuku Park Tower made famous by Sofia Coppola's *Lost in Translation*. 'We were all pretty smashed by the time Liz suggested karaoke'. The team suspected that Truss had not slept when she was downstairs waiting for them all at 6 a.m. the next morning. With sore heads all round, having only got in less than two hours before, Truss joked to her struggling aides, "well you look awful", when they finally made it down to the lobby.

No sooner had they returned to London it was wheels up again for New York for the annual United Nations General Assembly. Before the summit started there was the obligatory photoshoot. An English-made Mini had been acquired for her to pose with, promoting British car sales across the pond. But when she arrived, aides say her face fell. 'Let's put this under Brooklyn Bridge for the shot,' she suggested. 'Poor Joe Watts had his head in his hands, you could see him just trying to work out how the hell that was going to happen. You can't just park a car under Brooklyn Bridge,' recalls a colleague. An official was ordered into the Mini and drove it to what she thought was a better spot for the photo nearby, as aides panicked. Eventually Truss got a picture, but she was not happy. 'In the car into the City she was reviewing the shots, and was very down on them. We all thought they were great; you had the Mini, you had her, you had the skyline – it was a pretty good shot.' 'She wasn't upset with her staff per se, but you could just tell she saw it as a wasted opportunity. She was strangely cut up about that one,' recalls another Trade official. A double-page spread of the image in that week's *Daily Express* may have allayed some concerns.

But Truss had bigger matters on her mind as she arrived in New York. Johnson was to meet President Trump the following afternoon and that was all that mattered. 'I have to get into that bilat,' she told her private office and Spads; 'get me in the room for the Trump meeting.' But overtures to No. 10 had fallen on deaf ears. With every possible lever pulled by Truss's team, they were yet to get her in the room. Frantic phone calls to Lister, Cain and Political Secretary Ben Gascoigne were all met with a firm no. An aide recalls: 'She was putting pressure on all of us to speak to everyone and sort it out, but by the night before it was clear we were getting nowhere.' On the morning of Tuesday 24 September Truss was due to speak at a business breakfast with the PM; a change of tack was needed. 'I need to speak to Boris first thing,' Truss told aides that evening. Wanting to look the part, she instructed a very junior official from her private office to book her a blow-dry in her hotel room for 7 a.m.

That same morning a political bomb detonated in Westminster. The government had been defeated in the Supreme Court, with an attempt to suspend Parliament to avoid Brexit rows ruled illegal by the highest judges in the land. As Lady Hale read her withering verdict in London, Johnson's entire government wobbled under mounting calls to resign. The PM was mobbed by the travelling press pack, holed up in his hotel suite working out a response. Down the corridor Truss was having a crisis too: the hairdresser had failed to turn up. The young Private Secretary responsible for organising had got 'absolutely smashed' the night before and been found hugging the lavatory of a New York dive bar in the wee hours, but the team had tried to cover for him. 'Liz had probably overestimated the powers of this lad in his twenties in terms of sorting out a blow-dry in a foreign city, or indeed knowing what a blow-dry was,' one official recalls. 'It's safe to say he was not flavour of the month that day though. A few weeks later he got booted off to somewhere else in Whitehall.' A frantic Truss turned up at Sophie Jarvis's room to borrow her hairdryer 'absolutely seething', and still livid that she had not yet wangled her way into the Trump meeting. 'You can't have Lighthizer in there and not me,' she complained.

Over at Hudson Yards – a development designed in part by Brit Thomas Heatherwick – the PM's business breakfast was a carnival of chaos. Appearing for the first time publicly since the Supreme Court news had dropped, Johnson was met by shouts from broadcasters, full of questions as the British arrived to meet and greet some of the most powerful executives in New York. While some aides desperately tried to keep Truss away from the baying press pack, others tried to keep her on track with meeting people like billionaire BlackRock boss Larry Fink. 'There were certain people she just had to meet that day, but she had absolutely no interest. There were serious big cheeses there but she only wanted to collar Boris.'

With Johnson ushered to waiting cameras to address the TV news back home, Truss missed her moment before his speech. And after he addressed the news from London during his remarks, the PM was mobbed by business people, wanting their 30 seconds with power. A witness recalls: 'Liz was watching like a hawk for the entire half-hour he was talking. Eventually Boris's security people got in there to ease him out because he was on a time constraint, so they began to pull him away towards a back entrance. And Liz just follows the entourage.' With Liz disappearing for ten minutes down a back staircase, her team were left bewildered as to where she had gone. 'Finally she emerged back in the room like the cat that got the cream,' says an aide. 'She was grinning ear to ear when she told us, "We're in. I've sorted it and none of you fuckers did anything!" And she was absolutely correct. Liz knew she would get Boris to say yes if she could just get in front of him, and so she did and he folded after two minutes. It was genuinely impressive.' Where officials stood in her path, Truss the wrecking ball had struck again.

With the invitation secured, a scramble for accreditation from the United Nations HQ, where the talks were due to take place later that day, followed. With Johnson and Trump at the top of a diplomatic horseshoe, Truss was nestled between Ambassador Karen Pierce and Chief of Staff Eddie Lister in the third-best seat on the British side. Sources say very little trade was actually discussed in the meeting, and that every time Trump brought conversation around to it, Johnson wanted to talk about Iran. But that seemed to matter little to Truss. As she came out of the meeting, the first thing she said to her team was 'get the pictures'.

Battle-scarred from her time with Defra and Justice, isolated at the Treasury, Truss vowed upon entering the Department of International Trade (DIT) that she was not going to repeat the mistakes of her earlier career. But at the beginning of her tenure at the DIT, it looked like she was on a similar path. The trade establishment were not as snooty as the lawyers Truss encountered at Justice, but it appears Truss had alienated them just as quickly. Officials used words like 'unclubbable' and 'cold front' to describe their new boss, and were quick to bombard her with technical discussions to try to bamboozle her.

In the first three months of the job, Truss's free-trade, free-market ideology cut up rough with the 'trade bods' and the diplomats still reconciling with the loss of the European comfort blanket. 'It should be noted that none of them knew a damn thing about doing a trade deal either, as they were all still in shorts the last time Britain cut an independent trade deal,' one official dryly recalls. But by Christmas 2019 Truss had swotted up on the subject and was starting to get the better of them. 'She started to surprise them in terms of the details of which she had a grasp, down to particular tariff lines or digital data terms. It was clear she was doing her homework and it started to pay off and she grew in confidence almost by the day.'

An insider recalls: 'An official would come forward and say on this particular technical detail, we want to do X, and she would let them blather on before coming back hard and saying, "why would we do that when that doesn't match with our free trade ideology? I want to do Y, regardless of the domestic blow-back, and I want to do it on this particular minor technical detail." It made for some lively scenes.' 'A couple of people made the fatal mistake of mansplaining the complexities of WTO [World Trade Organization] rules one too many times and were swiftly eased out,' one DIT source added. Another colleague at the DIT said: 'She's quite a good Secretary of State. She was very, very clear with what she wanted: US, Australia, New Zealand, Japan and Trans-Pacific Partnership.'

Officials were moved on, allies brought in and heavy artillery outsourced by once again bringing Tufton Street think-tank figures into government advisory positions. The early days at Trade saw a significant restructuring of the department; the new minister was not afraid to tell officials where she thought they were failing or undermining her agenda.

While Truss was finding her feet in the department, Westminster was focusing on Boris Johnson's Brexit battle. The

PM's refusal to rule out a 'no-deal' Brexit sparked howls of protest from Remain-backing MPs. Among those Tories who clashed with Johnson was Amber Rudd, the Work and Pensions Secretary, who quit the Cabinet in protest in September 2019. Truss was one of the beneficiaries of her demise: Rudd's departure left a vacancy in the Government Equalities Office. Truss was duly given the added title of 'Minister for Women and Equalities' to add to her existing Trade brief. Johnson congratulated his new Equalities Minister on her appointment with a cricketing metaphor, saying: 'Liz, I know you are more of a Ben Stokes, but in this role I need you to be more Geoffrey Boycott. Block everything.' Truss instead marked the appointment by drawing up plans for a major speech in which she planned to defend 'women's rights' against calls to strengthen protections for transgender individuals. The hard-hitting intervention was canned by No. 10, who were uneasy with the blunt nature of Truss's comments. Undaunted, Truss was to exploit the role skilfully over the next three years, using it to rail against Whitehall's 'woke brigade' in successive speeches and op-eds. She scrapped plans to reform the gender recognition process but presided over the collapse of the government's LGBT Advisory Panel.

A month after Truss's appointment, Johnson finally secured the election he craved. Having failed to pass his revised deal before the first Brexit extension deadline of 31 October, the PM agreed to a second extension on negotiations with the EU. An exhausted Commons finally threw in the towel, voting by 438 votes to 20 to support a dissolution of Parliament; the Lords duly followed suit.

In the frantic six weeks that followed, Truss played a marginal role, being largely confined to the so-called 'Red Wall' Labour strongholds in the north. She was, according to one CCHQ insider, 'persona non grata'. Disliked and distrusted by Cummings and Cain, she played little role in the broadcast 'air war', much to her dismay.

Truss's only moment of note was an intensely embarrassing one. Near the end of the campaign, Jeremy Corbyn held a press conference to reveal 451 pages of uncensored minutes from talks between the UK's Department for International Trade and the US Trade Representative. The leaked files suggested that the US wanted 'total market access' after the UK left the EU. Waving aloft pages of documents, the Labour leader claimed they proved Boris Johnson had lied when he said that the NHS would not be part of any future trade talks. 'He tried to cover it up in a secret agenda,' Corbyn claimed, 'and today it has been exposed.' An adviser at the Trade Department was held responsible for the leak in Whitehall. They had forwarded reams of papers from their secure government email account to a Hotmail one run by Liam Fox. Fox's account was then hacked, with the blame aimed at Russian state actors. The documents subsequently ended up in the hands of the Labour press office. The aide was sidelined and then quietly drummed out of the department, with Truss left 'personally embarrassed' by the episode, according to a DIT source. Luckily for Truss, the effects of Corbyn's 'bombshell' proved to ultimately be negligible. Two weeks later, Boris Johnson led the Tories to victory. His party won 365 seats, as dozens of 'Red Wall' constituencies went blue for the first time. It was the biggest Conservative majority for over 30 years: Johnson was triumphant. But overseas in China, a mystery virus was starting to spread.

Just weeks before the pandemic engulfed Britain, Johnson reshuffled his team in a February post-election shake-up. Truss had been spooked by reports throughout the winter that Michael Gove was set to head a new 'super Trade department' comprising the Foreign Office, Business and DIT ministries. 'Liz took that really personally,' says one ally. Her aides were bombarded with phone calls when such stories appeared, demanding to know from where they had originated. Having alienated No. 10 throughout the last six months, Truss now tried desperately to rebuild bridges and smooth over past tensions. 'She could have probably thought about that before to make her life easier,' says one involved. 'It wasn't until she almost got chopped that alarm bells started ringing.' Another adds: 'I don't think Lee [Cain] and Dom [Cummings] ever warmed to her. I think there was a distrust there.' 'She really did think she was going to get the bullet,' one friend says.

Despite briefings from the centre that Truss would be axed, the PM had little truck with the idea being floated by his advisers to a number of papers. On the day of the reshuffle itself, members of Truss's team were preparing to be moved to another department. 'She really wanted to stay on trade, it was a positive agenda, she suited it,' says a friend of Truss. But the unexpected resignation of Chancellor Sajid Javid killed any such plans. Javid quit the Cabinet over Cummings' demands that he fire his advisers; in his place came Rishi Sunak, Truss's one-time pal. She herself spent reshuffle day nervously waiting hours for the call from No. 10, having been one of the last to be summoned. When she came back into the department, she batted away calls from her private office for a speech and instead summoned Chesterfield to her office. 'I'm not leaving, but you are,' Truss told the worried aide, who assumed she was being fired. But having earned her spurs on the political attack team at the 2019 Election, Chesterfield was promoted to the Treasury under Sunak. One ally recalls that Truss 'liked Nerissa, and was never going to try to stop anyone going on to a massive job. She was delighted for her.' That left Truss with just the support of Jarvis – who Cummings had 'put the fear of God into over speaking to the press'. Three years later that original team would be on opposing sides of a bloody battle for No. 10.

To replace Chesterfield, Truss turned to an old ally: Jason Stein, her former Treasury official. He had left the civil service in November 2018 to become a special adviser to Amber Rudd, the then-Work and Pensions Secretary. After her resignation in September 2019, Stein spent a few lively months spinning for Prince Andrew at the Palace, before jumping ship to Finsbury, the PR and lobbying firm run by silky Europhile Roland Rudd – brother of his old boss Amber. Mystery surrounds exactly why he left Andrew's service in a hurry. The version of events Stein tells is that he had advised the Prince not to do the now notorious *Newsnight* interview and was ignored so walked. Either way he had clashed heavily during his time at the Palace with Simon Case, then-Private Secretary to Prince William – and soon to be the Cabinet Secretary. Their firefight on the royal front would come back to haunt the pair in later years. But it was Stein's reputation as a troublemaker under Amber Rudd that stopped him becoming Chesterfield's replacement in early 2020. It was seared in the memory of Lee Cain – a fellow Whitehall fire-starter during the dying days of May, but now in charge of communications at No. 10. With a poacher-turned-gamekeeper in charge of hiring, Stein was promptly blocked by Downing Street from becoming Truss's special adviser. The next plan was put to the sword by the Trade department Permanent Secretary John Alty, who vetoed Stein coming in as a civil service Director of Comms – a role Stein was underqualified for, given its largely managerial nature.

Determined to get Stein in, Truss sought a backdoor route instead. She signed off Finsbury to be external contractors – ignoring advice from officials that they were not on a Whitehall-approved list. On a mammoth £80,000 per quarter contract, for six months, it was expensive. But Truss was waging a political battle royale against the National Farmers' Union (NFU) over post-Brexit trade deals. The powerful lobby group had allies around the Cabinet table in the form of Environment Secretary George Eustice and his predecessor Michael Gove. Fighting the civil service, the opposition and her own colleagues was too much for her on her own, reasoned Truss, and she pressed on with Stein's hire.

Chesterfield's replacement was instead handpicked by Downing Street. Traditionally ministers have some degree of control over who their closest political aides are, but after the

2019 Election victory, a massive centralisation of power was going on. In January 2020, Dominic Cummings, the No. 10 Chief of Staff in all but name, had put out a call for 'weirdos and misfits' to come and work for the government, with limited success. The unorthodox job advert had been placed on his personal blog while the PM was away on holiday. Paul Stephenson, now of Hanbury Strategy, was drafted in to oversee the recruitment of private sector figures as special advisers, rather than using the traditional Spad breeding ground of CCHQ or Parliament. Crucially, they would answer to Cummings first and foremost. A website, spadjobs.uk, was set up, with candidates urged to 'go through a rigorous process' including speechwriting and telephone interviews, before being grilled by a selection board chaired by Stephenson. One of the few successful applicants was Adam Jones, a speechwriter at HSBC. After a brief initiation in No. 10 he was despatched to Trade to keep an eye on Truss.

It was a rocky start for Truss and Jones, although they would become close colleagues. Her early enthusiasm for a free trade deal with America had earned her the enmity of the NFU. The voice of 55,000 British farmers, it launched a vociferous campaign in tandem with the *Mail on Sunday* in spring 2020, urging ministers to 'Save Our Family Farms' by resisting an avalanche of chlorine-washed chicken and other inferior food products that they feared would be sold if such a deal was passed. 'She had no idea who the guy [Jones] was,' remarks one long-serving aide. 'He was thrust on her in the middle of this massive battle. She was getting battered day in day out by the NFU, the *Mail* and she had Cummings and Cain trying to kill her and briefing she was going to get sacked at every turn. Adam arrived in that department green as the grass and was totally out of his depth.'

The hire was indicative of No. 10's distrust of Truss. An insider recalls: 'They were really trying to kill her. I think Cummings and Cain really hated her. Frankly this is where

Gove turned on her too. Throughout 2020 she was seriously worried about her Cabinet job.' When Cummings hit the headlines with his Barnard Castle lockdown-breaking escapades in May 2020, Truss was one of the few Cabinet ministers to refuse to do a centrally ordered tweet in support of his unorthodox Rose Garden press conference. And in July a leaked letter Truss had written to Sunak, warning that delaying the implementation of new EU trading laws until the following year risked major smuggling threats and could break international law, only made relations with No. 10 worse. Within days of being sent, the letter had found its way to Business Insider – a relatively unknown outfit for such a targeted and damaging leak. The fact it was CC'd to Michael Gove heightened paranoia in Truss circles, but she got the full blame from No. 10 for the leak – something she ferociously denies to this day.

Cummings would blog in 2022: 'Truss is the only minister I shouted at in No. 10. The reason was her compulsive pathological leaking. As soon as she left any meeting she would call people like Harry Cole (the *Sun*) and blurt out what had been said. This routinely caused chaos and often damaged the UK. I called her over to No. 10. I sat in that tiny little room near the Cabinet room next to the loos (G39). I said to her: what are you doing leaking everything, stop, focus on your real job where you're failing to grip your department, focus on that … The eyes had a thousand-yard stare. "What do you mean the real job?" she said. It was pointless to go on. For her, leaking to the media *was* the "real" job.' Truss tells a different version of events involving her haranguing both Cummings and the PM at that particular showdown over their soft stance on Chinese tech giant Huawei being allowed into British Telecom's infrastructure. But recollections certainly vary.

Cummings would soon be gone. An insider recalls: 'Things started to change when Dan Rosenfield came in; she [Truss] was quite clever. She knew that Rosenfield would try to grip the process so she went straight to Rosenfield and said, "we need to establish a trade committee".' One source cites Truss as telling Rosenfield: 'Dan, you like process, I need process, and there is no way currently for me to speak to the PM on this stuff.' The Global Britain (Strategy) Committee was set up in early 2021 but soon became locked in the same tensions as the wider Cabinet. Nevertheless, it helped strengthen the ties between Truss and the centre.

One of Truss's fears about accepting the DIT job was the level of travel. 'She was mostly upset because she thought she would be away from the kids,' one friend said. As it happened, the pandemic curtailed international travel, with negotiations switching to Zoom. Many of the early stages of talks with Japan, New Zealand and Australia took place from the front room of the Truss family home in Greenwich, with a hastily ordered Union flag couriered down to south-east London. 'The whole lockdown experience was interesting to her because it made her much closer to her family,' says a friend. 'It was the first time that they've spent all day, every day together and they grew much, much closer.' Discussions with international counterparts at strange hours were interjected with *Come Dine with Me* contests against Hugh and the children.

Having escaped the messiest aspects of the Brexit civil wars hidden away in the Treasury, Truss found her foreign-facing DIT role to be a similar blessing as she avoided responsibility for the horrors of Covid. Denied a seat on the relevant Cabinet committees and deeply distrusted by No. 10 chiefs Cummings and Cain, Truss did not have to present a single Covid press conference. She thus evaded the fate of Cabinet rivals like Matt Hancock, who, as Health Secretary, became the face of the government response. At the beginning of the pandemic, Truss was the eighth most popular Cabinet minister among Tory members. Twelve months later she was the most popular of all, comfortably ahead of Sunak who was in second place.[1]

It was in these times of Covid that Truss began to seriously ponder her frustrations and perceived failings of Johnson's administration with her closest allies. Long walks in Greenwich Park forged a powerful pact with her old ally Kwasi Kwarteng, who had moved two streets over and by January 2021 was in the Cabinet as Business Secretary. He recalls: 'We talked about the government, how the government could be better. We had been talking about the government as you would expect as friends, mostly since I became a secretary of state. And we could see that there was no economic strategy. We were raising taxes like it was getting out of fashion. There was no real growth plan. And we didn't think we were pro-business enough. Really we were talking about government, growth, and making a pro-business culture for ages.' Allies say it was in those lockdown days, during the walks in the park, that 'a tacit deal' was done. If Truss was going all the way, Kwarteng would be her number 2 and biggest advocate. With Brexit negotiator David Frost and Truss ally James Cleverly also living in the leafy corner of south-east London, what would be known as the 'Greenwich Set' was born.

Throughout all of 2020 Truss's ambitions for future trade deals were getting bogged down in the fights over food standards and chlorinated chicken. Truss told the department: 'We need to go out campaigning on the free trade, and the capitalist elements of trade deals, and talk about the benefits for the UK.' Stein and Head of News at the Department Joe Watts – a former Lobby hack who had known Truss since his days as a cub reporter on the *Eastern Daily Press* – honed her 'Trade = Jobs' mantra that was hammered every single day, alongside a true-blue defence of the ideology underpinning it.

In a conscious effort to recreate the cries of 'Cheap Bread!' that tore down the Corn Laws in the 1840s, Truss tried to directly link her free trade to voters' wallets. One war-weary veteran recalls: 'In a pitched battle you had the NFU, lots of farming-backed Tory MPs, Labour and the *Daily Mail* group, who were conscious of their proprietor Lord Rothermere's vast farming interests. And on the other side you had Liz saying, "these trade deals are going to create loads of jobs for people; why do you want to rob them off those opportunities?"' Truss began to continuously shape every trade deal discussion in the narrative of a Brexit 'win', or opportunity, both to the public but crucially also to the Prime Minister. Colleagues say her performance in the role at Cabinet through 2020 was 'fairly lacklustre'. But as Johnson began to see 'wins' that could be punted, he quickly warmed to her aggression towards the protectionists. 'She played to his vanity for sure,' one aide concedes. 'At the end of the day what PM doesn't want to sit there with the leaders of Japan and Australia and say "Look at this big win we've achieved." She knew what she was doing.'

Those who worked with Truss at the time said her defence of free trade at Chatham House in October 2020 encapsulated the orders she was handing out. In words that can be read as an instruction to her own negotiators, she said: 'Richard Cobden came to conclude trade was "God's diplomacy". In that spirit, I urged my newly appointed Board of Trade earlier this month to make the case around the world as the Cobden, Peel and Bright of the twenty-first century – and to re-establish the UK as a major voice in global trade.' She continued: 'If so many of us can see that free trade is a force for good, why do some people treat it like the source of all evil? … Free trade is a lean, green, value-creating machine. It has lifted billions out of poverty across the world, led to a cleaner environment and put food on people's plates. It helps developing, and developed, nations alike.'

And addressing the claims of the NFU with support from the unlikely alliance of the *Mail* and the *Guardian*, she continued: 'We have legislated to ban the import of chlorinated chicken and hormone-fed beef. And I can assure anyone worried about such food entering our markets that our standards are not up for grabs. But we cannot have blanket bans on any food produced differently from the UK, which would have a devastating effect on economies which we want to see benefit from free trade.'

Despite warm words from Donald Trump in the White House – and even a signed copy for Truss of his book *The Art of the Deal* that read 'Secretary, let's get a huge deal' – the UK–US trade talks were bogged down. One of Truss's allies now admits that 'Too much store was set by a US trade deal as the gold standard.' By the time Trump was replaced with Biden in January 2021, hopes of a US trade deal any time soon were dead. This was privately accepted long before it was in public. Instead, the main free trade struggle of the Johnson years concerned Britain's major Antipodean ally. Australia, Japan and New Zealand would be a path for the UK to join the vast Trans-Pacific Partnership, but only if tariff-free trade with Australia could be shown to work. To achieve this, Truss would have to build the first Free Trade Agreement entirely from scratch.

The battle over Australia fell to three major Cabinet characters: Truss, Michael Gove and George Eustice, all of whom had served as Defra Secretary. George Eustice, the incumbent minister, was a close ally of Gove, who faced constant jibes from Truss's supporters that he was living in his predecessor's shadow with Truss's old rival pulling his strings. 'Given his devout brexitiness it was odd quite how far Gove went the other way on Free Trade,' one minister recalls. 'He was determined to put a spanner in the works of every deal and would just turn up to Trade Strategy meetings spouting NFU lines.' In a reference to the NFU president Minette Batters, they added: 'We might as well have had Minette in the room.'

Truss also felt she was negotiating without any clear mandate from the PM and Cabinet; rather than thrashing out issues beforehand, arguments were only being held once a deal had been agreed. 'It was totally unsustainable,' says one No. 10 Spad. 'Dan [Rosenfield] got that and the committee was set up.' Another official involved in the negotiations added: 'The whole thing was done in reverse. The DIT negotiated aspects of a trade deal and No. 10 decided whether to approve it or not. Rather than "here's what I want you to negotiate". It was classic Boris.'

At the Cabinet table and in the press a very public debate played out between what the *Spectator*'s Katy Balls called the 'Waitrose protectionists' and the 'Lidl free marketeers', characterised as being between those who wish to prioritise British farmers at a higher price and those who want their constituents to benefit from cheaper produce on the supermarket shelf.[2] The terms started to appear in columns in 2021, but had been widely used by a frustrated Truss for months. At times of particular stress she was also heard dubbing Gove, Eustice, Zac Goldsmith and others the 'axis of evil'; another example of her love of a pithy shorthand such as 'enemies of enterprise'. 'The negotiations were as much about negotiating with other countries as our own government,' allies say.

There were yet more press blunders too. A bizarre briefing to the *Telegraph* in April 2021, citing 'sources in her department', claimed they would seat Truss's Australian counterpart, Dan Tehan, in an 'uncomfortable chair' in the Foreign Office's famous Locarno room 'so he has to deal with her directly for nine hours'. The briefing, aimed at expediting the 'glacially slow' talks, caused an outcry in the Australian press. Truss was forced to text Tehan to rectify the situation, insisting whoever had briefed the paper did not speak for her; Adam Jones later privately confessed responsibility.

Yet the biggest roadblock to the deal was not the Australian side, but the Cabinet itself. Gove explains his position thus: 'I felt that this was a potential watering down of animal welfare and environmental standards, that this was important to Defra: George Eustice was fighting for them. Yes, there was a geopolitical imperative to get those deals which we understood but my argument was that we were dealing with the Australians as we were dealing with the EU and my anxiety was that in our anxiety to get a deal we weren't necessarily being as tough as we should have been. It did get quite tense in some of the conversations because for Liz this was absolutely central. Getting the first new FTA was really, really important. There

George and I were quibbling over things that she doesn't seem to consider particularly important. Her view was, "UK agriculture should just be more competitive and stop bellyaching and Michael why are you worrying about all this green stuff and the Australians mutilating sheep when they're young? There is a great prize here." And my argument was we had painstakingly built up a reputation on standards and environmental protection that those things meant UK agriculture was not just respected but had a competitive edge overall. If we eroded that so people thought that farmers were no longer able to maintain that premium position, then that would be bad for brand UK as well as being bad in itself.'

The debate over Australia came down to a crunch meeting in May 2021. Britain was due to host the G7 in Cornwall the following month, with Scott Morrison pencilled in to attend. It was clear that both sides were working towards that deadline. A 'zero tariff / zero quota' quid pro quo had been agreed with the EU already, so Eustice was fighting an uphill battle to suggest that the UK should trade with a Commonwealth ally on worse terms. In the end, Truss was the victor but it came with a hefty caveat. In a classic Johnson move to try to keep everyone happy, the transition to free trade with Australians would be staggered over 15 years; quotas and tariffs would be reduced gradually to avoid an influx of cheaper meat coming into the British market. Prices at the tills were not the explosive political issue they were to become 18 months later, but even with this caveat it was hard to paint the battle as anything other than a comprehensive victory for Truss – and free trade. Gove admits: 'George and I accepted that in terms of what the Prime Minister wanted to achieve, Liz had won the argument. We've made the best case that we could but I think Liz was very irritated that we were trying to point out the same pitfalls.' 'Better late than never,' Truss would claim in June when the deal was agreed by a hand-shake between Johnson and Morrison in the Downing Street garden.

In an interview with the *Sun* the day the deal was agreed, Truss had been up literally all night, fuelled on six expressos and a few glasses of Australian white wine. While her aides and officials looked ready to flag at 11 a.m. the next morning, Truss was hyperactive. She told the paper, 'Everyone's a winner' when asked if she was enjoying her vanquishing of her Cabinet foes. 'This is our first post-Brexit deal that we've negotiated from scratch,' she beamed – 'the first entirely British-shaped deal. The PM is a massive proponent of free trade. Of course, George is a winner too,' she teased with a smirk.

Truss's allies say she knew full well she would be long gone before ground was made on any subsequent US deal, so she took the early win – and the selfies to back it up. 'They've shot their bolt way too early' was her succinct verdict on the NFU to staff. 'They're worried about the US deal, the US deal isn't going to happen. Why they are so worried about Australia and New Zealand is beyond me.' An aide adds: 'She said the Australia deal is the hardest thing she's ever got through. She was negotiating with the Australians, she was negotiating with her own department and she was negotiating with her own government. There really was a kind of massive sense of self satisfaction.'

A former official involved in the talks says: 'In terms of the fight she had with the NFU, she probably won. They underestimated her and she fought a good fight.' Another DIT source adds: 'the farmers thought they could scream bloody murder and chlorinated chicken, and that would be enough. Under another politician it probably would have but she just put her fingers in her ears and carried on talking to the Aussies.' The Australia trade deal was officially signed in December 2021; a similar agreement with New Zealand was finalised two months later.

At the DIT, Truss exploited her seven years of ministerial experience to the fullest extent. She became much more adept at operating the machinery of government and surrounding herself with allies. Sonia Khan recalls: 'When we moved on to the DIT, she didn't get on with the Private Secretary there so I think within a week there was a new Private Secretary. And it's like "Wow that was a quick process, you've made a quick judgement call about this person." I hadn't seen that side of Liz. I think the only people who she doesn't get on with are the people that don't give their all to the job when she does, 24/7.' Truss overhauled the painfully mis-acronymed Strategic Trade Advisory Group (STAG), reinforced the department's own board, relaunched the Board of Trade and bolstered the Trade Advisory Groups (TAG) too. Think-tank allies like Mark Littlewood of the IEA and Robert Colville of the Centre for Policy Studies served on STAG; the new Board of Trade was sprinkled with Brexiteers such as ex-MEP Daniel Hannan and former Australian premier Tony Abbott. Truss also brought in businessman Dominic Johnson, who co-founded Somerset Capital with Jacob Rees-Mogg, as a non-executive director in December 2020. Working from a desk in the department, he helped push the Truss agenda through the bureaucratic machine.

Such appointments had to be balanced in line with Whitehall rules; though Truss loathed the NFU, they also received a spot on STAG. But Matt Kilcoyne, who was appointed to the same body in October 2020, says that having their voice in the room meant Truss's free trade arguments were heard by the attendant officials. 'If various producer interests, such as the Farmers' Union, are calling for protections and the retention of tariffs and quotas, at levels that would be detrimental to consumer interests – we could make that point. Sometimes, the green representative would say that he wanted the government to divest from various things. And we'd make the point that that would come with higher costs to consumers on bills and just reiterate to civil servants that there was a divergence of opinion on various issues, and that they had to take those into account. We didn't force the agenda in one way or another. It just made sure the consumer interests were taken into account, not just producer interests.'

A surer touch in Whitehall was matched in Westminster too. Truss encouraged an increase in the number of Trade Envoys – unpaid roles for MPs or peers to sponsor engagement with a country or region. In the words of Kilcoyne: 'Backbench MPs suddenly became interested in the trade agenda because they were made the trade envoy to Tanzania or South Africa or whatever … that's 35 people who she had like a weekly call with. That's a very good way of building a base and a group of people who know who you are and know what you think and know why you think it and who you get to reward … and the PM agreed because you had to vote with the government, you'd have to quit as a Trade Envoy.'

Truss certainly had her critics during her time at the DIT. Some outside and inside her own party suggested she merely rolled over existing deals, like that with the EU, prompting accusations that she was running the 'Department for cut and paste' or that DIT stood for 'the Department for Instagramming Truss'. Even her allies would admit that the deals were far from seismic game-changers as the UK wrestled with its post-Brexit identity. But Truss's energy and initiative certainly impressed many. Former aide Kirsty Buchanan admitted to the BBC that Truss's deals didn't always match her hype: 'Some of that is true but what made that genuinely brilliant from a political point of view is the complete kind of shamelessness with which she rode that. Her boosterism had incredible cut-through in a time where it was all full of doomsters and naysayers … to actually have that kind of full-throttle unabashed unashamed support for Brexit and its consequences made her much beloved of the Conservative Party members … it was the making of Truss 2.0 and it was the building of her confidence but what it really did was cement her relationship with the party.'

But there were other clear wins too, alongside the Australian deal, such as the Japan deal in August 2020. One involved in the negotiations says: 'The Japanese are quite inflexible, they're not very humorous, they don't do flirtation. It didn't work on them.' But Truss played a personal role and helped strike the first agreement that went further than any accords the EU had struck with a non-member state, albeit only marginally on some aspects of data. Yet as Politico noted at the time: 'the substance of the deal is almost as important as its political implications – showing that the dream of Global Britain is alive and well'. After three months of negotiations, it was the first independent deal the UK had signed after leaving the EU. It also laid the groundwork for Britain to join the Comprehensive and Progressive Agreement for Trans-Pacific Partnership (CPTPP), a trade bloc of 11 nations. A win was chalked up, a precedent was set and domestically it was exactly the sort of good news that the government needed after months of dire Covid headlines. Crucially, the PM was impressed, remarking to friends that Truss had 'made a silk purse from a sow's ear and showed great éclat'. After leaving office, Boris Johnson said of his successor: 'She did a bang-up job at DIT and even if many of the deals were rollovers there was plenty of extra value for the UK – and she sold her achievements so well.'

Whereas earlier in her career Truss had been steamrolled or cut out by rivals, this time she had rolled the pitch, brought reinforcements and fought in the gutter. It was the playbook that would ultimately win her the premiership.

At the DIT, Truss had had her first proper experience of international diplomacy too. Her entire political career up until that point had focused exclusively on domestic affairs: local government, public sector reform, taxation. Beyond the scarring 'Enemies of the People' episode she'd had little involvement in any of the Brexit shenanigans that bogged down Theresa May's government, and she'd never made a major speech in Parliament about foreign affairs. Rory Stewart even claims she once told him she found the whole subject area 'boring'. But, having once proposed reviewing Trident and axing the navy's aircraft carriers at Reform, she now embraced a more hawkish, binary view of the world. According to Kilcoyne: 'She fundamentally gets, as we saw when she moved into the FCDO [Foreign, Commonwealth and Development Office], that the world has split into spheres now.'

The issue that best demonstrated this was China, whose education system had so previously enamoured Truss. By 2020, George Osborne's 'Golden Era' was truly over, following the Hong Kong crackdown and Beijing's treatment of Uyghur Muslims in Xinjiang. Many backbench Conservative MPs wanted a tougher line on China than their leader – a self-proclaimed Sinophile – was willing to countenance. As the minister responsible for international trade, Truss found herself at the centre of several of these fights. In December 2020 anti-China Tory MPs sprung the so-called 'genocide amendment' on her department's Trade Bill. If adopted, it would had given British courts a role in determining whether genocide is happening in Xinjiang province. Dominic Raab and the Foreign Office were resolutely opposed, but Truss was privately content to support the measure. Ahead of the crunch Commons vote in January, Raab's team organised a frantic ring-round of rebel Tory MPs to cut their numbers; Truss was also roped in. One supporter of the 'genocide amendment' recalls just how lacklustre Truss's efforts were in such calls. 'It was the most half-hearted ministerial phone call of all time. It was just "Are you voting for this or not?" and the response was "Well, actually, I am going to vote for this amendment." "Yeah, I kind of understand" and that was the end of the call.' Throughout the row, Truss publicly supported the Foreign Office and dutifully trooped through the voting lobby to vote the amendment down. The government squeaked home by 319 votes to 308.

Truss's aide Sophie Jarvis is credited with having hardened her stance on Beijing. Jarvis, who ran Truss's parliamentary outreach, was a key backchannel between the minister and the China hawks like Sir Iain Duncan Smith. 'I've never seen someone who can network a room better than Sophie,' says Matt Kilcoyne. 'And she's a true believer, she used to watch Reagan's

"Shining City on a Hill" speech and Thatcherite videos.' 'We had a pretty strong hatred of the Heseltines of this world.' Such connections would later prove to be invaluable in the 2022 leadership race when Duncan Smith lobbied MPs on Truss's behalf to get her through the parliamentary rounds.

By summer 2021, Truss was in a strong position in the Cabinet and tipped for higher things. No. 10 and rival Cabinet ministers became highly suspicious that Truss was taking the parliamentary outreach a little too far. Press reports branded Mayfair's 5 Hertford Street Team Truss's 'unofficial headquarters' where she plied favourable MPs with champagne in so-called 'Fizz with Liz' sessions. 'She was not exactly subtle about what she was doing,' noted one Boris ally.

But for all the trade deals and hawkish posturing, what guaranteed her promotion to the Foreign Office wasn't international issues but domestic politics. After months of lockdown and a summer recess, in September 2021 the Cabinet met around the table for the first face-to-face meetings in months. Plans for a National Insurance hike had leaked to the *Sun* and *The Times* in early July, and tensions had mounted throughout the summer recess. Hosting a press conference that July to mark 'freedom day', the lifting of the last of the pandemic restrictions, the PM had refused to rule out hiking the tax on employees and employers in a classically Johnsonian denial. Asked by one of the authors if he was planning to increase National Insurance contributions (NICs), the PM obfuscated: 'On the long-awaited plans to deal with social care and how to cover all that, a problem that has bedevilled governments for at least three decades, you've just got to wait a little bit longer. I'm sorry about that, but it won't be too long, it won't be too long now, I assure you.'

A 1.25-percentage-point raid on workers' wallets through National Insurance contributions had been cooking through June and July. After almost a year and half of Covid largesse when it came to spending, Chancellor Rishi Sunak had drawn a line on the PM's latest demands for cash to fix the Covid-crippled NHS. It was Johnson's attempt to make good on his promise to fix the black hole in social care funding, made on the steps of Downing Street as he entered office in 2019. 'Boris wanted more cash, and Rishi called his bluff on putting up taxes,' as one Cabinet minister put it.

Johnson had hoped to get the whole thing done and dusted before the summer recess. But Covid reared its head yet again, with the announcement delayed after newish Health Secretary Sajid Javid tested positive just hours after meeting the PM and the Chancellor in the Cabinet room to sign off the hike. That delay gave time for the sceptical Tory MPs and Cabinet Ministers – including Truss and Kwarteng – to stir up opposition to the plan. Parliament breaking up for the summer took some sting out of the rebellion, but the scene was set as MPs sloped back to Westminster in early September. Johnson called a Cabinet meeting to rubber stamp the tax hike on the 7th, but Truss was not going to go along with it quietly. Ahead of the Tuesday showdown, battle lines were drawn via an unprecedented amount of briefing in the Sunday papers two days before.

On Sunday 5th, it appeared that even the *Sunday Telegraph* could not believe the politically explosive gear they had plastered across their front page. Political Editor Ed Malnick breathlessly reported: 'On Saturday night, in a particularly extraordinary intervention, a Cabinet minister said: "Putting up National Insurance would be morally, economically and politically wrong. It kicks in at a low level and there are all kinds of exemptions which benefit the rich. If you get all your income from investments and property you don't pay a penny but if you work your guts out for minimum wage you get clobbered."' The astonishing tirade continued: 'After all that's happened in the last 18 months they can't seriously be thinking about a tax raid on supermarket workers and nurses so the children of Surrey homeowners can receive bigger inheritances. It makes a total mockery of the levelling-up agenda and Red Wallers will be up in arms. That's before you even get to the fact that a couple of years ago we promised not to do it.'

Over in the *Sunday Express*, it fell to Jacob Rees-Mogg to hammer home the point that raising NICs was a direct breach of the Conservatives' landslide-winning 2019 manifesto. He did not hide behind the cloak of anonymity, quoting George H. W. Bush's 'Read my lips: no new taxes.' His pointed column spelled out that Bush later broke that vow and subsequently lost the 1992 presidential election. As he put it: 'Voters remembered these words after President Bush had forgotten them.'

While Rees-Mogg often got away with sailing close to the wind, within 10 Downing Street there was little doubt over the identity of the *Telegraph*'s anonymous Cabinet minister. One insider recalls: 'It didn't take a leak inquiry to work out who had planted that one.' Truss herself had already warned the Chief Whip and Dan Rosenfield that she would be speaking out against a NICs rise at the first opportunity around the Cabinet table. Adam Jones had organised the incendiary briefing, texting Malnick the quote in full, but with the full blessing of the boss. Inside No. 10, Truss was placed firmly on resignation watch. Some of her closest allies, including Jason Stein, were already urging caution, warning she had made her point and that any further petrol on the fire could force her into a corner where she would have to quit.

But Team Boris had a cunning plan to ensure Truss did not walk: Truss got the tip that she was in line for major promotion in the coming weeks. Scottish Secretary Alister Jack had become increasingly close to Johnson and had counselled the PM on his planned reshuffle that summer. A senior Tory explains: 'Jack was despatched to basically say don't go overboard, hold tight, a big job is coming.' A source close to Truss says: 'She told the Chief Whip and she told Boris how against this [the NICs hike] she was and said very clearly "I'm going to make my point in Cabinet."' Shortly after that, Alister Jack called her and said, "Look Liz you're gonna get a massive job in two weeks' time, a massive job. You would be well advised to shut the fuck up."'

Come the morning of Tuesday 7 September, the stage was set. But Truss was nowhere to be seen. Panic ensued in the ante-room of the Cabinet when it was clear the Trade Secretary had not turned up for the traditional pre-coffee chit-chat ahead of the 09:30 meeting. 'They all thought she was resigning,' an official recalls. 'They called her office about 15 times: "Where is Liz, where is Liz?" Poor Adam Jones was getting it in the neck, as she was not answering her mobile.' With the time zones playing havoc on trade talks with New Zealand, Truss was stuck at the department and ended up arriving at 10 Downing Street 15 minutes after the start of the meeting. She slipped in just ahead of the main business of the day: approval to break the Tory manifesto and hike a tax on workers' wages and employers' cash flow.

But did Jack's message cut through to Truss? She had already told the PM to his face that she thought this was a 'madness', and most around the table had read as much in the press. Truss's turn to speak saw a marked increase in the tension around the table, as 30 colleagues watched her turn to Sunak directly in the meeting and say: 'this is a mistake'. A witness present recalls: 'It wasn't a long speech, it didn't even seem that prepared. But she made the Conservative case: "I don't think we should be raising taxes and I don't think this is the right thing to do. It's going to increase the burden on people and I don't think we should be doing that."'

One witness says Truss's argument was: 'First of all, we've promised not to raise taxes in our manifesto and this isn't even Budget time. We don't have to do this now. The OBR forecasts change by tens of billions every week so we don't know how we need to raise this, or whether you can still allocate this £13 billion from general taxation. Why on earth are we doing this now? The one thing that people know the Tories for is low taxes; this is just putting a massive target on our backs.'

After Truss had spoken, witnesses say the PM claimed: 'I completely agree with everything you've just said.' 'Great,' said Truss, but the PM insisted there was no other way to pay for the funding than by raising National Insurance. An aide who saw her shortly after the meeting, recalls: 'She was particularly irritated because you had the ridiculous charade of Boris piping up at the back end of Cabinet and basically agreeing with her, saying how awful it was but he had no choice. She just thought it was ridiculous that Boris basically let Rishi flex his muscles like that and bully him into doing it. It was Rishi basically throwing his weight around saying I'll only do the spending if you put up taxes, and the PM went along with it. She thought it was insane. End of, so she spoke out against it.'

Several ministers privately let it be known they were against the measures, but in the end just three spoke out that day. The prospect of a reshuffle loomed large, but Jacob Rees-Mogg and Lord Frost both sounded the alarm around the table. 'I am genuinely shocked if anyone thinks the answer to the question is more borrowing,' Sunak told the gathering in response. It was a line he would later repeat until he was blue in the face while running for leader. But a massive dividing line was set up that morning between himself and Truss. 'Rishi hated it,' says another present. 'You could see him rolling around in his seat.' 'The Chancellor was not quite tutting but he clearly wanted to,' says another Cabinet minister. 'I kind of admire her for doing it,' says one Boris ally in the room. 'Obviously it was disloyal and they briefed it out, but she had a bit of eloquence in the way she would be disloyal. It wasn't chippy, she didn't do the big-I-am, but she made it clear she cared about this. And then she shut up.'

The Business Secretary Kwasi Kwarteng, who sat on his hands during the meeting, recalls: 'She opposed the National Insurance rise in Cabinet, she actually did that, we were all very British but there was a lot of concern.' Other Cabinet members recollect silently cheering on Truss, as Sunak squirmed. Kwarteng went on: 'I remember joking to Priti Patel: the National Insurance tax, we used to call it the jobs tax, and we were laughing and we were thinking no; but we were bound by collective responsibility. The Chancellor knows the books, but time and time again we were raising taxes and were disincentivising investment and we had exactly the same view on that. Something had to change.'

Despite her protestations in the Cabinet, Truss didn't comment further. 'She really never fucked us publicly on this,' a No. 10 official admitted. 'She said [her piece] in private and on and off the record and then sucked it up.' Perhaps Alister Jack's plan had worked after all; Truss did not resign. While Truss and Rees-Mogg bowed to collective responsibility, Frost resigned by Christmas citing his disillusion with the direction of travel of his old friend Boris. Kwarteng remembers the NICs rise being a key moment that Truss turned on Boris too: 'Their answer to everything was to put up more taxes, and that was what Rishi was saying. We put up National Insurance, we were going to put up corporation tax. In the end we had a windfall tax, which I said was crazy. Liz said windfall taxes are a surprise tax, so we were talking about this for months. I think the Sunak/Johnson relationship was a disaster. I think Rishi Sunak was very much a creature of the Treasury. He was described to me as the head boy of the Treasury.'

The next morning's papers were brutal. 'Boris rolled the dice on his premiership yesterday', said the *Sun*. 'The PM tore up his 2019 manifesto to launch the biggest tax hike in a generation on wages and shareholder profits.' 'Tax burden will rise to highest in 70 years', noted *The Times*. The *Mail* was succinct in its summary: 'Opposition crumbles amid reshuffle talk.' In the end it would be less than a fortnight before Alister Jack's warning came good ... but not before Sunak had tried to exact his revenge.

2021

DIPLOMACY

On Sunday 12 September 2021 the reshuffle whiteboard was out once again in the PM's Downing Street office. The culling of the team before the Party Conference was nailed on, but there were still 'moving parts'. Foreign Secretary Dominic Raab was determined not to be landed with the blame for that summer's disastrous withdrawal from Afghanistan. Following the tensions over National Insurance that led to Rishi Sunak contemplating resignation with his closest team, there were even some inside No. 10 who wanted the Chancellor demoted. In reality Johnson told friends he never seriously considered such a move. One close confidante says: 'The tragedy at the time was Boris still liked and admired Rishi and believed in him. Even though the evidence became thinner and thinner and thinner, Boris kept thinking that he was going to come good, but he never did.'

While the PM was never genuinely contemplating sacking Sunak, he was ready to clip his wings. For more than a year, the telegenic Chancellor was the crown prince of Tory politics, the obvious heir apparent with few major rivals. So Johnson resolved to address that by promoting one of Sunak's likely competitors. In the final 48 hours of planning, the PM finally showed the plans to his now distrusted neighbour. As the pair eyeballed the moves, allies of the PM claim there was some obvious discomfort from the younger man: 'Hmm, are we sure about Liz to Foreign Secretary?' A few moments later he came round for another go: 'Are we sure about that? Is that going to work?' Of course he could see her as a threat. 'He tried to get her taken out,' says an insider, 'repeatedly.' But the matter was closed: Liz Truss would be the new Foreign Secretary.

Despite ripping up the Tory manifesto on National Insurance, Johnson was at this point fresh off the boost of the vaccine rollout, with another 10 years in power being discussed openly by senior Tories. Britain was open for business while other countries in Europe lingered in semi-lockdowns. The week of the reshuffle a Cabinet minister told *The Times*: 'Boris will want to go on and on. The stuff Dom Cummings was saying about him going off into the sunset was nonsense. He's very competitive. He wants to go on for longer than Thatcher.' Johnson himself told author Sebastian Payne in a book released that month that his goal of 'levelling up' was 'going to take a while, it's going to take ten years'. The comments were immediately interpreted as the starting pistol for the 2024 election campaign, when the PM insisted that voters would see a 'great, great project' making progress. Johnson's grip on history looked firm when Tory candidate Jill Mortimer thumped Labour in the Hartlepool by-election in May of that year – another symbolic brick of the Red Wall turning blue, even after a brutal pandemic slump in the polls for the Tories. But the warning signs were there when his party fell short of a similar upset in Batley and Spen that July.

Hubristically or otherwise, Johnson felt powerful enough to sack more than a dozen colleagues. Some Cabinet casualties were obvious: Gavin Williamson had been a dead man walking at Education after the botched handling of schools during the pandemic and a litany of exams fiascos; ousted Housing Secretary Robert Jenrick was a lucky cat that ran out of lives after a number of scandals that might have ended careers in a less brazen age. More surprising sackings included Justice

Secretary Robert Buckland – who might have thought he was safe after the departure of Dominic Cummings, who found him an irritating obstruction on terror and crime reforms. Long-term Boris-ally Amanda Milling was relieved as Party Chairman, with Oliver Dowden never forgiving Johnson for his demotion from Culture to be Milling's replacement.

But the row over what to do about Dominic Raab was what dominated the reshuffle. The dust had barely settled on August's bungled Kabul evacuation, in which thousands of foreign citizens and vulnerable Afghans fled the country as the Taliban prepared to take the capital from the Americans. Soon the Ministry of Defence and the Foreign Office were at loggerheads as to who was to blame. The FCDO charge sheet was not looking good for the Foreign Secretary or his Permanent Under-Secretary, Sir Philip Barton, who were both on holiday when Kabul fell to the Taliban. Raab was pilloried in the press but rejected calls to resign; four weeks later, in a classic Whitehall move, he was fired by promotion to Deputy PM.

Kwasi Kwarteng is scathing about his rival member of the 2010 intake: 'You've got to remember Dominic Raab had fucked up right? I mean, it was a disaster what he had done. And we could not be all British about it and say, "well he was unlucky"; he didn't respond to the Foreign Minister of Afghanistan when his capital had fallen to the Taliban. He was in Crete, and he had not responded to the call. That was kinda serious and there was a view that Raab had to go. You've got a foreign secretary who didn't see it was his job to answer the phone. The idea that Raab could stay in that job was highly questionable. And then who was the person to get the job? Someone who'd been in international Trade and travelled around the world for two and a half years. That was a natural promotion.'

And so 11 years after taking her first step onto the ministerial ladder, at the age of 47, Liz Truss was at last given a Great Office of State. She entered the marble finery and questionable colonial art of King Charles Street as just the second-ever female Foreign Secretary, and the first Tory woman. For once, her promotion was met with a reassessment from the commentariat: the betting markets now made her joint-second favourite as Johnson's successor, behind Sunak but alongside Gove. When asked if she had previously wanted the post, one friend says, 'She didn't, but she grew to want it', adding that her strategy at Trade had been about 'getting that promotion to Foreign Sec or Chancellor. It was about being in position to make that massive leap to be a serious candidate and then she made the massive leap in September.'

Truss kept the additional bauble of Equalities Minister and enjoyed the luxury of not one but two grace-and-favour homes: the Carlton Gardens townhouse in London and the Chevening estate in Kent. The latter was subject to a long-running row between Truss and Raab about who got to enjoy the 115-room house: eventually, a time-share-style compromise was brokered to soften the blow of Raab's sacking. Despite their differences, she let Michael Gove take the house at Carlton Gardens, preferring to stay in Greenwich. Gove had recently split from his wife, the columnist Sarah Vine, and the act of kindness was typical of the complicated friendship and rivalry between him and Truss.

Truss wasted no time in using her preferred medium of Instagram to herald her new success, posting a photo of her striding purposefully forward outside her new department, red bag in hand, sandwiched between two mandarins. It would be the first of many: in her first five months as Foreign Secretary, more than seven hundred pictures of Truss were uploaded on the government's official Flickr account: one for every five hours in the job. It was more than any other minister; her rival George Eustice appeared in just three.

The new Foreign Secretary received a fillip within her first 24 hours, after news was announced overnight of the AUKUS submarine pact with the Americans and her old friends the Australians. Two weeks into post and Truss received another accolade: she again topped the ConservativeHome league table of Tory members in October, but this time with a whopping 15-point gap on her closest rival. The 83 per cent approval rating for the newly appointed Foreign Secretary was broadly in keeping with previous polls, but the gap to second was owing to Rishi Sunak's slide down to fifth, owing to the NICs fall-out.[1]

A return to the United Nations General Assembly within two weeks of her starting the job needed none of her previous scrambles to get in the room with the United States leadership. Early meetings with her counterpart Antony Blinken included preliminary steps to circumnavigate US embargos on Iran to be able to pay the ransom Iran was demanding for the release of British mum Nazanin Zaghari-Ratcliffe, as well as doomed attempts to kickstart trade talks that had faltered since Biden replaced Trump in the White House. Truss was not alone either as a new Foreign Minister on the world stage; forging close early friendships with fellow newbies Mélanie Joly of Canada, Annalena Baerbock of Germany and Yoshimasa Hayashi of Japan. A source says: 'You had many new faces around the table and all of them were forward-looking diplomats who wanted to get stuff done.' Those early friendships would become vital in later months as tensions on the Russian border with Ukraine intensified.

An over-ambitious briefing to the travelling pack about discussions with Blinken about joining the United States–Mexico–Canada Trade Agreement was the only blip on an otherwise faultless debut on the world stage in the new job. Meetings with the Biden administration at the White House finally dashed any hopes of a US trade deal in the coming years, however, with an offer to restart formal trade talks rejected by the Americans. While Johnson returned home, Truss continued to Mexico where some witnesses recall a bleary-eyed Truss rather overdoing the celebrations of her promotion and having to be coaxed into a full schedule of visits in Mexico City the next morning.[2]

Within weeks, though, the vast majority of the Foreign Secretary's 'bandwidth' was taken up by the growing intelligence picture of Putin's massive troop build-up in the west of Russia, looking poised to invade Ukraine. 'We had good intel, and the rest of the world bar America did not – or they did not necessarily believe what they were seeing, or want to believe it,' a source says. An early decision to 'get the machine in place' to start arming Ukraine was made by Truss, Johnson and the Defence Secretary Ben Wallace in the early autumn.

There was also a decision to try to 'flush out the Russians': something pushed heavily by Truss. This included an unprecedented declassification of intelligence material that was released to the public about what Putin was planning. 'We needed to catch the Kremlin off guard,' a Truss ally argues. 'There were plans for puppet regimes, for cyber attacks and we wanted the Russians to know we knew what they were up to.' These efforts prevented the Kremlin from repeating the playbook of deniability it used during incursions into the Donbas region in 2014. A Foreign Office Strategic Communications hub that had been mothballed after the Cold War was reactivated to counter Russian propaganda. By December's meeting of the G7 Foreign Ministers in Liverpool, Truss was taking a leading role in paving the way for the threat of united sanctions against Moscow as well as cajoling the Western powers into preparing to arm Ukraine with lethal aid, which Britain began to do officially at the turn of the year.

Truss's 356-day tenure at the Foreign Office continued to bolster her credentials within the party. Given the domestic strife, it helped at times that Truss was so often out of the country. But she never let a visit go to waste, playing to the crowd back home. Pictures of her posing on top of a tank in the style of Maggie Thatcher during a visit to Estonia delighted Tory members but were mocked by her detractors.

Truss's status as a grassroots' favourite was cemented by her warm reception at October's Conservative Party Conference.

Her conference speech was packed for once, and she started to draw larger crowds for fringe events. At the LGBT Tories disco Truss snapped selfies and danced along to Beyoncé with admiring glitter-decked fans, with her husband Hugh and the Australian High Commissioner both jiving along in tow. Unsurprisingly, talk began to circulate of another leadership campaign, with Truss flashing some leg to her small-state allies at an IEA fringe event: 'There are people who say it's inevitable that because of Covid we are going to have a fundamentally bigger state ... I think those people are fundamentally wrong.' Her every move was scrutinised, including a new haircut that was described by sketch-writer Quentin Letts as 'Hillary Clinton meets Michael Fabricant'. When she quoted Margaret Thatcher in her speech to the grassroots, saying 'when people are free to choose, they choose freedom', the *Daily Mail* asked: is this 'the new Iron Lady?'

It was no surprise then the following month when the *Mail on Sunday* reported that a new 'Liz for Leader' WhatsApp group for Red Wall Tory MPs had been launched.[3] Though officially denied, it was clear the party was being courted. Truss kept up her social media game, posting pictures of her striding purposefully on the world stage. Her Christmas Instagram post was so grand that some in Westminster suggested she had given up on her ambitions to be the Prime Minister and was making a pitch to be Queen instead. A 1,500-word profile by Truss's former aide Kirsty Buchanan in the *Sunday Times* that December poured petrol on the rumours. Buchanan quoted an ally of Truss discussing her chances to succeed Johnson, saying, 'if he goes out on a low then MPs will want to replace him with the polar opposite, someone who is seen as managerial, steady and competent'. One prophetic MP told her: 'Make no mistake about it, if she makes the final two in a leadership ballot and goes to the membership, she will win.'

But if she was to get the top job, Truss needed to restore the fortunes of the Foreign Office, then still reeling from the Taliban debacle. The department was 'knackered after Afghanistan' says one former aide; 'the whole place was quite weary, bits of it were underpowered'. The new minister had both privately and publicly signalled her willingness to embrace a harder line on China at the DIT; now she was in a position to make that happen. Her impact was shown in the two Foreign Office reports she oversaw on Hong Kong, then in the midst of a Beijing crackdown. These reports have been published every six months since 1997 to give a public update on the Sino-British Joint Declaration. The first under Truss's tenure was published in December 2021 and was regarded by Tory hawks as 'abysmal'. The second, in March 2022, was much tougher in its condemnation and was published in the same week it was announced that serving UK judges would be withdrawn from the Hong Kong Court of Final Appeal. An ally says Truss needed time to grow into the role: 'You see this pattern repeated with Truss where she goes in, she's very unconfident, not sure what she's doing and then actually quite quickly gets into it.'

There were also press reports suggesting that Dame Caroline Wilson, Britain's ambassador to Beijing, was insufficiently hard-line on Xinjiang. In November, *The Times* recounted a meeting in October 2020 between the pair in Truss's previous role. The paper quoted an 'ally of Truss' as saying, 'Wilson ended their discussion by asking why the UK couldn't treat China "like we treat the French".' According to the source, Truss retorted: 'Because the French aren't committing genocide.' Days later, the *Mail on Sunday* followed it up with a prominent story that claimed: 'Our woman in Beijing' had been 'lobbying Cabinet ministers for appeasement with China', citing sources who accused Wilson of sending letters to ministers at the National Security Council that 'effectively argue for the appeasement of China'. The move 'risks putting Dame Caroline at odds' with Truss, 'one of the most hawkish members of the Cabinet on China'.

Such reports were clearly part of an organised strategy to boost Truss's credentials as a tough-talking operator, willing to go further than the 'official' No. 10 line. Three months into her role, she laid out her vision for a so-called 'Network of Liberty' in a speech at Chatham House. 'I want to see all freedom-loving nations calling time on introspection, protectionism, and isolationism,' she declared, stressing the UK's support for more economic partnerships, security ties and tech leadership. One ally explains that the 'Network of liberty was basically all about increasing economic alliances between existing friends but also reaching out to new friends like Mexico and Indonesia.' Truss subsequently told the *Atlantic* that the G7 needed to become 'more institutionalised' and turned into an 'economic NATO' to defend its members from Chinese economic coercion. Her stance appealed to various factions of the parliamentary party; an ally of Truss notes that: 'When you get people as diverse as Damian Green or Tom Tugendhat or Iain Duncan Smith or a good number from the 2019 intake all complaining about China, you know you need to take it seriously.'

While China was one issue through which Truss could endear herself to new party allies, Europe was another. The resignation of Brexit chief Lord Frost from the Cabinet in December saw Truss given additional responsibility for negotiations on the Northern Ireland Protocol. Typically, the Foreign Secretary saw the opportunity in this extra burden, viewing it as a chance to build bridges with Brexiteers on the right of the party. Members of the European Research Group (ERG) were impressed by Truss's bullish approach and would later give her the crucial votes that got her into the final two of the leadership race in 2022. But critics said she was too close to the Brexit hardliners, allowing them to set the government's hardline EU policy to begin legislation to unilaterally tear up the trade terms in Northern Ireland, which had been agreed just two years previously.

A senior Cabinet minister lamented that while the Tory Party had a 'strong stomach for confrontation with the EU, the worry was we hadn't thought through the end game. At the court of tribunal, our case will be so weak, once we've played every card, we will be told, right you have had your fun, but you have got to comply with the original terms of the protocol.' Cabinet colleagues including Sunak and Michael Gove urged further negotiations rather than bellicose threats to walk away. One ex-Minister says: 'There were things that we could have won in negotiation, but could not if we bet everything on one spin of the roulette wheel.' While rumours about Sunak's leadership ambitions meant he largely kept his doubts private, Gove raised concerns with the PM on at least two occasions over Truss and the ERG's hardline approach to talks with Brussels.

With foreign affairs, Ukraine diplomacy, the Commonwealth, international development, Brexit negotiations, women, equalities and representing South West Norfolk, Truss's many duties reflected her growing power base in government. And her team correspondingly swelled to a record seven special advisers in January – the most for any Foreign Secretary – just one short of Sunak's combined No. 10 and 11 unit. Existing aides Sophie Jarvis, Adam Jones and policy brain Jamie Hope were joined by Lord Frost's Brexit wonks Hugh Bennett and Christopher Jenkins; a new press secretary Sarah Ludlow; and Reuben Solomon, a full-time digital aide. As well as being a reflection of her increased status, this team would provide the core of Truss's leadership bid just six months later. The size of her entourage certainly did not go unnoticed, and there were frequent clashes in the department between the Spads and more civil servants. Westminster troublemaker Guido Fawkes quickly pointed out the obvious empire building too.

Now on to her second major job, with extensive travel, Truss was very particular about what she expected from officials on a foreign trip. While not a formal 'rider' in the style of a travelling celebrity, orders were sent ahead to embassies around the world with details of what the Foreign Secretary would expect on a visit:

- Double espressos served in a flat white-sized takeaway cup.
- No big-brand coffee, independent producers only, except Pret if in the UK.
- No pre-made or plastic-packed sandwiches – nothing to be served that has not been freshly prepared.
- Bagels or sushi for lunch – absolutely no mayonnaise on anything, ever.
- A bottle of Sauvignon Blanc provided in the fridge of any overnight accommodation.

Former aide Kirsty Buchanan once remarked: 'She drinks about 42,000 espressos a day or she used to when I worked for her … she would sit there with a massive meatball sub or eat three croissants for breakfast. She would carb up; frankly no woman in her 40s should be eating that much and getting away with it.' Other aides note a long-suffering espresso machine was lugged from department to department each reshuffle, while another former staffer was at pains to point out that under no circumstances was the Foreign Secretary to be served fruit for breakfast.

As Truss's team and demands expanded, so did her list of enemies. It was around this time that someone purporting to be a senior civil servant at the Foreign Office began an anonymous letter-writing campaign to prominent foreign editors at national newspapers. These poison-pen notes were withering in their assessment of Truss's handling of the department, as well as of her behaviour on the diplomatic circuit. While we've treated them with extreme caution, the notes contained a level of detail that pointed to a Foreign Office insider with access to Truss's closest aides, and that tallies with widespread discussion in diplomatic circles. Particular anger focused on Truss's demands to rip up pre-arranged schedules as well as factor hair appointments into her diary. One such note read: 'At the same time as No. 10 were throwing parties, Truss was making the most of escaping abroad. She grew her entourage from the normal three to five, to as many as eighteen, so more of her "advisers" and favoured junior staff could party with her. The drinking began at the airport and continued on the plane ... her main advisers drank two bottles of champagne on a four-hour flight. On the ground the FS [Foreign Secretary] would drink well past midnight ... and be incapable of working the next day. On several trips, Truss would cancel/attempt to cancel important parts of her programme, alienating foreign representatives, due to her hangover or to restart the party. For example she left the HMS *Queen Elizabeth* reception where she was guest of honour after 15 minutes in order to go drinking in Mumbai. Embassy staff began to organise different programmes to match her focus on Instagram, and the next drink. She tried to cut out Ambassadors to hide her behaviour, only to be reminded that this was a breach of the ministerial code.' The letters would recommend journalists target specific Freedom of Information requests to the Foreign Office to back up their claims, begging for help in removing 'a cynical and incompetent disgrace' from government.

It was clear that some of the foreign policy establishment had little time for Truss, but the sentiment was reciprocated. She is said to have found her mandarins to be a little *Yes Minister* and was suspicious of their instincts. Some of her aides shared this disdain for officialdom, with Sophie Jarvis performing a rendition of David Bowie's 'China Girl' at one FCO staff karaoke night to 'piss off' her pro-China colleagues. Another aide said Truss 'cut up rough' against the Foreign Office's 'culture of secrecy' and being overly 'pale, male, stale'. Many officials, though, did impress Truss: her Principal Private Secretary Nick Catsaras would accompany her from the FCDO to No. 10, as would some senior officials with intelligence backgrounds.

One minister who worked under Truss said of her relationship with civil servants: 'She doesn't like people second guessing her. If someone brings her some information and says "here's some stuff, what's your decision?" and she says "My decision is this" and they think "Oh we don't like that decision" and they re-present it a month later and basically say "I know we asked you about X. Well we've been thinking about it and we'd like you to reconsider", she's just like "No, I've made my decision. Don't just come back to me to say that wasn't the answer we were expecting." I've seen that and it genuinely pisses her off – don't keep asking the question.'

When she first got to the Foreign Office, Truss tasked her private office with setting up briefing breakfasts to MPs, cross-party, to explain the long-term stuff she was doing – as well as meeting more potential supporters. The minister recalls: 'About a month later she turns around and says how are we getting on with all those briefing breakfasts? An official piped up: "There's a submission coming to you on that, Foreign Secretary." And she said: "I didn't ask for a fucking submission, I asked for briefing breakfasts. Just get the breakfast sorted."'

And Truss certainly disliked the equidistant posturing of some of her diplomatic corps. On China, one colleague recalls her unique brand of diplomacy when resisting a suggestion that London could not antagonise Beijing too much in order to maintain cooperation on climate change. 'Liz was having none of that, she said: "No, no. We're fucking going after them. They're doing too many things in too many places too often. That's it and we will deal with the consequences if they try and freeze us out of this and freeze out of that."' The insider says she gave short shrift to trying to please everyone in the tinder-box of the Middle East. 'One official would say "well we've got to balance, we've got to say this with the Israelis, we've got to say this with the Palestinians, this with the Saudis and Liz is firmly like: nope, some people matter to us a lot and we've got to lean into those relationships. So the Gulf and Israel, fucking lean in hard."'

Despite her difficulties with some officials, as 2022 dawned, Truss was in a much more secure position than her political chief. Boris Johnson's ratings had tumbled in growing fury over lockdown parties alleged to have been held in No. 10 during the Covid lockdowns of 2020 and 2021. Outwardly Truss remained a model of public loyalty, telling the BBC in January that Johnson was 'absolutely' the man to lead the Tories into the next election. Asked about her own ambitions she replied, 'there is no contest, there is no discussion'.[4] But behind the scenes, Truss supporters' overt campaigning drew the wrath of Johnson's closest team. Not least the day they were caught red-handed by the Chief Whip openly plotting against the PM.

In early January, Chief Whip Mark Spencer was hosting Scottish Secretary Alister Jack on a day's shooting in an estate in Devon. Between drives the tweed-clad pair were in a Land Rover with others, when Jack's phone rang. As he was behind the wheel, Jack answered on the built-in handsfree. On the other end was the inescapable boom of Kwasi Kwarteng, voicing fears the PM was on his knees: 'If it all goes wrong, what happens? Are you a Liz guy?' Kwarteng asked Jack, with the eavesdropping Chief Whip flitting between silent laughter and seething incredulity. 'No, no, no I am not,' replied Jack. 'Oh,' said a disheartened Kwarteng, 'so you are a Rishi guy?' 'No, let's be clear Kwasi, I am a Boris guy,' hit back Jack. 'And furthermore I have the Chief Whip in the car with me.'

'It was a proper middle-stump bowl,' recalls one passenger. 'He [Kwarteng] didn't know what to say.' A few dead pheasants later, and the pair were back in the Land Rover only for Truss herself to call, insisting that Kwarteng had got carried away and was not canvassing Cabinet support on her orders. But her card was marked in No. 10 from that day, despite the public protestations of loyalty. 'Rishi got a lot of stick for quitting, but everyone could see Liz was lining up her ducks for months,' one Boris ally recalled to one of the authors months later. 'Kwasi properly shit himself though; you can't not see the funny side of it.'

There was also a conversation in January on the joint defence ministers' trip to Australia on 'What happens if the balloon goes up?' One of those present characterises Truss's view thus: 'She was never going to move against Boris no matter what. She remained 100 per cent loyal; it was the right thing ethically, politically, personally to stick by Boris.' But around this time Truss herself took soundings among friends in her vast room at the Foreign Office. She was blunt and to the point, telling one visitor: 'I think I would be a very good Prime Minister, there are just two problems: I am weird and I don't have any friends. How can you help me fix that?'

By the end of January, Johnson was in serious trouble. 'He was bleeding out,' his closest allies accepted. Most of the revelations in late November and December about 'Partygate' had focused on the behaviour of Downing Street staff. Johnson told the House of Commons that he was 'sickened' and 'furious' for the 'impression that has been given that staff in Downing Street take this less than seriously'. He added that 'I have been repeatedly assured that the rules were not broken' and later told broadcasters that 'I certainly broke no rules.' An investigation into the claims was started by senior mandarin Sue Gray. But the following month Johnson was forced to admit that he had attended an event in May 2020 at a time when mixing between two households was banned.

Ukraine briefly looked like it might offer Johnson some respite. He was hailed as a hero in Kyiv, thanks to Britain's role in coordinating the international efforts to repel Russia's invasion. In early February Truss travelled to Moscow to meet her counterpart Sergey Lavrov: the first time a British minister had travelled there since the Salisbury attacks in 2018. Foreign Office staff were divided on the wisdom of the trip, but Truss insisted. 'The trip was a signal,' one ally said. 'We just wanted to ramp it up as much as possible, collectively as allies, to let the Russians know if they did this, there would be severe consequences. Of course there were varying degrees of hope or scepticism about how likely the Russians were to change their tactics. But it was important to show not only the Russians, but the wider world, that we were being very clear, and maximise the sense that there was an alliance that was going to step up if Ukraine was invaded.'

Arriving at the Kremlin and led into an ante-room, Truss and her entourage, including security advisers and Adam Jones, were stripped of their phones and cut off from the outside world. It left her at the mercy of Moscow's spin-doctors, who were quick to try to paint Truss as a novice in international affairs. Following a frosty bilateral in which both ministers talked over each other, Lavrov claimed that he had referred to the Voronezh and Rostov regions, two Russian provinces where Russian troops are deployed, whereupon his counterpart replied: 'the UK will never recognise Russian sovereignty over these regions'. It led to much mockery but allies of Truss are quick to describe this account as 'bullshit'. One says that Lavrov had actually 'muttered to her in English during the meeting [and] she misheard him. She knows Rostov is in Russia, rather than Ukraine, but the Russians seized on this and briefed it out. It's just the nature of what they do.' Another says that after Lavrov listed the two provinces, Truss replied: '"Look, I'm mindful of what you're saying; we will never accept your supremacy over Ukraine." And then they spun it as "Oh, she doesn't know." And it was obviously misinterpreted.'

The surreal encounter was followed by a bizarre press conference between the two in which Lavrov described their discussions as like a 'conversation of a mute and a deaf person' and then appeared to walk out. But, away from the cameras, the Russian actually waited for Truss and held the door open for her. There then followed 'quite a cordial but very weird lunch' consisting of borscht and vodka, which Lavrov gulped down, in between drags on his cigarette. Both politicians took the chance to quiz the other on what their respective political systems were and even 'traded a few laughs about how different it all was'. It was all 'very strange' according to one in the room, 'and the food was crap'. Truss left with the impression Lavrov was actually isolated from Putin's decision making and was nothing more than a 'superannuated spokesman'. A diplomatic source said: 'It was clear from that lunch that he is not very influential, he wasn't one of the key instigators. In fact, there's some suspicion that he didn't know what was planned.' Whether he was clueless or simply lying, Lavrov still insisted Russia had no plans to invade.

Truss herself was the public voice of realism, warning in a Sky interview on 15 February that 'we could be on the brink of a war in Europe'. And so it transpired nine days later, when Putin gave the order to send over 100,000 men across the border. Truss was at home in Greenwich when Nick Catsaras called her at 3.30 a.m. on 25 February to say simply 'it's started'. Having listened to Lavrov's lies just over two weeks previously, Truss wasted no time in summoning the Russian ambassador to her office. After listening to him 'spouting the usual propaganda' she ended the meeting early and dismissed him after just ten minutes, having told him he 'should be ashamed of himself'.[5]

Truss was an enthusiastic supporter of Kyiv's cause from the beginning of the crisis. She remonstrated with friends who thought a negotiated settlement was inevitable, arguing both publicly and privately that such talk amounted to little more than appeasement. Her credibility was bolstered by the weaponry, particularly the portable anti-tank missiles that proved so effective in the early weeks of the war, that Britain had been sending Ukraine for months during the worsening climate. Boris Johnson heaped praise on Truss's role in those months, saying, 'she was always terrific on Ukraine'. But Truss did sometimes overstep the mark in her enthusiasm, such as in her BBC interview on the first Sunday of the crisis. Asked whether she would back anyone wanting to volunteer to help the Ukrainians fighting for their freedom, she told Sophie Raworth: 'That is something people can make their own decisions about. The people of Ukraine are fighting for freedom and democracy, not just for Ukraine, but for the whole of Europe. Absolutely, if people want to support that struggle, I would support them in doing that.' An aide suggested she had not been briefed properly beforehand and that week 'she had been up till three, four in the morning' working on the UK's response, but No. 10 were forced to distance themselves from the comments the following day.

Nevertheless, reflecting on his Foreign Secretary's role, ex-PM Johnson says: 'She and Ben Wallace had a great relationship and a great partnership, and I think that was a real benefit to the UK. Other governments faffed around. They worried about humiliating Putin and other such nonsense. She was very clear and focused and got good results in the G7 and elsewhere.'

Though dominating most of her time, Russia was not the only major moment of Truss's short tenure as Foreign Secretary. In March 2022 she scored a diplomatic triumph that had eluded her four predecessors, securing the release of Nazanin Zaghari-Ratcliffe and Anoosheh Ashoori from Iran. Truss made the deal after the Tehran regime agreed that the £393.8 million paid in parallel for her release would 'only be available for humanitarian purposes'. An old debt was settled after a loosening of American objections, negotiated by Truss and her counterpart Blinken. Nazanin's husband Richard Ratcliffe later wrote: 'she delivered on her promise to us'.[6] Standing on the tarmac at RAF Brize Norton in Oxfordshire waiting with the families and loved ones, Truss had succeeded where Johnson, Hunt and Raab had failed. After six long years separated from her mother, Zaghari-Ratcliffe's daughter Gabriella chatted away with the Foreign Secretary. 'We had a chat about the tooth fairy,' Truss would reveal. 'Her tooth was coming out so she was very keen to make sure she was fully compensated.' She says that moment was the 'most privileged moment' of her ten years in government. In a rare comment about her emotion, she told *The Times*: 'To meet them, to see them all safe on British soil, it was an amazing moment. Just to see particularly Gabriella and her joy and her excitement to be with her mum again, it was just beautiful.'

Back in Westminster, leadership speculation went nuclear when the Metropolitan Police announced in April that a criminal investigation into 'Partygate' would serve up both Johnson and, surprisingly, Rishi Sunak with a fixed penalty notice for breaching Covid laws. Both refused to resign. Sunak endured an especially hellish 20 days between his much-mocked Spring Statement and the day he was fined, with a series of revelations about his wife's non-domiciled tax status, his own use of a US Green Card and dire figures for the UK economy. It was Sunak's first moment caught in a proper scandal – something that Truss had been used to for 16 years since the Mark Field story first broke. 'She had more than a decade to toughen up on Rishi, and that showed in the leadership election,' a friend would later remark. With Johnson and Sunak both reeling from Partygate, the House of Commons called for an inquiry into whether the PM had deliberately misled the House. A Privileges Committee investigation was duly established; the following month the Met concluded its own probe on 19 May. Six days later, Gray's full unredacted report was released, damning the government still further.

On a roll, in May 2022 Truss announced the finalised plans to overhaul the Northern Ireland Protocol in order to preserve the Good Friday Agreement. At Stormont the DUP were refusing to join the power-sharing administration until changes were made. To the delight of them and their allies in the ERG, Truss went ahead with their proposed measure to rip up the 2019 deal struck between Britain and the EU should a negotiated deal with Brussels fall through. This would include freeing the movement of UK-made goods from 'unnecessary bureaucracy' and regulatory barriers. It prompted a furious response from the European Commission, which hinted darkly that it would respond with 'all measures at its disposal' if Truss pushed on with such plans, raising the spectre of an EU trade war. 'On Northern Ireland she was impressively robust,' says Boris Johnson. 'She saw the sensitivities but she also saw that there is simply no need for the checks that the EU have been imposing. Liz got the main point straight off the bat – that there is no future in just relying on negotiations with the Commission. She saw that we must stop our United Kingdom being slowly and invisibly hauled apart. She saw that we must protect the integrity of the UK internal market – and the only way to do that is with a Bill in Parliament, with notwithstanding clauses and all the rest of it. And she saw that we could do that without the slightest threat to traffic in goods or anything else north-south in the island of Ireland.'

It did not escape notice that Truss's proposals kept the ERG happy, just at the time that leadership speculation had begun to intensify in the spring. One Tory MP says: 'It wasn't just the case that she was delivering something that the ERG wanted, she was delivering it in cooperation with the ERG, in that the Protocol Bill was co-designed by Bill Cash and everyone else ... more energy and time was spent finetuning a bill with a backbench caucus than with other ministers.'

Truss's final two months in post were dominated by domestic leadership concerns: things were not getting any easier for Johnson. After Partygate in the winter came the local elections in the spring. The one-time invincible Tory electioneer lost almost five hundred council seats and scraped just 30 per cent of the national vote. A no-confidence vote was inevitable and by the beginning of June, the crucial threshold of 54 MPs' letters was hit. Asked by an aide on the morning of the vote if the PM would keep the number of critics under a hundred, Truss replied: 'No chance, it's way worse than that. He's really in trouble. He's going to win, but the mood is very bad.' Truss was a model of public loyalty, though privately she began to have tentative conversations about running, even as she told aides that Johnson would likely survive, which he did, winning 211 to 148. Key lines were drawn up, stressing her main messages, ahead of such a bid.

Events never let up for Johnson. A combination of two by-election defeats in Wakefield, and Tiverton and Honiton, a fortnight later saw Party Chairman Oliver Dowden – a key Sunak supporter – resigning. At the end of June came allegations in the *Sun* about the behaviour of Deputy Chief Whip Chris Pincher at the Carlton Club. He quit, beginning his letter: 'Last night I drank far too much.' It subsequently emerged that Johnson had ignored previous complaints over Pincher's appointment, prompting a Cabinet revolt at the beginning of July. Truss largely avoided the last fortnight of domestic drama by dint of her diplomatic duties. In the last 10 days of June, she was on a whistlestop tour of the globe, attending the Commonwealth Heads of Government Meeting in Kigali, the G7 Leaders' Summit in the Bavarian Alps and then the NATO summit in Madrid. But it was clear an end game was approaching.

With Johnson hanging by a thread, on Monday 4 July Truss flew to Switzerland for a Ukrainian recovery conference. Landing back in London that night she was still adamant that the political Houdini would find an escape route. Her aides disagreed, as did Thérèse Coffey, who urged the Foreign Secretary not to fly to Bali that week for the G20. After a glum and stormy meeting of the Cabinet on Tuesday morning, Truss was in a meeting with the ERG regarding Northern Ireland when the news of Sajid Javid's resignation pinged onto phones at 18:02, just minutes after the PM had issued a public apology for reappointing Pincher while knowing of concerns about his behaviour. Iain Duncan Smith announced the departure of the Health Secretary to the room before declaring, 'but let's carry on'. Only when news broke of Rishi Sunak's departure at 18:11 did IDS declare: 'Ok, we need to stop this meeting.'

With SW1 in meltdown, Adam Jones quickly texted political editors to confirm Truss was not going anywhere and the PM maintained her support. There was a major concern in the team that the PM would offer her the Chancellorship; an offer that would explicitly bind Truss to Johnson's side. If she took the offer, she would go down with the ship; if she declined, it would look like rank disloyalty. As she prepared to leave for Indonesia her aides repeatedly warned, 'do not accept Chancellor'. Truss was torn, knowing she would have to accept should she be asked to serve. Back in Greenwich she nervously watched her phone while having dinner with Hugh, but no call from No. 10 would come. Allies of Johnson say that while the thought was briefly considered, in the end he felt it would be too destabilising to have a new Chancellor and a new Foreign Secretary during the Ukraine crisis, so he gave the job to Nadhim Zahawi instead. At that point he was still trying to cling on, but that would become moot by Wednesday as minister after minister resigned.

Truss was sitting in a beachside villa in Bali when Johnson bowed to the inevitable early on Thursday morning. Even then though she was still torn on whether to come back. From her beach-hut-style suite, she watched her friend and boss resign at midday, UK time, before anguished phone calls, walking up and down the shore. The G20 Foreign Ministers gathering was on Friday, with a rematch showdown planned with Sergey Lavrov and crucial meeting with US counterpart Antony Blinken scheduled for that day. A source said: 'Even on Thursday morning the Foreign Secretary was still insisting that she had to stay, she was in full diplomatic mode.' Another source said: 'In the end it was Adam who had to be quite brutal, and literally said, "Liz, wake the fuck up and get back here."' After fellow G20 leaders, including Mélanie Joly, told Truss, 'shouldn't you be in London?', she decided to head back following a brief meeting with the Indonesians. But with the crew of the government's plane forced into a mandatory rest period after the 18-hour flight there, it was not until late on Thursday evening that she could take off. Her anguish was made worse by a long stopover in Dubai, where whispered calls were made holed up at the front of the plane, deeply suspicious of the prying ears of a junior civil servant with a reputation for leaking who was travelling with her on the government jet. 'We get her back for [what felt like] the longest plane journey in history by Friday night,' recalls one of the rapidly forming campaign team back in London. With hours lost and her rivals for the Tory crown already up and running, early calls were made on Friday evening to key right-wingers such as Iain Duncan Smith, Sir Bill Cash and John Redwood from her ministerial car racing back from Stansted. Back in Blighty finally, it was clear Truss was playing catch-up …

July 2022

UNITE THE RIGHT

While there had been few explicit discussions about the leadership in the months prior to Johnson's resignation, the assumption was 'she would always run', according to one insider. By Saturday morning Team Truss of old were in her Greenwich home. Ruth Porter and Jason Stein hurriedly negotiated a leave of absence from Finsbury; Adam Jones and Jamie Hope were huddled round laptops in the kitchen. But Sophie Jarvis was stuck trying to get a phone signal on a Swedish campervan holiday. Hot off the back of three summits, the team began to panic at how little they had done to prepare. One present that afternoon says: 'She really wasn't ready to go at all. That first day was utter chaos. People were charging around going "logo", "tagline", "video", "website". There was a sense of dread early in the day but no one vocalised it.' Another added: 'On the Friday after Boris resigned there was a real feeling of "Fuck, have we not prepared this properly, have we left this too late, can we actually win this thing?"'

In the sweltering summer heat Jones and Stein were put to work in the back garden clearing weeds and the remnants of months of building work to make it presentable enough to shoot a video. Hope began crunching the numbers on a tax package. Digital aide Reuben Solomon was hastily building a website, but would soon depart for a wedding in Italy, leaving a freelancer to film the campaign video. Pressure was heaped on the team that afternoon as Rishi Sunak dropped his slick online ad, which many suspected had been filmed and edited months in advance. Looking back, one adviser says: 'There was honestly nothing done. There's no bank account. We have no money. There's no MPs. We have no comms, we have no policy, we have no video, there's nothing.' Claims from rival camps that Truss had spent months secretly organising her campaign, including setting up a bank account in March, were met with incredulity by Truss's team. Indeed, with donors already reaching out and expressing interest, the lack of a campaign bank account was a major issue in the early days. Multi-millionaire Brexit-backer Jon Moynihan offered an early £20,000 and ended up becoming the campaign's main fundraiser. With his accounting hat on, Hugh O'Leary stepped in to talk to startup bank Monzo to arrange an account, but after delays in getting it open, Stein had to call in a favour from his firm Finsbury, for whom Monzo were a client, to speed things up.

Local neighbour James Cleverly and long-term ally Thérèse Coffey turned up on Saturday afternoon, and along with Porter began ringing MPs. Meanwhile a policy team was set up in Truss's daughter's bedroom. At the kitchen table, Jones and Truss sat down to begin writing an op-ed for Monday's *Telegraph* outlining the campaign from scratch. 'Liz said very early that day, "Let's not go ballistic on the tax stuff, there is no need."' 'It was clear that Rishi would have his hands tied on tax so we could own that ground without over-promising,' a campaign source explains. 'It wasn't a tactical decision to abandon the NICs rise, that's just what Liz had been arguing for months and the policy was never in doubt. As for the corporation tax, putting that up was one of the few things she hates more than mayonnaise.' Hope was despatched to 'do the numbers' and, fuelled by Vietnamese Banh Mi sandwiches, the team cooked up a policy vision over an 18-hour day. But even at that early point it was clear Truss's vision of tax cuts went significantly further than what would actually be announced in the campaign.

On Saturday evening Truss left to see Kwasi Kwarteng, with the MPs in Greenwich swelling to include Chloe Smith, Ranil Jayawardena and Wendy Morton. Porter sat in a stairwell for most of the evening organising more supporters, with Jarvis also working the phones from her Nordic caravan. Sitting in Kwarteng's garden two streets over, the pair cemented the informal pact they had agreed in Greenwich Park on those walks through lockdown. A friend of Truss recalls: 'He said: "Look, I'm not going to do that grubby thing of asking for a job. But you know where I am." He basically never even needed to say it; it was obvious he was on board and where he fitted in.' Kwarteng himself recalls: 'She came around to my house and asked, "Are you gonna back me?" And I said, "Yes". I didn't ask for anything. I actually said to her expressly don't do any deals with me because you need flexibility to do deals with other people.' In reference to Blair and Brown's infamous alliance, said to be forged in an Islington restaurant, another friend said: 'It wasn't exactly Granita, but neither of them left with anything other than the impression he would be her Chancellor.' The Greenwich Set had their first alliance. More good news for Truss came through that evening as Ben Wallace, the only leadership rival ahead of her in the ConservativeHome rankings, ruled himself out of the running for the top job after being begged by his teenage children not to go for the top job.

On Sunday morning a young videographer arrived at Truss's house to shoot the all-important launch video. 'Do you have any idea what this is?' barked a Westminster veteran at the outsider. 'Not really', came the unnerving reply. Over a number of takes in the garden, Truss began trailing her key message on tax cuts and promising to 'deliver, deliver, deliver'. 'Rishi was already trying to talk to people that are never going to vote Conservative in his video, we went straight for the membership and gave them what they wanted to hear,' says one aide. Truss told the camera: 'As PM, I will lead a government committed to core Conservative principles. Low taxes, a firm grip on spending and driving growth in the economy. We need a PM with experience who can hit the ground running from day one. I will work day and night to lead a party and government that puts more money in your pocket.'

She was even more explicit to Tory MPs in the *Telegraph* piece that went live on Sunday evening: 'I will fight the election as a Conservative and govern as a Conservative. Under my leadership, I would start cutting taxes from day one to take immediate action to help people deal with the cost of living. This is the clear and decisive leadership I would bring into Downing Street. Colleagues know I mean what I say and only make promises I can keep. I can be trusted to deliver.' And the message was rammed home by Kwarteng, who told the *Sun*: 'We have had a lot of tax rises and we can't tax our way to prosperity. No country has ever done that. What we can't do is simply load our economy with lots of different taxes. I think there has to be a reset and there has to be a new path. Liz's basic instinct on tax is right. She doesn't think people should be paying increasingly higher taxes to pay for higher spending.' In a dig at Sunak, he added: 'We can't simply be accountants trying to balance the books the whole time. We have got to look at growth as well.' With Sunak already hitting out at 'fairytales' that 'unfunded' tax cuts would lead to an economic boom, the dividing lines were drawn.

One Monday 11 July, a campaign HQ was set up in the Westminster office of Watford MP Dean Russell. MPs soon arriving to pledge loyalty included 2019 Red Wall poster girl Dehenna Davison and former TV presenter Rob Butler. Ministers James Heappey and Vicky Ford added some heft to the line-up. Four days after Johnson announced his intention to resign, the 1922 Committee that morning announced the rules by which his successor would be elected. Ballots of Tory MPs would be held over the following ten days, until a final two could be presented to the members ahead of a new PM being announced in early September. The team had until 4 p.m. the next day to hit the target of 20 names, and until Wednesday to get 30. By this point Truss was back to back in 15-minute meetings with MPs, hammering home her message that only a united right-wing flank could stop Sunak. Her team worked round the clock: Porter later told friends that she had undertaken 21 consecutive 18-hour days at the start of the campaign.

On Tuesday morning Truss and Thérèse Coffey went to Johnson's first awkward Cabinet meeting since he'd announced he was resigning with the official nomination papers tucked into Coffey's folder. Approaching Cabinet colleagues, Coffey asked them to add their name under hers as an official seconder. Home Secretary Priti Patel, who was still pondering a tilt at the job herself, refused. But the defining moment of the early campaign would come on the doorstep of No. 10 minutes later.

Ultra-Boris backers Nadine Dorries and Jacob Rees-Mogg broke usual protocol at the end of the meeting to stand in front of the famous black door, unleash a monstering of Rishi Sunak and show their support for Truss. Declaring 'she's probably a stronger Brexiteer than both of us,' Dorries added: 'she has consistently argued for low-tax policies.' Rees-Mogg chimed in: 'I'm also going to be backing Liz Truss. As Nadine said, I think she's a stronger Brexiteer than either of us and that's really important. When we discussed taxation, Liz was always opposed to Rishi's higher taxes.' Without saying it, a clear signal was given to the rump of Tory MPs who were outraged by Johnson's ousting and were looking for a continuity candidate. It also went some way to soothe fears of the hardline Brexiteers about backing a former Lib Dem and Remain campaigner as PM. 'It was a bat signal for the right, and we couldn't have been happier with how it landed,' one Truss ally put it.

Dorries and Rees-Mogg would become the two key attack dogs of the early campaign, at times infuriating colleagues with brutal assaults on Sunak designed to paint him as a backstabber who had brought down Johnson. In Tuesday morning's *Mail*, Rees-Mogg wrote: 'Liz has rejected the path that Rishi Sunak wanted to take us on. She opposed his breaking of our manifesto promise with the National Insurance hike when the British people had barely recovered from the shock of the pandemic. She opposed his raising the tax burden to the highest since the socialism of 1950s Labour. While the economy was at its most fragile, she opposed his 30 per cent rise in corporation tax, which will deter investment and economic growth when we need it most.' Dorries' preferred weapon was Twitter, where she accused Sunak of using 'dirty tricks, a stitch-up or dark arts. Take your pick.' She claimed: 'Team Rishi wants the candidate they know they can definitely beat in the final two and that is Jeremy Hunt.'

It was brutal, but effective. That Tuesday, Boris-ally James Cleverly came out publicly for Truss after spending the weekend in her kitchen, and former leader Iain Duncan Smith joined the camp, bringing three decades of parliamentary experience to the team. While the hardline Brexiteers in the ERG were mostly supporting Suella Braverman, an exhausting call-and-meeting schedule with right-wingers like Bill Cash and Mark Francois was underway to secure their second preference if Braverman crashed out. Efforts to win over other Cabinet Ministers Dominic Raab and Grant Shapps proved trickier. However, friends of Truss say Raab told her on Tuesday evening he would be sitting the race out and not backing anyone due to his role as Deputy Prime Minister.

So it came as a surprise to see him take to the stage to endorse Sunak at the former Chancellor's slick Westminster launch the next morning. Shapps was on the stage too, prompting a campaign source to vow privately to journalists on Tuesday 'their careers are over. If you're on the stage you're in a grave.' The chaotic Truss camp was still days away from being able to put together a launch event, but the numbers were there; she formally became a candidate at 4 p.m. on Tuesday afternoon. The rivals were Sunak, insurgent Kemi Badenoch, right-winger Braverman, moderate Tom Tugendhat, Chancellor Nadhim Zahawi, 2019 loser Jeremy Hunt, and popular if vague Penny Mordaunt.

In the first ballot that Wednesday, Truss came third with 50 votes, one more than her whip, Graham Stuart, had predicted in the sweepstake as the voting closed. 'Not too bad', was the verdict of the candidate but Penny Mordaunt's 67 votes were a major worry. However, it was clear that, unlike in 2019, there was no clear frontrunner among MPs in this leadership race. Whereas Boris Johnson had won over a third of MPs in the first round three years previously – thus guaranteeing he would be in the final two – Rishi Sunak won less than 25 per cent of MPs, topping the ballot with 88 of 357 votes cast. Fourth, fifth and sixth went to Kemi Badenoch, Tom Tugendhat and Suella Braverman with 40, 37 and 32 MPs respectively. Both Nadhim Zahawi and Jeremy Hunt, the runner-up three years previously, were eliminated after dismal showings.

Hunt texted Truss that evening: 'Hi Liz, congratulations on getting nearly three times more colleagues than me! I have been thinking hard about what to do next as I rather sensed things were not going my way. You have been a brilliant foreign secretary speaking on matters of principle with clarity and conviction and as a former FS have made me proud, especially when I heard you in Versailles. I have no doubt you would make a fine PM but I am afraid I have decided to support Rishi. Tough call and all best wishes for the rest of the campaign.' Sharing the missive with disgust, Truss remarked to her team: 'Another nail in Rishi's coffin.'

Throughout that first week, it looked at times as though Truss might struggle to make the final two despite her years of Cabinet experience against her rivals. Banging a red, white and blue, pro-military, low-tax drum, Mordaunt had beaten Truss by 17 MPs to second place: to surpass her, it was imperative that Truss 'unite the right' to knock her out. Again and again, her aides hammered home the message to wavering doubters: 'only Liz can make the final two and only Liz can represent your wing of the party'. While preaching unity, Truss aides also sought to destroy Mordaunt's chances. The gloves were going to have to come off if they were to stay in the game. 'It was obvious Rishi was going through, but it took a while to focus everyone's energy on not fighting him, but seeing off Penny and Kemi,' a senior aide on the campaign said.

With Truss's future in the balance, fellow Greenwich-set resident, Lord Frost, was despatched on the airwaves on the morning of Thursday 14 September. Appearing on Julia Hartley-Brewer's TalkTV show, Frost eviscerated Mordaunt, his deputy during the Brexit talks. He told his host: 'I'm sorry to say this, she did not master the necessary detail in the negotiations last year. She wouldn't always deliver tough messages to the European Union when that was necessary and I'm afraid she wasn't fully accountable or always visible. Sometimes I didn't even know where she was. I'm afraid this became such a problem that after 6 months I had to ask the PM to move her on and find somebody else to support me. From the basis of what I saw, I would have grave reservations.' Other Truss outriders were quick to row in behind Frost. Simon Clarke, the Chief Secretary to the Treasury, tweeted: 'Lord Frost's warning is a really serious one. Conservatives – and, far more importantly, our country – need a leader who is tested and ready.' Some within Team Truss were irritated, however, by Frost's refusal to go public with his support for Truss, which he preferred to hold for his *Telegraph* column the following day. Others, though, were more willing, with two more ministers, Ed Argar and Tom Pursglove, declaring their support.

But when the results of the second ballot came through that afternoon, it was clear Truss had more to do to stop Mordaunt's growing momentum. Aides scrambled to spin that Truss had secured the largest percentage increase in her vote, but the result was flat. As Ronald Reagan himself had said: if you're explain-ing, you're losing. Rishi Sunak came top again with 101 MPs, followed by Mordaunt on 83, Truss on 64, Badenoch on 49 and Tugendhat on 32. Suella Braverman, the most right-wing candi-date and favourite of the ERG, was eliminated with 27 supporters. The Truss team swung into action, urging Braverman backers to endorse their candidate. 'If the right doesn't rally it's a Penny versus Rishi final,' warned Jonathan Gullis to fellow 2019-ers on WhatsApp. Truss herself held talks with Braverman within minutes of the vote. In her Commons office she cut a deal that likely guaranteed her a slot in the final two. Braverman asked for the job of Home Secretary as the price of endorsing Truss and publicly urging her fellow hardliners in the ERG to support her in the final two rounds of voting. Truss promptly bit her arm off.

That night Chairman Mark Francois messaged the ERG WhatsApp group: 'Suella has put in a very creditable showing in this contest, even outpolling the current Chancellor of the Exchequer in the first round. Nevertheless, she unfortunately did not manage to advance further today – and she has, this evening, declared her support for Liz Truss to become our next Prime Minister. As a result – and as previously agreed – I do hope that all of our Group will now feel able to unite firmly behind Liz, to help deliver the vital Northern Ireland Protocol Bill, expand on the opportunities offered by Brexit and secure the future of the Conservative Party.' Braverman herself added: 'Kemi is a great woman and a friend. She could do a fantastic job as PM one day but we need to look realistically at her numbers. Liz and Kemi are not both going to make it into the final two. So a decision needs to be made to back one of them. The one we should back, I'd argue, is the one who can get to the final round: Liz can, Kemi cannot. Liz is undeniably the better-placed candidate to get to the voluntary party round, and fight there for the things that all three of us believe. And it's exactly our common beliefs which must come before the ambitions of any one of us. Liz, additionally, is ready now to be PM. She won't need to learn on the job. And the job is hard and needs to be done properly. The party has had a difficult six years and stability is urgently and swiftly needed.'

But any celebration was short-lived, as a spanner in the works came in a phone call from Channel 4 to Jones, confirming Rishi Sunak would appear in their live TV debate on the Friday night. While Tugendhat, Mordaunt and Badenoch had been obviously eager to raise their profiles, Sunak had been holding out. Now with Truss flatlining, it was clear that the former Chancellor was turning the screw.

'At first we thought C4 were pulling a fast one,' a campaign source revealed. 'We presumed they were bullshitting to try to get us to say yes.' Backchannel communications had been set up between the two camps with Stein speaking to ex-Truss Spad Nerissa Chesterfield, who had become a key member of Sunak's inner circle as his trusted press secretary. The news that came back from Chesterfield sent the campaign into a spin: 'We found out that they actually were in. We were third, we couldn't run from it. We had no time to do debate prep, and we didn't really do any. And the result was inevitable.'

Early on Friday morning, lecterns were acquired and a hastily organised debate prep session got underway at 11 Lord North Street. The Westminster townhouse owned by Tory peer Greville Howard had been the scene of leadership intrigue for decades. Back in 1995, Michael Portillo's abortive putsch against John Major was rumbled when an eagle-eyed *Sun* journalist spotted a BT engineer installing dozens of phone lines at the property, in order to call dozens of MPs. It had also been handed over to Iain Duncan Smith, Andrea Leadsom and ultimately Boris Johnson as an HQ for their successive tilts at the Tory crown. Truss's team were amused to find a cupboard full of retro desk phones when they moved in, a remnant from Portillo's short residency. But despite the belated practice session, Truss gave a poor performance that evening, replete with robotic gestures and stilted answers that her supporters had hoped she had shed earlier in her career. Her choice of outfit also divided opinion, with her white blouse fronted with a tied bow and a blue blazer identical to Margaret Thatcher's 1979 Election broadcast. While Twitter and the lefty commentators quickly mocked, one source on the campaign hit back: 'You forget that the people that are actually going to decide the next Prime Minister, really, really, really like Margaret Thatcher.'

Truss that night was described by aides as 'furious', despite their warm words of praise. While they tried to keep up the mood, feedback was pouring in from Tory MPs. Veteran back-bencher Richard Drax texted Truss to say: 'Having spent many years in TV can I please give u some tips … u r too wooden … no humanity there … drop the shoulders … slow the voice … and smile! U r a nice looking lady but u look far too serious … and imagine u R the PM … u need to ooze more confidence … forget the others. ur the PM. PS and for God's don't waffle!!!! R.' The uninvited assessment prompted Thérèse Coffey to threaten to take a 'stiletto to him'. The candidate herself drove straight from Channel 4 to Chevening for a long-standing social engagement on the Saturday with husband Hugh's family and on the advice of her aides deleted Twitter from her phone.

By the morning of Saturday 16 July there was a major wobble among Truss supporters. 'There was a bit of a melt-down,' an aide admits. 'Cabinet-level supporters were voicing concern, even Kwasi and Cleverly were getting jumpy. Some of the team had a bit of a flap.' A hurried line was prepared to be sent to supporters to hammer home to waverers, as the poor debate performance stalled further endorsements. MPs were instructed to try to spin her stern performance on its head: 'Liz is a serious person for serious times. In less than 2 months' time, this person will have the nuclear codes. She has the substance, the depth, not the froth. Liz has delivered in every department she has led. Rishi's growth plan isn't working, we cannot tax our way to growth and she has the plan.' The campaign was split on whether she should hit the Sunday-morning TV shows in a bid to gain some ground, but the idea was quickly batted away by Stein and Jones. Instead of a public fightback, the response to the debate played out in the shadows of the political dark arts …

For several days the team had been plotting what one insider called a 'monster hit' on Mordaunt. A supporter of the campaign had passed them leaked civil service policy papers from Mordaunt's time at the Equalities Office that showed she at best did not resist softening of the law to allow it easier for people to identify as Trans without medical approval. In the Channel 4 debate, amid claims she was 'too woke to be PM', Mordaunt had publicly claimed she never supported gender self-identification. But the document now in the hands of Team Truss showed, while serving as Equalities Minister, Mordaunt was in favour of removing at least one medical requirement needed by transgender people. Adam Jones had told a journalist at the debate, the team 'knew Mordaunt was lying. We have the docs to prove it too.' By Saturday night they were plastered across the *Sunday Times* and *Mail on Sunday*. Within hours the Cabinet Office had triggered a leak inquiry, but as so often is the way in Whitehall, the culprit was never identified – publicly, at least. Despite lashing out at 'toxic briefings', Mordaunt's team knew she had taken a direct hit.

The mood lifted dramatically on Sunday morning with the moral boost of seeing their number-one rival on the rack. After a day off and a decent night's sleep, Truss was also in better spirits. Walking into her kitchen in Greenwich where her debate prep team were waiting, she clapped her hands and said, 'Right, what do I need to do?' The eight-hour session was led by Aylesbury MP Rob Butler, who had a long career at the BBC and Channel 5 as a newsreader, before becoming a communications coach by trade. With Stein again playing Rishi, and Jones Penny, Butler took Truss back to basics. Over and over they practised her quips, tone and speed, with the practice continuing in the car to the ITV studios, where the next round of debates was being filmed. 'She was still practising in the green room,' says one aide, 'and it showed. She walked in there and kicked the shit out of Sunak.'

The debate was bloody, with Truss far sharper than that Friday's disaster: 'Rishi, you have raised taxes to the highest level in 70 years, that is not going to drive growth; you raised National Insurance, even though people like me opposed it in Cabinet at the time; the fact is that raising taxes will choke off growth.' When he hit back with a grin to ask what she 'regretted the most' out of being a Liberal Democrat or Remainer, Truss's death stare was brutal: 'I was not someone who was born into the Conservative Party; I went to a comprehensive school, but my fundamental belief and the reason I am a Conservative is I saw kids at my school being let down, and not get the opportunities, not get the proper educational standards you may have got at your school Rishi.' The Winchester boy was no longer smiling. After the show Sunak himself turned to Truss in the wings, to ask: 'Why are we doing this?'

Despite the headlines being dominated by Sunak's attacks on Truss's 'fairytale' offer of tax cuts, the Truss camp was hugely relieved with how the second bout had gone. 'It was one of the most spectacular recoveries I can remember,' a Cabinet minister recalls. 'She was so bad on Friday, and by Sunday I was actually cheering her.' One aide says: 'That was the night that the MPs finally realised the team knew what we were doing. All that week the Cabinet ministers backing her had been sounding off about the youth of the team, and the inexperience. That all went away that evening.' Alarmed Tory MPs were meanwhile urging candidates to call time on the remaining TV debates, fearing yet more damaging blue-on-blue attacks in public. Grimsby MP Lia Nici texted all five candidates, warning them 'not to do anymore' as 'every one of them has been awful ... the only people winning here are the opposition'. Such talk was music to the ears of Team Truss, given their candidate's mixed performance thus far.

Once again a backchannel was opened between the two camps. This time, though, they were in agreement: neither Sunak nor Truss would take part in the next scheduled face-off the following Tuesday, hosted by Sky News' feared interrogator Kay Burley.

With less than three days to go until the final round of voting, the attacks on Mordaunt were coming thick and fast. Anne-Marie Trevelyan – Truss's successor at Trade and a supporter of Tom Tugendhat – fired a fresh rocket on LBC, questioning Mordaunt's work ethic in her department. She told Nick Ferrari that she thought Mordaunt had gone AWOL from her day job as Trevelyan's deputy to instead plot her campaign, adding: 'There have been a number of times when she hasn't been available, which would have been useful, and other ministers have picked up the pieces, yes.' Trevelyan had privately promised Truss she was on board once her first-choice candidate was knocked out, which he duly was that evening. After stalling on Thursday, with the help of Braverman and the ERG, the momentum that Monday was clearly with Truss. When the third ballot results were declared, Tugendhat was eliminated with 31 votes leaving the final four of Sunak on 115, Mordaunt 82, Truss 71 and Badenoch on 58. With Truss just 11 votes behind Mordaunt, the jitters of the weekend died down. In a direct plea to Tugendhat's and Badenoch's supporters, she told *The Times* that evening: 'This is a pivotal moment for the country. I believe I'm the person who can do what it takes to turn our economy around and is capable of driving through the bold reforms and the bold decisions that are needed now. But, also to stand up to Vladimir Putin and aggressors around the world. I feel impelled to put myself forward for that reason.'

On Tuesday morning another deal was done. But one that would later be broken. At 10 a.m. Truss met with vanquished Tugendhat in the Foreign Secretary's Commons office and told him if he backed her and brought as many of his 30 supporters with him as he could, then this would be his office if she won.

With the offer of Foreign Secretary, and the deals with Kwarteng and Braverman, Truss had filled the great offices of state of her future administration before it was guaranteed she would even face the party membership. Friends say Tugendhat readily accepted the offer, but had just one caveat. Kemi Badenoch was a dear friend, and even though she had no hope of going through, Tugendhat wanted to vote for her in the fourth round that afternoon. Somewhat bemused, given she had just offered to make him the third most powerful person in the government, Truss agreed to the terms. However, Anne-Marie Trevelyan, who did back Truss that afternoon, was under the impression Tugendhat was fully signed up. The top three remained unchanged in the fourth ballot that afternoon: Sunak took first place with 118 MPs, Mordaunt took second with 92 and Truss completed the final three on 86. Despite a flurry of media interest, Badenoch, the anti-woke warrior, was eliminated with 59 supporters – the improvement of one since Tuesday's vote thought to be that of Tugendhat. Truss was left as the undisputed candidate of the right while Mordaunt, a proud liberal conservative, had failed to pick up more than a handful of Tugendhat's supporters, despite most of them coming from the left of the party. Badenoch's elimination left 59 MPs up for grabs: Truss only had to win seven more than Mordaunt to make the final two.

At 6 a.m. on Wednesday 20 July, Truss was clearly confident she was going to leapfrog Mordaunt. When her diary was sent over for the day, blocks of the afternoon were wiped out for photos with supporters, and a thank-you drink was planned for 7 p.m. Before a single vote was cast, aides were ordered to come up with a 'gameplan' for the following days, to be signed off that night. Not everything had gone to plan though, with Porter despatching Frances Truss back to Greenwich for more dresses and make-up. The 16-year-old had joined the campaign for the final days, and was put to work like anyone else. With Badenoch out, the calls to her scores of supporters carried on right up until 3 p.m. when the final ballot eventually closed. Rishi Sunak finished first with 137 MPs; Truss joined him as runner-up with 113 votes, having picked up 27 new supporters: more than twice as many as Mordaunt, who was eliminated with 105 votes.

Within minutes of the result, Simon Case, the Cabinet Secretary, was in touch with both finalists, offering them briefings on policy and forming a new government: 'Congratulations on reaching the final two. As in 2016 and 2019, the PM has authorised access talks for the final two candidates, so that you can [get] access to civil service briefing via me on issues such as government formation, government organisation and policy issues. You will no doubt now be very busy, but if you would like to take up access talks, please let me know and I will make myself available at your convenience. Simon.' And serious money started to be offered to the candidates. Tony Gallagher, the property mogul, got in touch via a Tory MP, who told the candidates that the 'BIG party donor, would like to meet or talk to you. He's v interested in housing policy. He is a potential £100,000 donor for your campaign.' After hours of well-wishers and drinks with the MPs and team on the House of Commons terrace, an exhausted but elated Truss had a more low-key celebration: a trip to Honest Burgers in Covent Garden.

August 2022

HOSTILE TAKEOVER

Arriving at Stoke-on-Trent's Victoria Hall ahead of their first head-to-head TV showdown, Rishi Sunak and Liz Truss did not say a word to one another. The campaign to convince 180,000 Tory members had only been going five days, and it had already got nasty. The first polling was in and YouGov had Truss ahead by a massive 24 points – with the Foreign Secretary polling 62 per cent to Sunak's 38. He would need a knockout blow that evening. In less than a week the two camps had exchanged scathing barbs, mostly under the cloak of anonymity and a degree of deniability via the press. Just that day a 'Sunak campaign member' had savaged Truss for playing up her Roundhay days, suggesting the school was worse than other former pupils remember: 'Liz Truss should not be rewriting history, particularly when it comes to education. Her unfounded allegations against her old school are nearly as ludicrous as her unfounded evidence for tax cuts.' But a 'supporter of Truss' hit back that 'she will take no lectures in educational standards from an L.A.-based, Goldman Sachs banker who went to a school for the uber elite'. They added, a trifle wishfully: 'This puerile nonsense has no place in a leadership race. Liz's team will be speaking to Rishi's team to ensure this contest remains a battle of ideas not a mud-slinging match.' Other such exchanges would take place that week on China, freeports and borrowing. In the battle for the Tory Party's soul, there was no love lost between the pair.

While Sunak arrived at Stoke 'like a coiled spring', Truss equally knew that night could shape the entire campaign. She had spent two days in debate prep with Rob Butler, Jason Stein and Jamie Hope, using a rented boardroom at Port Vale Football Club to maximise her practice time on the day. Again Stein played Sunak, but he never got quite as agitated as the real thing would do that night. Hectoring and interrupting, Sunak barely let Truss get a word in edgeways in the first half an hour of the BBC show. He rolled his eyes at her answers and butted in every few words, interrupting his rival 22 times in the first 12 minutes alone, according to Truss's team. One female Cabinet minister texted journalists that evening claiming 'that's what he was like in meetings'.

Sunak raged against 'the short-term sugar rush' of cutting National Insurance and 'unfunded and irresponsible' tax cuts, warning: 'Your own adviser has said they would lead to mortgage rates, interest rates, going up to 7 per cent. Can you imagine what that is going to do for everyone here, everyone watching? That's thousands of pounds on their mortgage bill, that is going to tip millions into misery and it means we have no chance of winning the next election.' 'Rishi, I don't believe this negative, declinist language,' Truss replied. 'Everyone thinks that putting up taxes at this moment is going to hurt the economy.'

Summing up the verdict of the commentariat after what had been a nasty debate, the narrative-shaping Politico website said: 'the foreign secretary did exactly what she needed to do. She came across as calm and focused in the face of a shoutier and more aggressive performance from Sunak, and managed to avoid any of the PR gaffes for which she has been known through parts of her ministerial career.' It added: 'Critics who wrote off the foreign secretary as wooden and error-prone early in the contest have been forced to eat their words. It's early days, but she appears on course for No. 10.'

However, it was what was said ringside before the debate had even ended that dominated the headlines the next day. A 'spokesman for Liz Truss' – on the record – told Steve Swinford of *The Times*: 'Rishi Sunak has tonight proven he is not fit for office. His aggressive mansplaining and shouty private school behaviour is desperate, unbecoming and is a gift to Labour.' That spokesman was Stein, who would later admit to friends he had 'seen red that night' and probably went a bit too far. But he was far from alone in pushing the toxic charge of 'mansplaining' that evening. 'Most women MPs have been subject to mansplaining and being talked over in debate', tweeted Truss's pal of 25 years Jackie Doyle-Price. 'Never a worse example than right now on the BBC.' Thérèse Coffey told the *FT*, 'people don't like the interrupting ... it started to look a bit like mansplaining'. But the charge of 'unfit for office' annoyed even Truss-supporting MPs, especially as it came just minutes after she had suggested she would be delighted to offer Sunak a job in her government should she win. Sunak's team swore revenge, citing that debate as the moment when a line was crossed that irretrievably damaged the tone of the contest. There was a noticeable increase in direct hostilities after Stoke, culminating some weeks later in Sunak's spokesman accusing Truss of being 'divorced from reality' and Dominic Raab warning that a Truss premiership would be 'electoral suicide' for the Tories.

By a twist of fate it would be the last time the pair went properly head to head in a full debate. The following day a live contest hosted by the *Sun* and TalkTV was abandoned after half an hour after host Kate McCann fainted live on air. But in the 29 minutes they were going at each other, Sunak was noticeably more emollient in his barbs, clearly stung by snap polls of Tory members overnight showing they were turned off by his BBC performance. The only remaining TV head-to-head was due to be hosted by Sky some weeks later, but would eventually be negotiated down by both camps to separate interviews with their candidates. And the 12 official Tory hustings never had the two candidates opposing each other from the stage. Sunak needed his big box office moment to turn round the polls, and had not got it.

Nor did he pull one back when the pair met again the following Friday in Leeds for the first membership grilling. Truss treated it like a homecoming, noting she had 'bought her first Whitney Houston record' round the corner, back in her days as 'a teenage controversialist'. By the time she said she wanted to 'channel the spirit of Don Revie', Leeds United's most celebrated manager, the crowd were loving it. Attacks on Keir Starmer the 'patronising plastic patriot' landed well too. Sunak was more polished but less convincing in his claim to be 'the most Northern Chancellor in history', having been born in Southampton and educated at Winchester and Oxford. Taking the mic, one Tory member accused Sunak of 'stabbing Boris in the back' in a painful moment of television viewing. Compared to the awkward Secretary of State who had generated nervous laughter eight years earlier with her conference speech about cheese, Truss the candidate looked unrecognisable. 'Leeds was the night I just remember looking at her and thinking, yep, she's gonna win this,' recalls one long-serving ally.

While Truss was cruising ahead of Sunak in the polls and the bookmakers' odds, the commanding lead masked a deeper chaos in the campaign. Efforts to 'scale up' from the two dozen staff that had got Truss into the final two were proving difficult. 'It was a bit of a mess,' a senior Truss aide admits. 'No one had actually been involved in a ground game before except Jason Stein, who had been on the Hunt campaign, and that was a disaster.' Senior Cabinet ministers began to voice their concerns to Truss that she needed to bring in some big guns. And there was an obvious candidate on the shelf who already had a ground campaign ready to go – because he had designed it for Penny Mordaunt. A veteran of Boris Johnson's 2019 campaign, Mark

Fullbrook was a Tory lifer who had worked for years with election guru Sir Lynton Crosby, as the 'F' in his CTF Partners lobbying firm. The fact he had backed Nadhim Zahawi and then Penny Mordaunt in the space of two weeks was overlooked for his obvious and available political skills. Zahawi, Brandon Lewis and Ben Wallace all fired off text messages to Truss directly recommending that she hire him, as did Kwarteng, who made clear that while Ruth Porter had done a good job stewarding the fledgling campaign so far, it was time for a 'heavyweight'. After repeated lobbying from his Cabinet contacts, Truss sent word: 'Mark, if you want to get hold of me you could just call.'

But the appointment caused some unease. Porter fought hard to keep the title of co-campaign coordinator while Jamie Hope had grave misgivings. Fullbrook had been in touch in early January from Libya, asking for the Foreign Office's help on behalf of some clients. A friend of Hope says: 'Jamie always thought he was a bit dodgy.' Jones was also suspicious of losing influence within the camp. 'The grown-ups have arrived,' said one Fullbrook ally when Truss ignored her team's concerns.

Fullbrook was tasked by Truss to 'grip this' and given carte blanche to whip the campaign into shape. As well as building a functioning team, now based in rented offices in Millbank Tower, a shock-and-awe campaign of big-name endorsements was drawn up. Tom Tugendhat was felt by Truss to have reneged on his end of their deal as he had still not publicly come out in support for her. Fullbrook quickly changed that with a big unveiling planned for the following Saturday. It followed Ben Wallace going public on the last Friday of July, with a brutal attack on Sunak. He accused the ex-Chancellor of a 'dereliction of duty' by resigning from the Treasury in the midst of a cost-of-living crisis. Brandon Lewis was lined up for the Sunday, again going for Sunak's jugular, suggesting he had put up 'huge resistance' to Truss's plan to fix the Northern Ireland Protocol. After Sunak's campaign had subsequently backed unilaterally tearing up trading rules in the province, the ex-NI Secretary hit out: 'It's good to see him coming round to see that is the way forward, because that doesn't quite reflect the experience I've had of the Treasury in the last year and a half.' He added that Sunak had seemed 'to want to keep the EU happy, and I've always felt that our focus should be on working to deliver for the people of the UK'.

All the while campaign attack dog Nadine Dorries kept pushing the Rishi backstabber narrative, writing in the *Mail on Sunday* on the 31 July: 'A tweet I posted last week highlighted Liz Truss's choice of £4.50 earrings and Rishi Sunak's decision to wear £450 Prada shoes to visit a Teesside building site, while also donning a £3,500 suit for a leadership debate. It caused a bit of a storm, to say the least … Rishi had been plotting against the most electorally successful Prime Minister the Conservative Party has known since the days of Margaret Thatcher. His actions made Michael Gove's betrayal of Boris Johnson during the 2016 leadership campaign appear like a rank amateur rehearsing for the role of Brutus in a village hall play.' At Boris Johnson's wedding party the day before the piece dropped, Dorries fielded calls from Team Truss during the reception over worries that she may have gone a bit too far; sipping a rum punch she politely and firmly told them there would be no toning it down.

Yet the biggest coup that week was one the campaign team had managed to keep under wraps for maximum impact. Penny Mordaunt had been speaking to both sides since her third-place finish and skewering by many of her colleagues. Her talks regarding an endorsement for Sunak had gone as far as requesting detailed policy documents, but trust was low. The fears of Sunak's advisers played out when they saw Mordaunt stride onto the stage to introduce Truss at the second membership hustings in Exeter on Monday 1 August. As political drama goes, that reveal would take some beating, coming as it did less than two weeks after Truss's supporters and aides detonated

Mordaunt's campaign in some of the most brutal political attacks of modern times. But with the promise of a Cabinet job, all it seems was forgiven. Penny certainly sang for her supper, heaping praise on Truss's 'graft, her authenticity, her determination, her ambition for this country, her consistency and sense of duty – she knows what she believes in, and her resolve to stand up against tyranny and fight for freedom. In short folks, to give us all hope. She for me is the hope candidate.' 'Hope of a big job' was the immediate joke vocalised by the cynical hacks watching from the sidelines. Two weeks after letting her team off the lead to take out Mordaunt, Truss gushed: 'She's a great person, she's a great politician, she's a great patriot and I'm proud to call her my friend.' But the endorsement was overshadowed by the campaign's moment of maximum danger that would begin when an embargo lifted at 10 p.m. that night.

Truss had been in a helicopter on her way to Exeter at lunchtime when her team claims she first became aware of a proposed policy due to go out that day. Buried in a puffed-up press release about clamping down on 'woke' civil servant group-think was a plan to introduce regional pay boards to allow different rates of penpusher pay in different parts of the country. It was an idea that had been kicking around Whitehall for years, but it was considered too toxic by George Osborne to even attempt it. It had last reared its head when the *Telegraph* reported Liz Truss had made the case for it at Cabinet in 2018, but the plan had come to nothing. Now there it was again under her name. While the release claimed it would only apply to new public sector contracts, the small print of the policy announcement said: 'This could save up to £8.8 billion per year. This is the potential savings if the system were to be adopted for all public sector workers in the long term.' The rather glib aside did not take into account that this massive figure would mean widening out the policy to reduce the pay of doctors, nurses, teachers, soldiers and firefighters outside of London rather than that of the civil service officials at which the rest of the release was taking aim.

A frantic text message exchange with the team back in London confirmed it had already been sent out to journalists at 10:02, under embargo until 22:00, leaving hacks 11 hours and 58 minutes to take the policy apart. And shred it they did. By the afternoon it was clear the policy was going to get monstered by the unions, Labour and, crucially, Sunak the following day.

If the reported chain of events holds true, it would reveal an astonishing lack of organisation at the heart of the campaign where junior staff were able to speak for a potential future PM without a single check or balance. But a campaign source insists: 'She was in the helicopter when belatedly she saw it for the first time. Her first order was to recall it, but Adam Jones argued that was impossible and Jamie Hope said it could be amended.' Truss was incandescent, her anger made worse by the radio headsets she was shouting into in the noisy chopper. At 5 p.m. an updated release was distributed by the campaign, adding supportive quotes and tweaking some of the figures. But, bizarrely, the £8 billion figure was kept in, meaning the key problem with the policy was still there in black and white. Later, insiders would admit: 'The mistake we made was not just pulling the whole thing that day, but letting it go to print. It would have been painful but less painful than crashing the whole thing down the following day.'

With predictable results in the next morning's press, Sunak's team had a field day. His attack dogs piled onto Twitter to slam the policy, marching in lockstep with the public sector unions who had erupted in fury. It was a totally unforced error, and one that Sunak would ensure caused maximum pain. At 11 Lord North Street the following morning an emergency meeting of Mark Fullbrook, Ruth Porter, Iain Duncan Smith and Jason Stein convened. The decision to jettison the policy was taken in less than two minutes and led by IDS. A statement was drafted and WhatsApped to the Lobby:

'Over the last few hours, there has been a wilful misrepresentation of our campaign. Current levels of public sector pay will absolutely be maintained – anything to suggest otherwise is simply wrong. Our hard-working front-line staff are the bedrock of society, and there will be no proposal taken forward on regional pay boards for civil servants or public sector workers.'

A campaign source says: 'It was brutal; Adam was still on the phone trying to spin it when Fullbrook basically took his gun and badge off him, pulling the plug right there.' The use of 'misrepresented' was disingenuous but the deed was done. Truss would repeat the claim on a visit later that day. The U-turn came quickly enough, but there is no denying the team had made their first strategic blunder of the campaign.

It was not a mistake Mark Fullbrook was prepared to allow the team to make again. He ordered that a new sign-off procedure be set up immediately to allow as many senior eyeballs as possible on anything going out from the campaign. And then he set a clear and firm rule: 'No more bloody policies.' It was a ruling that held. For the rest of the campaign the Truss team did not announce any new major promises, instead hammering home their tax-cutting mantra and defence-spending hike over and over again. A new WhatsApp group was set up called 'Announcements'. Nothing else was ever to go out in the campaign's name without the agreement of all members of the senior team in that group.

While the U-turn was embarrassing and revealed the disarray behind the scenes, the damage to membership support seemed non-existent. Kwasi Kwarteng puts it down to the fact many Tory members would actually support the proposal. 'It's controversial,' he says, but 'it's funny because that day I got two people independently saying to me, "So why should a teacher in Doncaster, where houses cost a third as much, get paid as much as a teacher in Basingstoke?" Our members, and actually the *Daily Telegraph*, the house journal, said, "Hang on a sec, maybe she had a point there." But she realised that this was not part of her policy. This is not part of our programme. And she did a very quick reversal of where she was.' But with Boris Johnson's administration blighted by endless U-turns, was this a bad omen for a future Truss administration? Kwarteng says not: 'All politicians at that level have to be realistic. I mean, look at Margaret Thatcher about the poll tax, she wasn't nimble at all. She said, "No, we've got to keep doing this" and it was a disaster and it brought her down. So you've got to be flexible, but you've got to have a strategic sense of where you want to go. And I think there's nobody in politics who has more of a strategic sense of what she wants than Liz Truss.'

With the Truss campaign making its first gaffe, MPs that had been out of the blocks early to back Sunak were cock-a-hoop. Re-emerging with a new impetus, one mocked: 'U turn if you want to, the lady's not for … oops! We need a Prime Minister who is a political signpost not a weathervane. #Ready4Rishi.' It was a welcome sliver of hope for Team Sunak, as was the change to the voting rules that was announced in late July. A major plank of their strategy had been to try to 'go long' to give them time to claw back membership support in the affluent south-east, against stronger support for Truss in the wider regional membership. That required ballots being sent to members as late as possible, and dragging the race out for as long as they could; it was a plan one Sunak-backing minister described as 'letting common sense prevail'. Therefore the campaign had been delighted by a quirk in the new CCHQ rules that technically let members change their mind on their vote. With both online and paper voting available, the leadership election process published by the party HQ stated that the last vote received would be the one that counted; therefore allowing members to vote by post, but modify that decision later online.

With the opportunity for Sunak to drag the race right through until September on a 'it's not too late to change your mind' ticket, Truss's campaign sensed danger. So they were massively relieved by the *Telegraph*'s front page on the day after the public sector pay bungle. The paper quoted spy chiefs at the government's National Cyber Security Centre, warning that the online change-your-vote loophole left the party vulnerable to hackers and malign actors attempting to influence the election of the next PM. The fact that the NCSC's parent body was ultimately the Foreign Office was not lost on Sunak's camp, yet the warning was near impossible to argue against. The first vote received by the party would now be the only one that counted, with Sunak's path to power narrowing by the day. When a video emerged on 5 August of him boasting to a crowd in Tunbridge Wells that he had diverted money back to the south-east from 'deprived urban areas' even the ex-Chancellor's most vocal supporters started to ease off.

A last throw of the dice for Sunak came on 8 August, when the Deputy PM Dominic Raab was wheeled out to try to finally move the dial. In a marked escalation of hostilities, a *Times* op-ed drafted for him by the Sunak campaign warned that Truss's tax plans were an 'electoral suicide note' with the Tories facing 'impotent oblivion'. Sunak's press team had a bet on whether Raab would put his name to their draft, but it came back within 15 minutes without a single change. In retaliation, Truss personally accused Raab of spreading 'portents of doom' and found him guilty of her cardinal sin: 'declinist talk'. In order to 'fuck with his head', sources say Truss signed off a mischievous briefing to the Sunday papers that Raab had been in line for a major Cabinet role in her administration before his attack in *The Times*. The fact that Raab popped up on the Sunday shows to claim he had 'seen every Jedi mind trick in the book before' would suggest some degree of success for the ruse to get into his head. Having started the campaign saying he would serve in a Truss government should she win, Sunak finally put that idea to bed on 9 August when his spokesman briefed the lobby that 'it seems she is divorced from reality'. Eleven days after Raab's 'electoral suicide' attack, Michael Gove came out for Rishi Sunak, suggesting Truss's campaign had been a 'holiday from reality'. Though the pair would have a drink before the end of the campaign to try to make peace, friends say Truss believed a line was crossed.

If some ministers had had their way, the campaign would have been significantly nastier. At least two ministers and four MPs backing Sunak briefed a number of journalists that Truss was having an affair with an aide; had been subject to formal complaints for her predatory behaviour towards a younger male staff member; and even a far-fetched tale that she was battling to contain the public revelation that a sex tape existed of her. A 'dirty dossier' of claims floated around the grubbier parts of Westminster, but never saw the light of day. To his credit Sunak instructed his most senior team that they were to go nowhere near any personal attacks on Truss's private life and warned that anyone who did would be shown the door. Revelations about Sunak's family's tax status, US Green Card and wife's business connections were noticeably absent from Truss's official campaign, despite the teams trading hammer blows every day.

A further scare for the Truss campaign came when the security services contacted the Foreign Secretary to warn that her personal mobile phone might have been 'compromised' by hackers – possibly working on behalf of a hostile state. She was forced to hand over her telephone and change her number, cutting her off towards the end of the campaign from MPs and supporters, but putting an end to unsolicited advice from others.

In a sign of just how badly Sunak's chances were crashing, on the evening of 12 August the first big-name defection from his camp was splashed across the *Telegraph*. The Welsh Secretary Robert Buckland publicly switched sides after receiving private assurances from Truss that she would scrap Dominic Raab's planned reforms of the European Convention on Human Rights should she win. Buckland had already written a scathing op-ed against the new proposed British Bill of Rights a week previously, prompting a furious complaint by Raab to Simon Case that Cabinet collective responsibility had been breached. Thousands of hours of work over two years by civil servants and lawyers preparing that bill were junked by Truss for the sake of campaign momentum.

Buoyed by early voting figures passed to the teams by CCHQ and the fact that her lead in the polls had barely flinched in weeks, Liz Truss gathered her top team at Chevening on 13 August to start building her Cabinet. The data showed that far from 'going long', more than half of Tory voters had voted by mid-August. A third had cast their vote within the first week of the ballot opening. It would be an uphill struggle for Sunak to turn it around, and transition talks with the civil service on his side were all but non-existent. Meanwhile Truss had appointed close ally Ranil Jayawardena to lead her talks with the Cabinet Office. With many of the big jobs already earmarked during the voting stages, Truss began to test some of the promises she had made earlier in the campaign. An approach to Suella Braverman over whether the deal to make her Home Secretary could be watered down to Justice was firmly rebuffed, but backchannels to Tom Tugendhat saw him agree to accept the Security Minister role as long as it had a seat at the top table. An original plan to make Iain Duncan Smith Chief Whip or Leader of the House of Commons was rejected by the grandee, who was determined to return to government running a department, or nothing. Truss chose nothing on those terms. Another member of the so-called Greenwich Set, James Cleverly, would instead be Foreign Secretary, with long-term ally Thérèse Coffey earmarked for Health but given a powerful cross-Whitehall role as Deputy PM. Wendy Morton, another MP who was at Greenwich that first weekend of the campaign, was given the nod as Chief Whip, with other jobs quickly filled up by devoted Truss loyalists. Simon Clarke would go to Levelling Up, Chris Philp would be Kwarteng's deputy at the Treasury, and Jacob Rees-Mogg was heading to Business.

A trickier question was what to do about vanquished leadership contenders Penny Mordaunt and Kemi Badenoch, both of whom wanted to run the Culture department. Mordaunt was ruled out immediately over her previous support for press regulation, while Truss was wary of giving Badenoch a base to develop her brand of woke warriordom that had so delighted party members. 'Why the fuck does everyone want DCMS,' Truss was heard to ask her team. 'Don't these people actually want to run a proper department?' While Badenoch also fancied Education with Equalities wrapped in, Truss preferred to hand over her old stomping ground of Trade. At the time, Nadine Dorries was still keen to stay at DCMS amid 'unfinished business' with the BBC. But she got cold feet after Truss made clear that initiatives like gambling reform and privatising Channel 4 would be taking a backburner in her push for growth. Dorries' late decision to head to the backbenchers plunged a brutal but well-organised reshuffle into confusion. Eventually Michelle Donelan would be offered the DCMS job, leaving a last-minute scramble for Education – with Kit Malthouse getting the call-up. 'Penny was the trickiest customer,' a source says; 'given all the stuff that came out about her in the campaign, there were lots of departments she just could not be put near. But frankly she's a brilliant Commons performer so the Leader of the House role was ideal.' Mordaunt did not see it that way, however, and it was left to her old campaign adviser Mark Fullbrook to convince her to take the job.

Next on the agenda was the hunt for a Chief of Staff. Lord Frost was the first to be ruled out, having done so himself before even being offered the job. Other Tory peers were considered but quickly dismissed, including Osbornite Lord Bridges and Lord Polak, the former boss of Conservative Friends of Israel. But approaches were made to, and rejected by, leading Westminster lobbyists Scott Colvin of Aviva and Michael Hayman of Seven Hills. 'Rightly or wrongly, Liz had decided that Ruth Porter was not going to be chief,' a campaign source says. 'Fullbrook was keen for it and eventually as about fifth choice he ended up being offered the job.' Given senior members of the campaign had raised concerns about his original appointment, the decision caused some bad blood in the team. But with the news leaked to *The Times* within hours of the appointment being agreed, there was no going back. 'Ultimately Liz came to the view that Fullbrook was popular with MPs and MPs matter and he got it and she's grown to like him,' a source said. A similar thought process saw Simon McGee – Boris Johnson's former FCDO press secretary turned private spin-doctor – hired as a civil servant to be Director of Communications. Adam Jones was given the title Political Director of Communications, with details of exactly how this awkward split would work left up in the air.

'By the end of August there was a growing resentment among Truss's original Spad team that they were being slow-boiled in the pan,' an insider says. Fullbrook's boasts to journalists that he had turned the campaign around had gone down very badly with the team that had got her through the MPs' stage, and morale was low. By the last weeks of August the civil service had turned Chevening into an alternative centre for government, with Cabinet Secretary Simon Case a regular fixture at the Kent estate on most days. 'Officials appeared out of nowhere, and suddenly it was all paperwork and processes. You had to book slots to see the boss and the state basically kicked in,' one long-time staffer complained. Sophie Jarvis would get her coveted title of Political Secretary, but she would answer to the Director of Political Strategy, Iain Carter. Remembering their battles at the Palace, Case had also tried to stop Truss appointing Jason Stein as a senior special adviser, though he and Stein eventually made peace in the tranquil surrounds of the Chevening estate. Meanwhile Porter was appointed Deputy Chief of Staff, and Jamie Hope the head of a shelled-out Policy Unit; a new economic adviser Matt Sinclair, formerly of the TaxPayers' Alliance, would eat up most of his job. The true power-broker in the team would be a souped-up civil service Principal Private Secretary Nick Catsaras, who Truss brought over from the Foreign Office.

The fate of Chancellor Nadhim Zahawi had been a running concern throughout the summer. While Zahawi had been helping Truss meet media figures such as Aidan Barclay ahead of the *Telegraph*'s key endorsement of her campaign, he was fighting a doomed battle to try to stay at the Treasury. Relations with Truss hit a rocky patch when his allies let it be known that he was looking at strengthening a windfall tax on energy bills, as the looming price cap rise began to dominate the news agenda in the last weeks of August. 'Liz and Kwasi hit the roof and kept on going,' a Treasury source said; 'they were livid and bombarded him with messages telling him to basically pack it in. It went against everything they were planning.' Another source said, 'You had the current Chancellor and his likely replacement going hammer and tongs at each other over what to do.' When Ofgem, on 26 August, confirmed that bills would hit more than £3,500 a year, crisis energy-planning meetings began to eclipse all other conversations at Chevening. Truss was locked in intimate talks with officials, Kwarteng and Clarke over how to solve the issue, with an initial plan of upping Rishi Sunak's £400 bailout to all families to £1,000 quickly deemed an inefficient mechanism. When Labour announced they would freeze bills at current rates, orders went out from Kwarteng for the campaign and its supporters not to bash the policy too hard – the clearest sign yet that Truss would have to attempt something of a similar scale within weeks. But Zahawi would ultimately play a clever game, choosing to open up the might of the Treasury to the campaign to help get an energy support package up and running. He organised meetings with Norwegian gas giant Equinor at Chevening, and flew to the United States to meet his American counterpart Janet Yellen in the last days of the campaign for further chats on behalf of Truss about increasing US gas supplies. 'Zahawi came good in the end and basically kept himself in a top-flight job by getting on board,' a campaign source says, reflecting on Zahawi's new post as minister for the Cabinet Office.

Subsequently, a number of Truss's aides would rue the personnel changes agreed at Chevening. 'I think it was the appointment of the Cabinet that was the problem,' says one. 'Wendy Morton should never have been Chief Whip, Kwasi should never have been Chancellor, Jacob Rees-Mogg should never have been Business. Suella, Ranil, couldn't put them on the media. The minute she put them in the Cabinet, it started to go wrong.' It was not just backroom and ministerial positions that were decided at Chevening. The seventeenth-century residence hosted much of the planning for the new administration's 'mini-Budget'. The fiscal statement – set for late September – was intended to set out how ministers would pay for its tax changes and energy price plans. Truss hosted a summit of supporters, including IEA economists Julian Jessop and Andrew Lilico, Boris Johnson's former adviser Gerard Lyons, Matt Sinclair, Truss's economic policy adviser, and Kwasi Kwarteng. The trio of Lilico, Lyons and Jessop were dubbed 'the Trussketeers', with the latter two presenting a paper aimed at supporting her growth agenda. It backed the idea that a new government needed to 'hit the ground running' but stressed the need to keep the financial markets onside.[1] 'The markets are nervous about the UK and about policy options,' they warned. 'If immediate economic policy announcements are handled badly then a market crash is possible.'[2] Such advice appears to have been disregarded, with several of Truss's aides suggesting she was cut off in this critical period from candid allies who would have been willing to interrogate some of the key assumptions of her mini-Budget. Instead – surrounded by a coterie of unquestioning civil servants in the splendid isolation of the Grade I listed residence – she ploughed on with the plans that would prove to be her undoing.

With a week to go, Sunak finally sent word via an intermediary that the game was up. Key Rishi supporter Robert Jenrick, with his eye on a job in Truss's government after serving as her PPS at Justice, had agreed to relay a message to Sunak at the behest of Simon Clarke. On 30 August Sunak had given an interview with the *FT* in which he warned it would be 'complacent and irresponsible not to be thinking about the risks to the public finances' when making tax-and-spend decisions. He told the paper: 'My general view in life: you can't take anything for granted.' Jenrick told Clarke to send word to Truss that the last-ditch interview was nothing more than a valedictory last stand and that the attack dogs would now be called off. A message from the defeated Sunak was passed on to Truss: 'We all need this government to succeed and the next few weeks are going to be crucial.' After seven brutal weeks at each other's throats, Liz emerged victorious.

At a celebratory dinner on the Sunday night at Chevening with campaign staff and their partners, Truss gently took aim at her new Chief of Staff in a toast: 'I want to thank Mark Fullbrook because I couldn't have done it without him, without the incredible infrastructure you put in around the country, and all that operational expertise that was all ready to go ... for Penny.' With good grace, he hit back: 'I've not always been a Liz guy but I know how good this team is because they beat me.' 'We beat you twice,' came the heckling reply from around the table, amid some soreness that Fullbrook was getting all the credit after originally backing both Zahawi and Mordaunt against them.

In a side room at Westminster's Queen Elizabeth II Conference Centre the next day there would be no rapprochement between Truss and Sunak. There was no handshake or hug when the result was given to the candidates privately ten minutes before the public announcement. With 81,326 votes to Sunak's 60,399, Truss had won 57 points to 43 – a dip from the initial 24-point lead the pollsters projected – and perhaps a sign Sunak was closing the gap towards the end. When Sir Graham Brady revealed Truss was the winner in front of the watching cameras, she brushed past her rival without so much as a glance. In her eagerness to get to the stage, husband Hugh O'Leary would barely get an acknowledgement either. 'During this leadership campaign, I campaigned as a Conservative and I will govern as a Conservative,' Truss told the crowd. 'I will deliver a bold plan to cut taxes and grow our economy. I will deliver on the energy crisis, dealing with people's energy bills, but also dealing with the long-term issues we have on energy supply. And I will deliver on the National Health Service.'

A few hours later, Truss and her team enjoyed a last moment of peace as they sipped champagne at their victory party on the roof of Deliveroo HQ in Blackfriars. At Admiralty House, the grand Whitehall residence traditionally handed to incoming PMs on the eve of entering Downing Street, Truss told the team that 'ties are back in No. 10', demanding they all smarten up as they take over the country. Little did they know that the dress code for their first two weeks in power would be altogether much darker ...

September 2022

28 DAYS LATER

Eight hours after Boris Johnson drove away from Downing Street into a golden sunrise, Liz Truss's convoy was detouring around south London trying to catch a break in the rain.

Her planned speech about Britain 'riding out the storm' took on a grim irony as she sat in the back of the armoured prime-ministerial Jaguar XJ for the first time. Back at No. 10 frantic aides were studying rain radar apps, after the order came down that the new Prime Minister would be making her speech outside, come what may. With the world's media waiting, a black bin bag was placed on top of her new lectern to protect the microphones from the latest downpour. For a politician who had carefully Instagrammed her way back from political oblivion it was an unfortunate introductory image to beam around the globe.

The traditional handover of power can usually be done in minutes with a short dash up the Mall from Westminster to Buckingham Palace for the outgoing PM and their successor. But Queen Elizabeth had not been seen publicly for weeks, and her 'mobility problems' were cited as a reason for the unprecedented 'kissing hands' between the Monarch and the new premier at Balmoral on Tuesday 6 September. With Thursday earmarked for Truss to finally unveil her work on a long-awaited energy bailout package – potentially the largest-ever peacetime market intervention by the British state – it was already shaping up to be an historic week.

At 12:10 Liz Truss curtsied in front of the frail 96-year-old Monarch, in front of a roaring fire in the Drawing Room at Balmoral. With Truss's landing delayed at Aberdeen airport due to fog, and more torrential rain hindering the 45-minute drive to the royal estate, you could be forgiven for thinking there was a divine conspiracy against the day's proceedings. During the wait, the Queen had more pressing business to attend to however. She picked up the phone to her racehorse trainer Clive Cox to talk through her horse Love Affairs' chances at Goodwood that afternoon. It won. Cox would later describe Her Majesty as 'sharp as a tack' on the call; a sentiment echoed by allies of both Johnson and Truss that day. 'It was clear it was bad, but not that bad. Mentally she was totally with it; she was clearly uncomfortable but she stood to greet her guests and was firing off questions about the political situation,' one source familiar with the day says. Johnson and the Monarch had laughed and joked through a 40-minute departure audience that went on longer than scheduled. Events, though, were more formal when Truss arrived, with the traditional kissing of the hand ceremony conducted underneath a portrait of that other great female sovereign, Queen Victoria. In what would be the last-ever statement released about Queen Elizabeth II's engagements, Buckingham Palace confirmed: 'The Queen received in audience The Right Honourable Elizabeth Truss MP today and requested her to form a new administration. Ms Truss accepted Her Majesty's offer and kissed hands upon her appointment as Prime Minister and First Lord of the Treasury.'

Back in Downing Street, meanwhile, the clear-out had begun. Ruth Porter, newly appointed Deputy Chief of Staff, was overheard describing the handover as 'a revolution', while her boss Mark Fullbrook vocalised the mantra of the new team: 'Hashtag GSD' – or 'Get Shit Done'. But even in the earliest hours of her premiership, aides were worried about the new PM's behaviour. Changing her mobile number for a third time in as many weeks left her isolated and cut off from external advice and MPs.

'Lots of people thought they were going to be working for the new PM when they arrived at work that day, and were brutally dispatched,' says one newly appointed member of Team Truss. And that included civil servants as well as political advisers. More than two dozen of Boris Johnson's officials were alerted via email at 9:30 a.m. that their services were no longer required and they would be moved to new roles either in the Cabinet Office or across Whitehall. Both those dismissed and those reassigned were ordered out of No. 10 by 11 a.m. that morning. Boxes for hastily clearing desks were distributed as the pubs of Whitehall quickly filled up with early morning sorrows to be drowned. As the pints flowed, anger mounted at Cabinet Secretary Simon Case, who had been at Chevening for weeks working on new floor plans and structures for No. 10, 'without so much as a word of warning' to some of his civil service colleagues. While it is not unusual to see some officials leave upon the formation of a new administration, the basis for some personnel decisions left No. 10 staff baffled. Aides suggest a mixture of obsession and hubris, with one early meeting paused as Truss asked 'for the room'. Every aide traipsed out, except private secretary Nick Catsaras. It was later discovered she had remonstrated with him 'because she'd seen a civil servant who used to work for Gove', one witness recalls.

But, as with her arrival at Trade and the Foreign Office, Truss was not averse to a sweeping clear-out of officials she considered to be 'NQOT' or 'not quite our type'. The sacking of long-standing Treasury Permanent Secretary Tom Scholar on day one would spark howls of derision once the news was released later in the week. But it was a decision made and communicated to the mandarin in the days before the handover as part of the new administration's war on 'Treasury Orthodoxy'. While ex-Whitehall panjandrums queued up to slam the decision and attacked Simon Case for not blocking the move, allies of the Cabinet Secretary insist he 'did put up a fight' about the decision but was overruled personally by the PM. And National Security Adviser Sir Stephen Lovegrove was also put out to pasture with a new role in procurement – a decision allies say Truss based upon his hostility to arming Ukraine in early 2021.

Even those officials who survived the cull faced upheaval. The No. 10 Policy Unit was all but disbanded, with new economic adviser Matt Sinclair and Jamie Hope left to run the show. 'The PM is the policy unit,' one aide remarked. 'Very few of the big ideas that come out from her are sort of bottom up: they're Liz Truss down.' The No. 10 Press Office was moved from its traditional powerbase on the same floor as the Cabinet room and PM's private office to a distant part of the building. Its old offices were then handed to new Deputy PM Thérèse Coffey, novice Chief Whip Wendy Morton and a beefed-up political unit. While new civil service Director of Communications Simon McGee would head up the team, Adam Jones, the political comms boss, insisted he would remain in the PM's private office, leaving him separate from the other spin-doctors. Some argue that the seeds of major communications failures in the coming weeks were sown in that early and unusual decision.

'Liz doesn't want a presidential-style No. 10,' Jones would later brief the papers. 'She wants it to be lean, professional and relentlessly focused on delivery – policy making and legislating. You'll see fewer prime-ministerial visits, fewer events in No. 10, and in its place more meetings on the economy, on energy and the things people really care about.' Defending the cull of civil servants, he would claim: 'The good ones will be deeply empowered by her. The civil service are always in the ascendancy with Liz as long as they actually do their job.' Nowhere would that be more clear than in the role Nick Catsaras would play – merging the traditional Principal Private Secretary job with responsibilities that might usually fall to a Chief of Staff. 'Nick is in everything, and all seeing,' said a colleague; 'by far the most powerful person in the building now.' Case would also quickly impress the PM, especially in the torrid days of royal upheaval that were soon to unfold, although his rapid transformation into a Truss ultra-loyalist would earn him the nickname Varys among some in No. 10, after the highly manipulative eunuch in *Game of Thrones* who manages to seamlessly retain power despite brutal politicking at court.

Concerns mounted early about the performance of new Chief Whip Wendy Morton, though. Truss had originally made 'a very generous offer' to Thérèse Coffey to take the job, including full Cabinet minister pay and 'a seat at the top table', as well as use of a flat in Admiralty House, according to one source involved in the negotiations. But Coffey had held out for a department and the Deputy PM job. '[Truss] wanted a woman,' the source says. 'She wanted Andrea Leadsom, but that didn't work, Anne-Marie Trevelyan didn't work, so eventually they went with Wendy. But it was clear from day one she had no clue how to do the job. Basic questions about what MPs were thinking were met with blank stares.'

Despite the significant shifts in personnel, it was the energy package that dominated the majority of the PM's first hours in the job. 'These are extraordinary times and it requires an extraordinary intervention from the government,' the PM was said to have told her team on arrival in No. 10. 'But we also must take action to ensure this doesn't happen again.' Despite long-held beliefs that the government should get out of the way, in one of her first moves as leader, Truss would spend multiple billions freezing the price of energy bills. 'A conscious decision was made to announce all the energy stuff separate from the tax cuts,' one ally claims. 'The first load was what we had to do, the second lot was what we wanted to do.' And it was that energy announcement that Truss pored over on the plane to Scotland with speech-writer Asa Bennett, a former *Telegraph* scribe, rather than the address she was due to give on the steps of No. 10 that same day.

With the reshuffle almost entirely completed during the final weeks of the campaign, there were few surprises on Tuesday evening, with the new top team all announced by nightfall. All meetings were immediately 'pared back' to a handful of officials and advisers, rather than the sprawling sessions under Johnson, and the new PM chose to make the Cabinet table her powerbase rather than the 'den' next door preferred by her predecessors. 'The PM basically set up shop from there [on] day one, and has conducted everything from there since,' one official remarks. Powered by an ever-present Pret double espresso, Truss was up until 1 a.m. on Wednesday morning working with her closest team on the energy bailout package. Gas supply was also high on the agenda on Tuesday evening in the first call with President Biden, where the pair discussed increasing US supply following on from Nadhim Zahawi's overtures in Washington the previous week. While the official No. 10 read-out of the call would state the pair 'reflected on the enduring strength of the Special Relationship', sources listening in suggest it was Biden who first used the phrase – with Truss having privately remarked that she dislikes the 'needy' British obsession with deploying the term.

Truss's so-called 'new way of doing things' was most evident at Wednesday morning's brief but initial meeting of the new Cabinet. Truss may not have been the oldest around the table, with her ten continuous years of ministerial office, eight at the top level, she was the most experienced. One disregarded minister from Johnson's Cabinet says: 'Looking at the composition of her [Cabinet] overall, I think her view is, "Look guys, there's only one boss around here. I don't want to have some patronising old bugger of whatever gender stroking his or her chin and saying 'well' … Liz's cabinet says: 'I'm the boss here.'"' They continue: 'There's lots of talented people, one or two not so talented people. But it's definitely more than *primus inter pares*. She is the most experienced. She is the one that has been around longest. And from Liz's point of view that's fair enough, she's made the choice to have people completely aligned with her.'

Prominent Cabinet figures such as Michael Gove, Grant Shapps and Sajid Javid had been culled: a decision that would come back to haunt Truss within weeks.

More noteworthy than 'a Cabinet of minnows', as one MP described it, was Truss's decision to banish almost every No. 10 official except Case and Catsaras from the Cabinet meeting. Traditionally, Chiefs of Staff, Directors of Communications, Press and Political Secretaries have all had a seat around the back of the Cabinet room. But early on Wednesday morning, Truss's Private Office made clear none of them were welcome. Crucially, the PM's Official Spokesman, whose job it is to give the press an official briefing of the meeting every week, and field tricky questions, was excluded. Any account they could give would be second hand, in a break with the established norms of Whitehall transparency. Given that this restrictive measure was clearly designed to clamp down on leaks, the irony of Truss deploying restrictive measures to clamp down on leaks was not lost on many senior Tories who knew she had long traded in Cabinet gossip as a currency. And the move was not without its critics. 'They will cock something up spectacularly eventually,' one seasoned Tory says. 'And when they do they will blame the comms, when actually if a comms person had been in the room at the time they would have been able to warn of the giant train wreck coming.' And if it was designed to stop leaks, then that plan lasted all of two hours. The *Sun* would report by Wednesday lunchtime that the Cabinet had agreed to pause controversial legislation drawn up by Boris Johnson's administration for a new 'Bill of Rights' that would allow the British Supreme Court to trump rulings from the European Court of Human Rights. A leak inquiry was ordered, but for once there were only ministers rather than aides to interview. News of the decision had not been passed to the press team before calls came in to No. 10 from the media – immediately rendering the new process dud.

Westminster awaited 12 noon on Wednesday 7 September with a morbid curiosity. Truss had never been a particularly strong Commons performer, as evidenced by her previous debuts in Cabinet roles, so it was a full House to see her first weekly duel with Labour's Sir Keir Starmer. In a back-and-forth about a windfall tax, Truss put the clearest blue water between a PM and the leader of the opposition for half a decade by doubling down on her opposition to taxing businesses, to the obvious delight of Starmer, who was used to Johnson's obfuscation. The opposition looked more than a little confused to have a PM actually attempt to answer the questions, and to give the answers they wanted to put on their leaflets. But it was the Tories who were waving their order papers by the time Truss got the better of Starmer, turning his attack that there was 'nothing new' about her new administration on its head with a punchy retort: 'Well there's nothing new about Labour wanting to put up taxes.' An impressive debut had Truss's backers cheered, and her doubters muted. Long-time supporter George Osborne tweeted: 'I suspect after that PMQs it's starting to dawn on Labour that they've made a mistake in underestimating Liz Truss.'

But there was no celebration in No. 10 that evening. As the new PM put the finishing touches to her energy package, the news from Balmoral was becoming increasingly grim.

Plans for the Queen to host a virtual Privy Council to swear in the new Cabinet were downgraded to a telephone meeting in the late afternoon, before being cancelled entirely by the early evening. Buckingham Palace released a woolly statement, explaining: 'after a full day yesterday, Her Majesty has this afternoon accepted doctors' advice to rest'. While Truss had left Balmoral just a day previously under the impression the Queen was 'very unwell but nothing imminent', according to a friend, that night it was quietly suggested to the new Downing Street team that they might have a black tie to hand in the drawer of their new desks. A sense of foreboding took hold overnight that the PM's landmark announcement might be about to become overshadowed.

In any other week, Truss's long-awaited energy package would have dominated the news for days. With an estimated £120 billion price tag, her price freeze would limit average annual household bills to £2,500 over the next two years – beyond the next election. It was the biggest-ever energy market intervention, with Truss later claiming in a Tory video: 'I saw the reports in the media about bills that were £5,000 or £6,000. And I just thought this isn't right, it was just very, very important that people did not have to worry any more about this winter and next winter. I think it was right that we took a decision as a country that we were going to make sure that the price was reasonable.' But in reality, the free marketeer at heart had taken some convincing to reach that stage. 'The whole thing was completely alien to her worldview,' one Tory MP close to her argues. 'She kicked the tyres on a lot of other ways of doing it first,' an ally admits.

Truss's initial plan drawn up at Chevening in late August was to more than double the £400 cost-of-living support package set out by Rishi Sunak to £1,000. But that plan was abandoned over claims that government IT infrastructure would not be able to change the payment level quickly enough before bills soared on 1 October, as well as fears the figure would quickly be seen as insufficient in the face of energy costs that had risen by five times in a year. Even while arguing against 'handouts' culture during the campaign, Truss was privately preparing to bow to the inevitable political pressure for a price freeze. But she warned advisers she 'only wanted to have to do this once' and to come up with a plan of sufficient scale. One source says: 'The key thing for the boss was she did not want to have to keep coming back to this every three or six months. For her it was "go once, go big – problem goes away".' But the scale of the intervention would stun her ideological allies, with even some in the Cabinet believing more targeted support could have been drawn up despite the febrile political climate.

In the very early hours of Thursday 8th, word reached Simon Case that Her Majesty was deeply unwell, with Truss informed before she appeared downstairs. But while Truss was practising her speech in the Cabinet room with aides at around 9 a.m., a stony-faced Cabinet Secretary entered and asked to see the PM alone in the den next door. Upon her return, Truss began frantically organising for black dresses to be fetched from Greenwich, having barely had time to move her personal wardrobe to Downing Street. For watching aides, the seriousness of the situation was abundantly clear: the Queen had taken a dramatic downturn. 'Case told her it was a matter of when not if. She knew it would be that day but she had to go to the Commons and pretend everything was normal,' said one eyewitness.

Having outlined her plans to MPs – fully aware that not a word of it would appear on the next day's front pages – Truss sat listening to Sir Keir Starmer's windy response at the despatch box when Nadhim Zahawi, the minister for the Cabinet Office, entered the chamber bearing a note. Buckingham Palace was due to issue a statement about the Queen's health, something the PM had been expecting but which Zahawi inadvertently alerted the world to. In the full glare of the press gallery, Zahawi then summoned Labour's deputy leader Angela Rayner to the area behind the Speaker's Chair where Simon Case was hoping to brief Starmer. As Starmer continued on, not a single pair of eyes or ears were on the leader of the opposition, as it became clear there was a major situation brewing. A note was passed to the Labour leader urging him to wrap things up and get out of the chamber, so he too could be told the Queen's death was probably imminent. Rayner would later tell LBC: 'The note was that the Queen is unwell ... I read between the lines on that because you don't get a note saying the Queen's unwell if she's got a bit of a cough and cold. I thought at that time that it's very serious.' By the time the statement dropped that the Queen's doctors were 'gravely concerned', the newswires and social media had put two and two together, thanks to the Commons drama.

Her Majesty died at 15:10. Truss was already working in the privacy of the No. 10 flat on what she would say. Seating space was short after Boris Johnson had taken almost all of the furniture, so some advisers were sitting on the floor at 16:30 when the news came from downstairs via Case that the Queen had died. Presented with proposed remarks drafted by the civil service 'clearly in about 1960', Truss and her team decided to try to write their own version of what she should say to the nation, and the world, in light of the news. Back on the steps of No. 10 by 18:50, her words that 'Queen Elizabeth II was the rock on which modern Britain was built' may have provided a headline, but the speech was not one for the ages. However, as the first public figure to utter the uncustomary words 'God Save the King', any criticism of her speech seemed fairly insignificant in the enormity of the moment. Boris Johnson quickly published his own tribute to 'Elizabeth the Great' on Twitter. He had been working on a speech for that moment since the 2019 Election, but was deprived of the Downing Street pulpit by just three days.

Several of Truss's new ministers were spotted shedding tears in the bars of Parliament while younger party staff led a chorus of the national anthem outside Buckingham Palace. Inside No. 10 the civil service machine whirred into action – with a well-planned 'Operation London Bridge' leaving political aides with nothing left to do but find their way around their new building and figure out how the computers worked.

King Charles III returned from Scotland on Friday 9 September, Liz Truss's second audience with a second Monarch swiftly following. A single pooled TV camera captured the first encounter between the novice premier and a brand-new sovereign at Buckingham Palace 'It's been so touching this afternoon when we arrived here, all those people,' began Charles. 'Your Majesty, my very greatest sympathies,' she replied. 'It was the moment I have been dreading, as I know a lot of people have,' he sighed. 'We'll try to keep everything going. Come, come have a seat.' The new Monarch and the minister did at least have something of a pre-existing relationship from her work at Defra and on COP26.

The Queen's passing put an immediate stop to 'normal' politics. Civil servants donned black attire; a period of national mourning was declared until 19 September – the day of the State Funeral. Courtiers and mandarins instead stepped in to temporarily run the show. While most in government respected this temporary cessation of hostilities, there were some hints of irritation at the restraints it imposed, given the ongoing cost-of-living crisis. And while Truss made no blunders – beyond a questionable curtsy to the King – the formality and strained environment did not play to the new PM's strengths. Solemn readings and official statements did little to introduce Truss to the nation beyond her awkward style of public speaking. More cynical observers quietly noted that the holes in the energy price package unveiled on the day of the Monarch's death could have blown up into major rows had the news agenda not been obliterated. Top of that list was the astonishing cost of the intervention and the fact that taxpayers would pick up the bill for years to come while energy firms continued to make vast profits.

Truss's plans to lift the ban on fracking and the bankers' bonus cap both leaked out during this period, with the latter story enraging the Palace. Aides were also forced to row back on a botched briefing to the Sunday papers that the PM would 'tour the UK' with King Charles. Downing Street claimed that Truss had never intended to accompany the new Monarch on walkabouts; instead, her role was confined to attending services of reflection in Scotland, Northern Ireland and Wales. Truss's team faced further difficult headlines after the *Sunday Times* revealed Mark Fullbrook had been questioned by the FBI as a witness about an ongoing investigation into an alleged criminal plot to bribe an American politician. It was not being suggested

Fullbrook was implicated in any bribery. A plan to pay Fullbrook as a secondee from his firm was quietly dropped after the arrangement was leaked a week later. While the Chief of Staff was quickly becoming a lightning rod for bad news, rather than fire him Truss instead gave him the nod to run her future general election campaign. It sparked fury among many senior Tories, who were hoping to keep 2019's winning strategist Isaac Levido.

Normal politics resumed on the evening of the Queen's spectacular State Funeral on Monday 19 September. Hot-footing it straight to Stansted Airport from Windsor Castle, Truss would finally visit somewhere other than a church or palace for the first time in days. While all living PMs had attended the service earlier in the day at Westminster Abbey, only John Major and Tony Blair, as Knights of the Garter, were also invited to the smaller service in Windsor. Eyewitnesses say there was a much friendlier bond that afternoon between the Blairs and Truss, after he had privately advised her at the Foreign Office. 'Major seemed to still be sulking about Brexit and ignored her,' according to one fellow mourner.

Still in black, Truss boarded a flight to New York, defying advice from some of her closest advisers to not leave the country ahead of the following Friday's delayed mini-Budget where her promised tax-cutting plans would finally be unveiled. 'It was damned if she did, damned if she didn't,' says one ally. 'If she had not gone there would have been a load of babbling about turning her back on the world stage.' Another aide says: 'It takes foreign secretaries a long time to get out of international mode.' The PM told the travelling press pack on board that the past 11 days had been 'a momentous period and a period of great grief and sadness in the UK ... from my own point of view I am hugely honoured to have been invited to form a government by Her Majesty the Queen in one of her last acts and since then I've had two audiences with His Majesty. And I have seen a huge outpouring of public warmth and support for him and the Royal Family.'

While Truss was pressing the flesh at the United Nations, an energy cost for businesses to match that for families was delivered on Wednesday, followed by a programme to tackle the backlog of care in the NHS on Thursday. Meanwhile Truss finally got her first meeting with US President Joe Biden as PM, on the fringes of the UN General Assembly. Though Biden had been in London on Sunday ahead of the funeral, the pair swiftly abandoned plans that had been announced for an off-camera bilateral in Downing Street, given the constraints the mourning period placed on what could actually be discussed. Rumours in Washington diplomatic circles that Truss had been the source of a scurrilous newspaper article after the previous year's COP26 summit in Glasgow regarding the President's alleged flatulence seemed not to have caused lasting damage to the Special Relationship.

The summit passed without major incident, but back home there was incredulity in Downing Street about parts of Friday's package and wincing at footage of Truss vowing she was 'prepared to be unpopular' as her fiscal policies hit home. The Budget in all but name would become the new administration's defining event; a mistake of epic proportions that would bring down the PM and her Chancellor. Some of Truss's closest advisers say her reaction to the Queen's death had a massive impact. The official mourning period, the massive upheaval of funeral planning, the lying in state and Truss's trips to all four parts of the UK meant many key advisers did not find out the full content of the planned statement until days before it was announced. One reflects: 'The whole thing just gave her this kind of sense of imperialism. She had come in and the energy price cap announcement had gone really well. The campaign despite being chaotic had ultimately gone well. And in the first few days there were just a load of "yes" people around her. Her Majesty had died so there was a complete pausing in politics, I think they just felt invincible. And to be fair, Kwasi was saying, "You have got to slow it all down, slow it all down." And nothing slowed down. And they went full head into this thing.'

Communication aides were shocked to discover the scale of the plans, remarking to each other: 'Why the fuck are we doing this bankers' bonus thing before Christmas?' But one admits: 'No one challenged her, she was like full-on prime-ministerial at that point.'

There had been warning signs: Truss told Laura Kuenssberg two days before she took office that she intended to tear up twenty years of attempts to detoxify the Tories as a party of the rich. 'To look at everything through the lens of redistribution I believe is wrong,' she had said, 'because what I'm about is about growing the economy and growing the economy benefits everybody.' In a clear hint that she would be going further on the tax cuts than she had proposed during the campaign, Truss told Kuenssberg: 'of course people at the top of the income distribution pay more tax, so inevitably when you cut taxes you tend to benefit people who are more likely to pay tax.' And so it proved on Friday 23 September when, in one of the most abrupt policy changes of an incumbent administration, Kwasi Kwarteng planted a bomb under what had been the Conservative's economic strategy since 2010. Out went Rishi Sunak's increases to the rates of National Insurance contributions and corporation tax; in came the lifting of the cap on bankers' bonuses. Taxes would be cut by £45 billion a year by 2026, with borrowing raised by £72 billion to fund the energy package for businesses and households. The new Chancellor made homes under £250,000 stamp-duty free, a doubling of the threshold, and extended the exemptions for first-time buyers.

The stamp duty move had leaked while Truss was in New York, and the other measures had been promised during the campaign. But there were bigger surprises to come. The Chancellor brought forward a 1p cut in the basic rate of income tax to April and scrapped the top rate of tax altogether for those on £150,000 or more. 'Jesus Christ!' one Tory MP was heard exclaiming from the public gallery when the 45p additional rate was abolished.

The shock was not confined to Parliament: at least one senior adviser in No. 10 only found out about the cut in the top rate of tax while watching live on television. 'Gobsmacked' was the reaction of another aide, who recalls seeing an 'elated' Treasury team returning from the Commons. 'There were two camps – the ones trying to be realistic and the ones that were ideological … none of us [in the former camp] were kept in the loop on it.' Some within No. 10 felt excluded by the Economic Unit being run by Matt Sinclair, Truss's Chief Economic Adviser and a fervent free-marketeer. 'There were not enough checks and balances,' complains one Truss aide. They contrasted Kwarteng's closest advisers with their more experienced counterparts who had served previous Tory chancellors. 'Usually, the Chancellor's team are economists who are trying to do politics. Kwasi's team were political aides trying to do economics. They were very good at splashing the *Telegraph* but they had no credibility in the City.' Indeed, the reaction to the mini-Budget in the Tory press was some of the most effusive received by a Chancellor, with Kwarteng and Sinclair photographed toasting their success at the Two Chairmen pub in Westminster that evening.

As one former Cabinet minister told the authors the week before the statement, '[Truss] is staking a lot on a particular IEA, TPA, ASI view of the world, that, if implemented sufficiently clearly, will give the economy the shot it needs. I think she thinks a bit like a surgeon who has seen a patient with various remedies that haven't really worked, so she thinks "let's get the biggest hypo possible, pack it full of adrenaline and pump it into the heart". Now either the patient will revive, *Pulp Fiction* style, or it won't. But that's the gamble. I think there's a one-in-three chance of it being a roaring success, but the odds are against it at the moment.' With Truss sacking the boss of the Treasury, Tom Scholar, and refusing to publish an independent assessment of her tax-cutting plans until November, the fuse was lit.

The political and market reaction was swift and damning. Within minutes of Kwarteng retaking his seat in the Commons, the pound began to plunge in value. Spooked City financiers ensured that Sterling plunged to below $1.09 by the end of the day – its lowest value since 1985 – while Kwarteng's cock-a-hoop Labour shadow Rachel Reeves dubbed it 'casino economics, gambling the mortgages and finances of every family in the country'. Shocked Tory MPs were incredulous at how Kwarteng had given their opponents the chance to paint them as the party of the rich on the eve of Labour's Party Conference. Colleagues of Truss dubbed it the 'kamiKwasi budget'; one former minister told the *Sunday Times* that 'Everyone who isn't mad hates it.' Labour's conference began that weekend and with the eyes of the country upon them, the party made hay; Leader Keir Starmer pledged to restore the 45p rate if elected to office. Kwarteng irritated Truss by going on television on Sunday morning and insisting there was 'more to come' with tax cuts. When the Asian markets opened on Monday, a Sterling fire-sale drove the pound to its lowest-ever rate of $1.035 against the dollar. It was a political and economic disaster.

The following day, the International Monetary Fund (IMF) piled in, warning that 'large and untargeted fiscal packages' were likely to deepen inequality. Truss herself blamed Tom Scholar for this and much of the resulting fall-out, privately telling aides of her suspicion that he 'had a hand in' the IMF's unusually forceful domestic intervention. A rush to dump UK government bonds forced a dramatic intervention by the Bank of England on Wednesday morning. With outrageously over-exposed pension funds claiming they were close to insolvency, the central bank promised to buy long-term bonds 'on whatever scale is necessary' to restore order in the market. Soon mortgage providers were not waiting for the Bank to hike up interest rates, but were instead withdrawing lending offers, with the likely repayment rates obliterating the relief of any stamp-duty saving. Six days after Kwarteng's statement, a YouGov survey had the Conservatives on a mere 21 per cent of the vote, with Labour ahead by a mammoth 33 points. It was published hours after Truss underwent a disastrous marathon of 24 local and regional BBC interviews, replete with a barrage of hostile questions, awkward pauses, stutters and unsatisfactory answers. By the time the Tories' own conference began three days later, Truss had plummeted to a score of -59-net popularity: lower than Boris Johnson or Jeremy Corbyn ever were. 'Trussterfuck' was the reaction from Fleet Street commentators. Though Truss had said she was prepared to be unpopular, the scale of the backlash stunned even the usually unemotional premier.

The fall-out did not help divisions within Truss's office either, with one aide openly admitting 'the team hate each other'. The predicted fault lines between the original – and younger – members of Team Truss and the new, older arrivals had fractured relationships. Fullbrook and Ruth Porter had been at odds virtually since day one, with supporters of each of them openly questioning what exactly it was that the other one did. Tensions between the libertarian, low-tax Matt Sinclair and the more cautious Jamie Hope got particularly bad in the wake of the 45p decision, as they did between Truss and Adam Jones, with the PM reprimanding him for 'the mess' at a pre-conference meeting. While Jones was apparently 'on the defensive' when faced with the accusation that 'the comms have been shit', Truss would make that view public, telling Laura Kuenssberg on the Sunday morning: 'I do accept we should have laid the ground better, I do accept that.' The PM added ominously for some in No. 10: 'I have learnt from that.'

Truss's first conference as leader started with her party in a mutinous mood, and as the conference began that Sunday, she found herself facing an old foe. Unfortunately for her, he is one of the best Tory communicators of his generation. Sitting yards away from the PM in the Kuenssberg studio was Michael Gove, who swiftly tore into the 45p tax cut. 'I don't believe it's right,' Gove told his host, claiming he was 'profoundly concerned' about the 'sheer risk' of the move as 'a display of the wrong values'. The intervention was particularly painful for Truss given she had tried to make peace with Gove less than a week ago. Amid their strange relationship of rivalry, Truss had organised a drink at No. 10 the previous Monday to try and neutralise Gove's inability to avoid politicking. Relieved that the rumours he would take over the Editorship of *The Times* had not borne fruit, Truss instead dangled the prospect of a key ambassadorship at him. Israel or China were high on the list of options available to her former boss, should he avoid causing too much trouble for her wobbly premiership. 'His answer was given live on camera sitting on that sofa,' says one friend.

Speaking to the authors in the days before the conference about Truss's tax plans, Gove said presciently: 'Liz herself has said she doesn't believe in redistribution per se; for what it's worth, no one cares what I think, but I take a different view and that was a difference, temperamental, ideological, whatever you want to call it. As I say, while I disagree with her on that and one or two other policy areas, I think her position is coherent, legitimate, principled. And to be fair to Liz, when something becomes too hot to handle she will drop it; she won't disavow it but she'll drop it.'

He was proved correct by Sunday evening. Alongside Gove, ex-Cabinet Ministers Grant Shapps, Julian Smith, Mel Stride and Damian Green – all of whom backed Rishi Sunak – had spent the day stirring up rebellion and were confident that more than 40 MPs backed their concerns. Green had been to see the PM in the afternoon to plead for a change of tack, to no avail. But it was the meeting with Sir Graham Brady, the chairman of the all-powerful 1922 Committee, that tipped the scales for Truss. Speaking to the Prime Minister at around 7 p.m., Brady warned that despite a majority of 71, she was in grave political danger should she not back down. He said she did not have the numbers to ram a tax cut for the richest 10 per cent through Parliament, and that trying to do so would likely bring her down. Truss's defence that the pound had returned to its pre-mini-Budget level, and the UK had the second-lowest debt ratio in the G7, would fall on deaf ears. After days of 'distraction' it was time to ditch the hated policy, and with it, a huge amount of political capital.

Truss summoned Kwarteng to her hotel suite at Birmingham Hyatt at 9:45 on Sunday evening. The Chancellor had been dining across town at the four-star Malmaison Hotel restaurant, eagerly awaiting his main course when an aide broke the news of the emergency talks. Discreetly raising four fingers and then five, the aide got the message to his boss, who made his excuses. Allies insist the decision to climb down had been a 'process he was involved in' throughout that day, but it was not until Kwarteng got back to the hotel that he knew it was over. Arriving on the 24th floor, he walked into the PM's suite to see her sitting behind the table with Fullbrook and Jason Stein. 'What's going on?' Kwarteng asked. 'The 45p rate, Kwasi, it's dead as a dodo,' Truss replied; 'we need to rip off the plaster.' Allies say Kwarteng 'agreed on the spot', and even accepted it would be him that would have to front the mess before his address to the party faithful scheduled for the following after-noon. A source says: 'The conference was a pressure cooker and the steam had to come out as soon as possible.' Before Kwarteng would get to his speech, however, an awkward broadcast media round lay ahead in the morning, with the pair agreeing the Cabinet would be told at 7 a.m. With that the Chancellor went to bed, while the PM slipped out to a drinks party hosted by Brady's 1922 Committee and the ConservativeHome blog at a nearby bar – managing to maintain a poker face throughout her remarks to dozens of MPs, without so much as a hint of the pending dawn surrender.

But the news was starting to permeate around the top floor of the Hyatt Hotel, where most Tory bigwigs were staying. Well-oiled Cabinet ministers were hosting drinks parties and whispers of a climbdown began to make their way to the ears of journalists. While the press team battled to insist that 'no final decision had been made', a story on the *Sun* website saying that the 45p abolition was dead detonated the febrile conference shortly after midnight. Instead of finding out from No. 10 that the policy was jettisoned, several of the most senior figures in the government learnt the news from Twitter at 12:20 a.m. Some ministers were angrier than others, with Party Chairman Jake Berry particularly aggrieved, having been sent out on the airwaves earlier that day to warn that any MP that voted against any measure in the mini-Budget faced deselection. 'U-turns after feeding colleagues to the dogs is exactly what did for Boris,' one senior Tory complained about Johnson's downfall. 'It's like they sat and watched the entire defenestration of the last lot and thought that was a successful way to run a government.'

While the blame game would soon begin, with the Prime Minister insisting 'it was a decision that the Chancellor made', in reality the decision to abolish the 45p rate was driven by Truss and Kwarteng together. 'She's always wanted to do it,' a former aide says. Large parts of the senior Downing Street team were kept in the dark about the original decision, in some cases until hours before the announcement. 'It came out of nowhere,' one official says. 'Truss and Kwarteng cooked it up together. We were as surprised as anyone else.' Even all-powerful official Nick Catsaras would plead ignorance to colleagues until very late in the week. It should also be noted that Truss's favourite think tank the IEA had put out a call for the 45p rate to be abolished in the days leading up to the statement. While that's far from suggesting she did it on their orders, it was clearly a joint bugbear. 'The whole Growth Plan was drawn up by Truss and Kwasi in lockstep,' another No. 10 insider says. 'Any other suggestion is just noise.' No. 10 spin-doctors were alerted to the 45p policy only after the decision to go ahead had been made. Privately, Cabinet ministers believe a simple focus group session should have put the idea to bed, but none was conducted during the mourning period. 'It was obviously a bad idea but they were excited. New team, new rules, they got over excited,' one Cabinet minister would claim privately at the Party Conference.

Asked shortly before taking up his appointment about how he saw the relationship between a Chancellor and the Prime Minister, Kwarteng insisted it should be one of subservience. Reflecting on his predecessors, he said: 'Hammond at least had the maturity, I would say, in the sense that the Prime Minister was in charge. He had the width and the experience to know that he was there, but the Prime Minister was the person who won the leadership, she was head of the government. And even though he had some frustrations, as we all know, he deferred to her. And realised that the Treasury was constitutionally subordinate.' Kwarteng cited rows between No. 10 and No. 11 over increasing NHS spending in 2018 as evidence of that, saying: 'I think the Treasury officials probably wanted to raise taxes to cover that. And No. 10 said no, Theresa said no, and they got their way.' But he was critical of the way in which Rishi Sunak had seen his role, saying: 'I think Rishi's relationship with Boris was very different.' Taking aim at the department he now runs, he added: 'In the meetings I was in, they were very much superior, the Treasury, they were the numbers people, they were the details people, and they indulged, they humoured the Prime Minister. I don't know whether they ran rings around him; they were very rude and the special advisers were very rude and they didn't give him any deference or respect.'

While relations between the long-term allies, friends and neighbours were as close as they had been between a Chancellor and PM since the days of Osborne and Cameron, the 45p climbdown row obviously put a huge strain on the pair. Though Kwarteng's team tried to put on a brave face, it was a painful blow as he had already trailed his speech to the Party Conference into the next day's papers. He was billed as saying, 'we must stay the course' and there would be no U-turns on his plans. Instead, taking to the stage on Monday afternoon, he despaired: 'What a day.' Even if a Chancellor is accepting that the Treasury is 'constitutionally subordinate' to No. 10, rarely was that relationship played out so nakedly as it was in Birmingham that day. Further tensions loomed as Truss pushed to solve the energy supply crisis in the UK for the coming decades. While the PM had been secretly meeting Norwegian oil executives and ministers in Chevening since late August, Kwarteng had been urging caution about massive borrowing for a long-term gas deal further spooking the markets. U-turns aside, the rest of the gathering was scarcely any better. Penny Mordaunt, the reluctant Commons leader, led a Cabinet revolt on the plan to raise benefits with earnings, rather than inflation, having told a boozy event on the first night: 'our policies are great but our comms is shit'. Home Secretary Suella Braverman opened a separate flank in the Cabinet civil war after claiming that the decision to drop the 45p tax cut amounted to a 'coup' and was a 'disappointing' climbdown. And at the LGBT Tories disco on the final night – an occasion at which Truss had been feted in 2021 – several MPs in the dingy smoking area of Birmingham's Reflex nightclub gathered around to laugh at pictures of Truss's scowling face in the early first edition of that day's *Telegraph*. Attendees cheered when New Labour's anthem, 'Things can only get better', came on, with one serving government aide being overheard shouting: 'No they fucking won't!'

Against such a backdrop, on a grey, wet Wednesday morning, Truss took to the Birmingham stage to try to reset her faltering premiership. The conference had brought the tensions among her team from below the surface into open warfare, with the political team at loggerheads.

As Truss entered the conference hall, after just 28 days in charge, she was already pleading with her party not to knife her as they had her two predecessors. 'Expectations are so low that mediocre would be a triumph', ran one headline in that day's *Times* newspaper. While platform oratory has never been Truss's forte, she delivered a composed speech that was by no means mediocre. Standing on stage at the same conference venue where eight years previously she had delivered her 'pork markets' *pièce de résistance*, she eschewed any mention of cheese and apples, instead turning her guns on the 'enemies of enterprise'. Summing up her economic priorities as 'growth, growth and growth', Truss took aim at members of the 'anti-growth coalition', which included 'Labour, the Lib Dems and the SNP, the militant unions, the vested interests dressed up as think tanks, the talking heads, the Brexit deniers and Extinction Rebellion'. Dividing the world into grifters versus grafters, her frustration was evident at those who 'prefer protesting to doing'. She accused them of moaning on Twitter over 'taking tough decisions' as 'they taxi from North London townhouses to the BBC studio to dismiss anyone challenging the status quo. From broadcast to podcast, they peddle the same old answers. It's always more taxes, more regulation and more meddling. Wrong, wrong, wrong.'

But her attacks could just as easily be levelled at her Tory critics. In a pointed dig at those working to undermine her leadership, the bruised PM said she knew 'how it feels to have your potential diminished by those who think they know better', adding that she was used to being treated differently 'for being female, or for not fitting in', making her only more 'determined to change things'. In a rare moment of self-reflection, she admitted: 'as the last few weeks have shown, it will be difficult. Whenever there is change, there is disruption. And not everyone will be in favour of change.' Urging her party not to give in 'to the voices of decline', she tied her entire fate as PM to the success of her economic plans. But having lost the faith of the markets, Truss was forced to prostrate herself before their wisdom. And in so doing, she would lose her agenda, her Chancellor, and ultimately, the premiership itself.

October 2022

INTO THE RED

Two days after Truss's conference speech, the Office for Budget Responsibility told Kwasi Kwarteng bluntly that there was a £72 billion black hole in the nation's finances as a direct result of his mini-Budget. The email sent to the Treasury by the OBR on Friday 7 October set in train two weeks of utter meltdown in Downing Street. The scale of the spending cuts that would be needed simply to stop debt interest bankrupting the country was not just eye-watering but politically impossible, even for a strong government. Yet, in spite of this, Truss told the House of Commons at her weekly PMQs session on Wednesday 12 October that she was 'not planning public spending reductions'. The line sparked panic among some of her No. 10 aides, who knew that while spending would – technically – go up, double-digit inflation would mean real-term spending cuts. Some even feared she might 'be done in for lying to the House' and face a parliamentary probe like her predecessor Boris Johnson.

Seemingly heedless of the mounting chaos at home, Kwarteng flew out to the IMF in Washington. There the Chancellor was subjected to a series of embarrassing meetings in which officials repeatedly attacked his government's plans on the world stage. With inflation rampant, the global experts held up Britain as an example of how not to handle the crisis. But the danger to

Kwarteng's career lay back in London. In his absence, the mandarins had turned the screw. Simon Case, the Cabinet Secretary, and James Bowler, Sir Tom Scholar's replacement as the head of the Treasury, urged Truss to jettison her plans to restore some stability. 'On October 13th and 14th we were being briefed that the UK was about to become a Third World country by the Treasury,' a Downing Street source says. 'Bowler, all the Treasury officials, Case, they all sat around the Cabinet table and said to the PM: "Unless you junk corporation tax, we are going to have the most catastrophic meltdown; it will take 20 years to recover." They scared the shit out of her basically.' Truss initially greeted the warning with incredulity, and 'railed against' what she considered a Bank of England and Treasury 'stitch-up'.

One No. 10 aide involved in the discussions recalls: 'Thursday 13th was terrible. They said the pound was basically going to crash to such a level that we would struggle to sell our debt in the way a Third World country does. Basically Britain was going to become like rubble. It was impossible to know who to believe at this stage.' Truss confessed privately that, despite her scepticism, 'the problem is the last time I ignored all these people they were right'. As the biggest revenue-raising element of the mini-Budget – some £18 billion a year by 2026 – corporation tax was in the official sights for a U-turn. But it would barely dent the size of the OBR's predicted black hole – with markets concluding the rest of the gap could not be filled with spending cuts alone. 'Corporation tax was sitting there and the Treasury bounced us into it by briefing the papers on that Wednesday night into Thursday,' the No. 10 source continues. 'Simon Case was pretty exercised about that, but she was boxed in and we had no choice. If we hadn't done an about-turn, the market would have slumped again, because they'd rallied on the back of reversing the corporation tax cut.'

With markets, officials and economists all panicking, political aides warned Truss that she would not have the numbers in the Commons to pass her tax cuts in a Finance Bill. Caught between the rock of mercenary traders in the City and the hard place of mutinous Tory MPs in Westminster, it began to dawn on Truss that her sticking to her tax-cut package risked her becoming the shortest-ever-serving Prime Minister in history. Away on holiday in Greece, the all-powerful boss of the backbench 1922 Committee, Sir Graham Brady, had made his disquiet known in a number of calls with Truss. Just as he had warned the PM during the Tory Conference that the 45p tax rate had to be scrapped if she wanted to survive, so he counselled Truss that Kwarteng had to be offered up as a sacrifice if her administration was to remain in any way credible. Deputy PM Thérèse Coffey was also said to be 'determined to get Kwasi', according to one source. Not that Truss needed much persuading. 'She put the knife through his shoulder blades while he was still in the departure lounge,' another source told us, a third adding: 'She was already thinking about it and then Brady, Wendy Morton, Thérèse and [Deputy Chief Whip] Craig Whittaker all told her to sack him. Senior officials were also desperate to get rid of Wendy and get Grant Shapps in. There was advice to move Thérèse to Chief Whip and make Grant the Health Secretary. But she ignored it and sacked Kwasi. She kept saying, "This is so painful, so painful."'

With Kwarteng summoned home early, shortly after he landed back at Heathrow on the morning of 14 October Twitter was already alive with the news that he was to be sacked after just 38 days in the job. At a brief meeting across the Cabinet table, Kwarteng attempted to warn the 'teary' PM that if she sacked him she would be next in line for the baying mob. 'They're already coming for me, Kwasi,' she feebly replied – a rare display of emotion from Truss, reflecting the scale of her betrayal of her closest ally. It was one of the shortest stints in the Treasury in more than two hundred years – a humiliation all too obvious to the former economic historian. Elected to Parliament on the same day in 2010, Kwarteng and Truss had been close friends for over a decade. They were co-authors, and co-founders and successive leaders of the Free Enterprise Group, as well as allies throughout the long years of May and Johnson. They had worked 'hand in glove' together and often in secret on their mini-Budget, and yet she dismissed him in a ruthless bid for self-survival. There was a surreal aftermath, according to No. 10 insiders, who recall Kwarteng wandering around the building 'chatting to people' even though he had just been fired.

Politically weakened, perhaps terminally, Truss now turned to Jeremy Hunt – the man whom she had mocked privately in her leadership race – to help calm her party. With this appointment of the embodiment of Tory orthodoxy, the Trussonomics revolution was over before it had even begun.

In their first call, Truss told Hunt she wanted a 'Dave-and-George-style relationship' in reference to the tight-knit partnership of Cameron and Osborne. Hunt told her: 'That's the only way I know how to work.' She replied: 'Look, we just need to be in lockstep. You've got freedom, I just need to know everything that is going on.' Hunt's allies boasted that he was the new CEO of the government to Truss's chairman, annoying some supporters of the PM. But others positively embraced the idea of Hunt being a new lightning rod for the painful decisions to come. A No. 10 official admitted: 'Basically the strategy was "Let Jeremy front all the bad shit." We were kind of laughing at this narrative that "Jeremy is the chief executive." Fine, fuck it, she's the PM, this keeps her in post. We just thought: use Jeremy as a human shield. We wanted him to own all the bad shit. And we thought it would work, to be honest. But it didn't.'

An hour after the appointment, Truss held an abject eight-minute press conference. She backtracked on her long-standing pledge to ease taxes on big business, admitting that she'd gone 'further and faster than markets were expecting'. Corporation tax would instead go up to 25 per cent in the spring: as per Rishi Sunak's old plan and in direct contradiction to what she said at her first PMQs. But after just eight minutes and taking four questions, Truss walked out – with MPs barely containing their rage that the awkward statement had made matters worse. Barely a third of Tory MPs bothered to dial into Thérèse Coffey's subsequent 'awful' conference call to explain the situation. The following day, on Saturday 15 October, the new Chancellor did the media rounds, telling Sky there would be less spending and warning the BBC that taxes wouldn't go down 'as quickly as people hope'. Amid jokes about Hunt being the 'real Prime Minister', the Chancellor met with his embattled leader at Chequers to rip up the last of her economic agenda.

By this point, Team Truss had turned on each other. There was widespread resentment of Mark Fullbrook, whose lobbying links prompted a series of negative newspaper stories. Tim Shipman in the *Sunday Times*[1] reported that Tory MPs had christened him 'Chief Wiggum' – a reference to the 'corpulent police chief in *The Simpsons* who is too lazy to fight crime' – while political aides mocked his decision to give them each a copy of *Total Competition: Lessons in Strategy from Formula One* by former F1 boss Ross Brawn. One aide who worked under Fullbrook raged: 'People ask what it was that he did wrong and I can't think of anything, because he just didn't do anything. He was just absent, he was never there. He was working from home half the time. He would constantly, at the end of meetings, be like, "Oh, Liz, can you sign this coffee cup for someone?"' Allies of Mr Fullbrook point to the illness and death of his father during his short time in the job to explain his absence.[2] Others in No. 10 speak further in his defence: 'He had a grip of what he was able to have a grip on,' says one aide. 'He wasn't kept in the loop – he was good for team morale. The problem was he wasn't used enough.' Another sympathetic aide suggests that after '40 years in Tory politics, maybe he was trying to leave a legacy' by taking up the role of Chief of Staff, adding: 'anyone would have struggled' to exert themselves over the warring factions.

Truss was also said to have regretted the appointment of Matt Sinclair as her Chief Economic Adviser. One source told the *Mail on Sunday* that 'he was always talking over her in meetings ... She said on one occasion that if he kept it up she would stab him in the leg.'[3] Another official complained they had 'never seen a structure in Downing Street as bad as this', even in the livelier days of Boris Johnson, while a senior Whitehall veteran of the past six administrations told a Spad that it was the 'worst No. 10 operation he could recall'. One staffer says: 'Ironically the operation post mini-Budget was better because basically Truss let everyone in the room. She realised the problem was she hadn't exposed anything to scrutiny. But by then we were fucked.'

The U-turn on corporation tax was not enough to abate the political pressures facing Truss. And a brutal briefing against Jason Stein that Sunday upset MPs further. The *Sunday Times* quoted a source close to Truss branding her former leadership rival and ex-Cabinet colleague Sajid Javid – who had reportedly just been sounded out by Truss's team itself about the Chancellor job – 'shit'.[4] Javid and his allies were furious and immediately demanded blood. Stein offered to resign when the story broke on the Saturday evening, but the PM refused to even countenance the suggestion, saying it was not a sackable offence. Across the Atlantic meanwhile, President Biden did his bit for his British ally, telling reporters at an Oregon ice cream shop that Truss's original economic policies had been 'a mistake' and that her reversal of tax-cutting plans was 'predictable'. That evening, as Hunt planned his speech to announce the U-turn the following day, the first Tory MPs went public with calls for Truss to go: Crispin Blunt, Andrew Bridgen and Jamie Wallis. Dozens more privately demanded the same, with an Opinium opinion poll that day forecasting a 411-seat Labour landslide.

Things got so bad that former Prime Minister Theresa May called Truss to offer advice, having been through the mill herself. A source says: 'Theresa called with three pearls of wisdom: firstly, fashion. She said wear more suits with smart tops that make you look more business-like. Secondly she said be more up front with mistakes that were made. And thirdly she had a pop at Liz's umming and ahh-ing at the press conference, and said she should have taken the broadcasters' questions first.' George Osborne was also in touch that weekend to tell Truss to say sorry more and do a reshuffle. Meanwhile Boris 'was constantly in touch', a source says, 'via WhatsApp from the beach' with helpful quips for PMQs and general advice. The ex-PM was also concerned that the *Daily Mail* Editor-in-Chief had been dropped from a new list of peers published that week, and found time to raise his concerns about this.

On Monday morning, Hunt gave an extraordinary statement to the nation. In seven minutes, he unceremoniously binned 'almost all' the mini-Budget pledges the Truss government had announced just a few weeks earlier. He binned the cut to dividend tax, the IR35 changes and the cut to the basic rate of income tax. Even the energy support plan – one of the few remaining positives of Truss's premiership – was to be significantly reduced, from two years to six months. Her free-market allies were furious: 'The light at the end of the economic tunnel has now been extinguished by this Chancellor,' claimed the TaxPayers' Alliance, while the IEA warned that 'higher corporate tax rates could deepen any forthcoming recession'. Hunt was due to make a further statement to the Commons that afternoon, but before that the Speaker of the House, Sir Lindsay Hoyle, accepted an Urgent Question on the economic turmoil. Instead of accepting the challenge herself, Truss instead sent Penny Mordaunt – another former rival whom she had defeated three months earlier – to stand in her place.

Having assured the House that Truss was not, in fact, 'hiding under a desk', Mordaunt's grave intonations concerning Truss's absence sparked fears about some kind of security scare. Concern turned to bemusement when it transpired that the Prime Minister was in fact mostly in political meetings, including one with Brady, actually on the parliamentary estate. Truss even turned up to watch the closing minutes of Mordaunt's speech before Hunt stood up to formally herald the death of Trussonomics from the despatch box. Mute throughout, Truss instead gave an uncomfortable interview that evening with the BBC in which she admitted that 'mistakes were made' but insisted: 'I will lead the Conservatives into the next general election.' Truss tried to bolster her flagging support among both wings of the party, meeting the One Nation caucus that Monday and the ERG the following day.

That Tuesday morning began with a joint operation from two Defence ministers on manoeuvres. Amid Hunt's talk of spending cuts, Ben Wallace and James Heappey insisted they would quit if Truss's pledge to boost defence spending to 3 per cent of GDP by the end of the decade was scrapped. The scale of the Treasury's proposed cuts list shocked even hardened Whitehall veterans. Unless some way could be found to fill the black hole, the entire prisons building programme, for example, was at risk, and one doomsday Treasury document even suggested cutting the capital budget for Education. One aide recalls: 'I remember sitting in a meeting with 86 different options to raise money. It was just insane; from the doable to the undoable. Like literal ceilings would have fallen on children. The one the Treasury really want is Defence. They hate Defence. And we would just constantly talk about Ben Wallace. How the Defence Secretary would resign if we went near it, and officials would say, "Well, so what?"'

Meanwhile the Tory press turned on Truss, with the *Mail* – previously her staunchest backer – declaring that morning she was 'in office but not in power'. The *Sun* labelled her 'The Ghost PM'; that week's *Spectator* cover had Truss disintegrating, under the title 'The lady vanishes'. Party discipline frayed even further, with backbencher Robert Largan writing a thinly veiled column on the dangers of dumpster fires, while Hunt's ally Steve Brine made a Freudian slip on *Politics Live*, suggesting Hunt was a 'fantastic Prime Minister'. In a last-ditch gamble, Fullbrook brought David Canzini back into No. 10, mere weeks after he'd left as Johnson's Deputy Chief of Staff. He joined the 'war room' of ultra-loyalists in Downing Street, desperately trying to shore up support among MPs. And as grumblings in Parliament grew ever louder, that evening Truss hosted a drinks reception for MPs attended by her daughters in a 'bizarre' belated charm offensive. But further trouble was brewing, with Javid still on the warpath, complaining to the Chief Whip about the *Sunday Times* briefing. The problem for Truss was exacerbated by the fact he had been drawn second for a question at the following day's PMQs, and was vowing to use it to attack her over the quote.

But the fireworks were not contained to Parliament. Ahead of the OBR's updated forecast, Truss was preparing to tell the forecasters that immigration rules would be liberalised, meaning they could factor in higher economic growth to their equations and reduce the size of the black hole. Treasury sums indicated that increasing high skilled migration over the rest of this decade could raise £14 billion, meaning fewer tax rises and spending cuts would be needed. However, Home Secretary Suella Braverman's hardline speech to the Party Conference, and her public declaration that she had 'concerns about having an open-borders migration policy with India', had spooked the OBR, as well as infuriating the Indian government and risking trade talks. The OBR put a £6 billion black mark next to Braverman's tough rejection of additional visas to meet job shortages in the UK. In a meeting on Tuesday evening, Truss ordered Braverman to publish a written ministerial statement saying she was clamping down on 'bogus illegal immigration and increasing high-skilled migrants, using a new growth visa'. In order to soothe the OBR, No. 10 wanted the Home Office to announce measures welcoming immigrants from key sectors like elite sport, science and IT. But Braverman cut up rough, warning the PM that such a move was hard for her to swallow. A source says she continued to resist the move 'even after the PM pointed out to the Home Secretary that £14 billion was similar to the size of the police budget'. The pair left on bad terms that evening, with No. 10 staff quietly putting the Home Secretary on resignation watch.

Matters did not improve on Wednesday 19 October. The day began with yet another U-turn, this time on protecting the pensions triple lock after Hunt suggested it could be axed to try to find savings. Enough MPs had made clear they would not vote for it, with Downing Street's power ebbing away in the face of rebellion after threatened rebellion. Sensing mortal danger, Truss also reluctantly agreed to suspend Stein after Javid refused to back down from his plan to out him in the Commons. With minutes to spare, Ruth Porter told Javid that Stein had been suspended, with a formal investigation by the Propriety and Ethics Team in Whitehall. Javid consequently pulled his planned question, but the news of the suspension was leaked regardless. Amid the infighting, Truss gave a solid but weary performance in which she insisted, 'I'm a fighter not a quitter', in a tortured echo of Peter Mandelson's words 21 years earlier.

Although she escaped a knockout blow in the Commons, the PM was hit by a baffling plot twist to the Braverman saga. While deciding what to do about the written ministerial statement on migration that she had been ordered to write, Braverman had emailed a copy of it accidentally to the office of Tory MP Andrew Stephenson instead of to her long-time ally John Hayes, from whom she was seeking advice. Using a private email address to boot, Braverman had breached the ministerial code twice. When word of the leak reached the Cabinet Office, Truss wasted no time: Braverman was to be sacked. A glowing letter from the PM offering the possibility of a future return to high office was shared with the Home Office so that the traditional exchange of letters could be coordinated. However Braverman, despite having been given the chance to go quietly, instead tweeted an incendiary missive all but calling for Truss to quit. It raged: 'Pretending we haven't made mistakes, carrying on as if everyone can't see that we have made them, and hoping that things will magically come right is not serious politics. I have made a mistake; I accept responsibility; I resign.' In another Truss administration record, Braverman was the shortest-serving minister in her office since 1834. A No. 10 source says: 'To be honest, we were quite happy. We wanted her gone for a while. Liz knew [giving her the position] was a mistake but a deal had been a deal.'

All this merely served as the pretext for the events of that Wednesday evening. The Labour Party had cleverly used an opposition day debate to put forward a motion on shale gas extraction – a mechanism that would allow the opposition to introduce a bill into the Commons banning the practice. The 2019 Conservative manifesto had promised a moratorium on fracking but Truss in her leadership pitch pledged to reverse that. Tory MPs were therefore put in a bind: did they support their new leader or the original pitch on which they were elected? The Whips' Office made it clear where they stood, writing an email to MPs to inform them that they were on an extremely strict three-line whip. 'This is not a motion on fracking,' read the email from Deputy Chief Whip Craig Whittaker. 'This is a confidence motion in the government.' It meant the administration would collapse if it lost and rebels would lose the whip. A third-tier issue with explosive political cut-through suddenly became the key determiner of confidence at a time of high tempers and low party discipline.

The dysfunctional Whips' operation of Boris Johnson's era had only worsened under his successor. By this point Truss had lost faith in Morton, with No. 10 staff openly referring to her as 'Wendy Moron'. Her Whips' operation was described as a 'shitshow', with its 'rag ratings' of red, amber or green, depending on their hostility towards Truss, seen as completely inaccurate: close supporters of Truss were on amber while Sunak allies were green. Fracking proved to be the straw that broke the camel's back. Shortly before the vote, Chris Skidmore – Truss's *Britannia Unchained* co-author and Net Zero guru –

announced he would not support the introduction of fracking, with several others following suit. With the Whips' Office fearing a rebellion of up to 60 MPs, the decision was taken to pull the plug. Minutes before MPs were due to go through the lobbies, Climate Minister Graham Stuart received a message from an aide to Wendy Morton that was later blamed on a 'junior No. 10 official'. In his winding-up speech, Stuart was instructed to tell the Commons from the despatch box: 'Quite clearly this is not a confidence vote.'

Confusion reigned supreme in Parliament as drama turned to farce, with MPs baffled as to whether they could rebel or not. The government won by 315 to 228 but it was a Pyrrhic victory. More than 40 Conservative MPs were listed as failing to back Liz Truss's government, with witnesses alleging ministers physically pulled some wavering Tories into the voting lobbies. Jacob Rees-Mogg reportedly suggested there could be a 'snap general election' if they failed to back the government.[5] Rumours abounded that Morton and her deputy Craig Whittaker had both resigned, with Whittaker quoted by onlookers as saying, 'I am fucking furious and I don't give a fuck any more.' Morton ran through the voting lobby in tears. For several hours No. 10 was unable to answer whether there was in fact a Chief Whip or not. It initially was reported that Truss had not voted for her own motion, but it subsequently transpired that she did indeed vote, and that she had forgotten to swipe her pass. Such an oversight was understandable in the circumstances, with Truss being barracked by her own MPs as she scuttled through the voting lobby.

As the drama unfolded all around him, one emotional Tory MP had had enough. Sir Charles Walker, the man who had beaten Truss to the Broxbourne nomination 18 years previously, stood in the central lobby of Parliament and told the rolling cameras that: 'I think it's a shambles and a disgrace. I think it is utterly appalling. I'm livid and, you know, I really shouldn't say this but I hope all those people that put Liz Truss in No. 10 – I hope it was worth it. I hope it was worth it for the ministerial red box. I hope it was worth it to sit around the Cabinet table, because the damage they have done to our party is extraordinary. I've had enough. I've had enough of talentless people putting their tick in the right box, not because it's in the national interest, but because it's in their own personal interest to achieve a ministerial position.' Many of his colleagues agreed. Truss returned to her Downing Street flat late that night. She cancelled a meeting with Hunt and instead pulled out a bottle of her favoured Sauvignon Blanc to share with her husband. Over a pork pie, the couple began to accept the inevitability of her resignation.

Arising early as usual, Truss began messaging aides from 5 a.m. onwards. They met together in No. 10, with the Prime Minister fearful that she had lost the support of every national newspaper except for the *Daily Express*, which enthused about her pensions plan. Despite the carnage of the previous night, the 'whip's report' was merely the fourth item on the planned agenda. Morton's performance left few impressed, as did her final words before leaving the meeting: 'Remember. I. Am. The. Chief. Whip.' A Truss confidant explains: 'She tried to sack Wendy and the whole Whip's office said if you sack Wendy, we'll go too. And that was that. She was done.'

The outward sign that the game was up was when Truss opted for an outfit change. Just as aides learnt that the Queen had died by the Prime Minister ordering dark clothes, they knew she was quitting when she swapped her red outfit for a dark blue one. Sir Graham Brady arrived in Downing Street shortly before midday to deliver the *coup de grâce*. He had received a cascade of letters, emails and WhatsApp messages overnight saying Truss had to go. Asked by Truss if the situation was retrievable, he replied, 'I don't think so, Prime Minister.' She concurred, 'I don't either.' And so, after a mere 44 days in office, Truss threw in the towel. At 1 p.m., she told political aides and No. 10 that she was going to resign. One onlooker told the

Sunday Times that Truss informed the assembled crowd that her position was not tenable. 'Politics is a blood sport,' she said, 'and I'm the fox.'[6]

After Truss telephoned the King, aides drew up her resignation speech. Hugh O'Leary left work to come to No. 10 and stand beside his wife outside the famous black door as she delivered her speech at 1:35 p.m. So rapid was the collapse that some of the marks indicating where the podium should go were still stuck to the pavement from her arrival speech six weeks earlier. Bowing to the inevitable, the woman who promised to 'deliver, deliver, deliver' was forced to stand on the steps of Downing Street and admit that 'I cannot deliver the mandate on which I was elected.' In front of the watching cameras and the eyes of a nation, she delivered the following 89-second statement:

'I came into office at a time of great economic and international instability. Families and businesses were worried about how to pay their bills. Putin's illegal war in Ukraine threatens the security of our whole continent. And our country had been held back for too long by low economic growth. I was elected by the Conservative Party with a mandate to change this. We delivered on energy bills and on cutting National Insurance. And we set out a vision for a low-tax, high-growth economy that would take advantage of the freedoms of Brexit. I recognise though, given the situation, I cannot deliver the mandate on which I was elected by the Conservative Party. I have therefore spoken to His Majesty The King to notify him that I am resigning as Leader of the Conservative Party. This morning I met the Chair of the 1922 Committee Sir Graham Brady. We have agreed there will be a leadership election to be completed in the next week. This will ensure we remain on a path to deliver our fiscal plans and maintain our country's economic stability and national security. I will remain as Prime Minister until a successor has been chosen. Thank you.'

In so doing, she became the shortest-serving premier in British political history, easily eclipsing George Canning's record of 119 days: a tenure only ended by his untimely death. There were tears among Truss's Downing Street staff at her resignation, but she reassured them – and herself – with the words: 'Don't worry, I'm relieved it's over … at least I've been Prime Minister.'

Epilogue

'THE PARTY WASN'T READY FOR THIS'

Seven weeks to the day after Liz Truss beat Rishi Sunak in the Tory leadership election, Conservative MPs crowned him their new leader, this time without risking another vote of the party membership. Sunak had predicted the damaging outcome of Truss's sweeping unfunded tax cuts; his prize was to try to fix it. Unrepentant to the end, Truss departed with a warning to her successor. On her last weekend in office, she gathered her dwindling band of MP supporters and aides at Chequers to thank them for their service. 'We were doing the right things,' she said in a goodbye speech. 'The problems that we face are not going to go away and we need to make difficult decisions to get our economy and country into the best place to take on our competitors and adversaries.' She told them she was proud of what they had tried to do 'but the party wasn't ready for this'.

Those that saw the Prime Minister during the height of the tax row, at the very moment the pound was sinking, were struck by her 'worryingly zen-like' demeanour. Even after the 45p climbdown, she sarcastically remarked to aides at the Party Conference: 'I don't know what happens – drama just seems to follow me wherever I go.' In reality, Truss and Kwarteng blundered into the tax-cut debacle through a mix of arrogance and impatience. They were eager to flaunt their radical convictions without doing the necessary groundwork first. The obvious parallel is with her first ministerial post at Education: she charged into the childcare brief armed with a reformist zeal and no time for critics, yet with insufficient support she was ultimately defeated by those notionally on her side. But as that and other experiences in her 10 years in office show, Truss could grow into a role – even if she has never fully got to grips with the drawbacks of her excessive enthusiasm.

The flashpoints of her short premiership are clear: the personnel and policy decisions taken at Chevening, the mini-Budget drawn up in secret and the subsequent U-turn played out brutally in public, the sacking of Kwasi Kwarteng and then the farce of the fracking vote. 'Frankly, it was hubris,' remarks one disillusioned aide, reflecting on that critical three-week transition period starting in mid-August when the tax cuts were being prepared. The advice of friendly economists was ignored; 'rolling the pitch' was never done properly. But the fatal error – and one that involves a question of honesty – was taken in the very first hours of her campaign to become PM. There was clearly a political decision taken in her kitchen at Greenwich that weekend in July to undersell to the membership the depth of her plans. A line can be drawn from that moment to the reaction of investors, who were caught off guard by the scale of Truss's ambitions.

The vast energy package and the sweeping tax cuts a fortnight later were clearly an attempt to offset doing something she knew she had to do politically, though begrudgingly, against what she wanted to do, unfettered and unchecked. Just because there was political consensus over freezing energy bills, it was complacent to believe there would be a blind eye turned to the price tag in the City. To then add more than £30 billion of tax cuts out of the blue was as reckless as it was naïve. It's hard to escape the verdict that the size of the bail-out was clearly such an anathema to her that she wildly overcompensated with the unfunded mini-Budget. It was a political misjudgement of monumental proportions and to spring it on a country already reeling from the shock of the death of the Monarch seemed tin-eared at best. So was the Truss administration doomed from the beginning? 'It just went from basically one extreme to the other: you couldn't get near her and no one had her phone number and then after the mini-Budget it was just chaos,' says one confidant. 'I'm just haunted by how badly it all went. It was just mental.'

As these chapters have illustrated, for a decade Truss had got away with trying to mix principle with pragmatism, alongside unashamed opportunism. When problems get too hot she junks them; from public sector pay reform during the leadership campaign, to the top-rate tax cut three months later at confer-ence. Yet crucially she is also a politician in a hurry who has only really succeeded when listening to advice. She turned her floundering leadership hopes around by putting herself in the hands of comms professionals for the debates, yet shut out media advisers from the decision-making processes that led to the mini-Budget blunder. As a result, those decisions consumed all of Truss's political capital, causing her government to take the heat for all of the country's economic woes. Despite presid-ing over the biggest-ever market intervention and government bail-out, she was painted as a 'trickle-down' zealot only serving the rich.

'Bouncebackability' is a quality that Truss's supporters say she has in spades, along with an inexhaustible work ethic and a nose for when to ditch a fight she is not going to win. Even Michael Gove admits: 'You don't serve under three Prime Ministers, you don't come back from the assaults and reverses she suffered at the MoJ, you don't come back from that, you don't become Prime Minister in a strongly contested field unless you are a good politician.' But in the end, despite that 'delightful Terminator-like quality' aides spoke of, the scale of the mistakes proved too large.

The case for the defence is that any Tory premier would strug-gle with the woes of their party and the country right now. Two separate sides were pinning their hopes on her: the right saw the zeal of a convert in her embrace of Brexit, while the Osbornites genuinely believed she was still one of them. During the leadership campaign George Osborne was said to have told a friend: 'What's not to like about Liz? She's a Remainer, she wants economic growth, we've spent the last three years worrying about other stuff like migration or levelling up, but the whole point of the Conservative Party is to generate economic prosperity.' After the first PMQs Osborne was mocking Labour for 'underestimating' his prodigy.

Any attempt to be all things to all people means that there are, inevitably, more people to disappoint. And in trying to please both sides of a warring party, Truss ended up unable to count on either side when things went south. In her first act as PM, on the steps of Downing Street, she said: 'as strong as the storm may be, I know that the British people are stronger'. In fact, the people never got a say: Truss was instead swept out by the bond markets and a ceaseless civil war within her party ranks. But when the public do get their say, their belated verdict looks likely to be damning.

It took the Conservative Party more than 15 years to even begin to recover from the defenestration of Margaret Thatcher, an election-winning leader brought down by her own side. Six years on from the Brexit referendum and after the removal of its poster boy Boris Johnson, there seems to be no end in sight to the internecine struggle that continues to plague the Tories; one that a weary public may prefer they finish in the semi-privacy of opposition. On to their fifth leader since taking power in 2010 and after the bloody battles of austerity, Brexit and Covid, many Conservatives seem simply too exhausted to win that elusive fifth term in office.

Rishi Sunak optimistically told MPs in the moments after he had been declared their leader that their party has never been more united on Europe. And he's right, to a degree. But the classic schism over EU membership that tore through the party for 20 years was actually masking deeper ideological splits. It was easier to see all problems through the prism of Leave or Remain, Eurosceptic or Europhile. Two camps came together under the Leave banner: the free marketeers who wanted to look beyond Europe, and the anti-immigration right. Those two camps are now at war. Remain was a broad church for the left of the party covering up the cracks between the social justice warriors who want more spending on benefits, and the reformers who do not believe that more money is the simple answer. In reality the Conservative Party is more fractured than it has been in decades, with a geographical divide offered between Johnson's 'Red Wallers' and the safer southern seats.

There is a sulphurous mood among some in Cabinet at the state of the party, while backbenchers seem hell-bent on becoming totally unmanageable by any Prime Minister. The Catch-22 any Tory PM will find themselves in rests on that fact. In order to turn the ship around, the PM needs to utilise that 70-seat majority gifted to them by Johnson. Yet the party is so divided, there appears to be no majority for any measure that might actually recover the situation. It looks to be a government unable to actually govern. After 12 years of Tory rule there are more than 50 sacked and embittered ex-ministers with nothing to lose. Meanwhile, younger and newer MPs are also jumpy, having been led into thinking that ditching Johnson would save their seats, only to find the party's woes have not ended with him.

Sunak faces many of the same problems as Truss, even if he is better at the presentation. As a Tory grandee from the right of the party warns, there is a 'genuine chance the Conservative Party splits irrevocably'. It is now facing up to a fresh round of spending cuts, but any attempt to save money on the welfare bill by not linking benefits to inflation is certain to trigger a revolt. Truss promised growth via sweeping supply side reforms – but the two biggest levers the government has to pull are planning reform and more immigration. Both are likely to enrage two different factions of the Tory coalition. Hugely increasing the level of net migration would push up overall GDP, but will be fiercely resisted by those in northern marginals and those on the right. Any significant moves to make it easier to build houses or roads will trigger a different side of the party, which has already successfully fought off Johnson's attempts to build more homes. Truss was right to say the problems faced have not been magicked away by a change of leader.

Rishi Sunak's fate now depends on whether the various rebel camps will back off from him in a way they did not for Truss. Only the extreme optimists think that will happen. 'They've taken the bat off Boris, broken it into pieces and given chunks to the different warring sides to beat each other with,' as one serving Cabinet minister put it. 'It's like *Lord of the Flies*.'

ENDNOTES

1975: 'Smart Alec'

1. 'Women with Balls', *Spectator*, 8 December 2018
2. *Spectator*, 1 December 2012
3. *The Times*, 2 September 2022
4. *The Times*, 2 September 2022

1993: Liberal Youth

1. *The Times*, 23 December 2021
2. *The Times*, 5 September 2022
3. *Daily Mail*, 3 September 2022
4. *Daily Mail*, 28 January 2022
5. *CNN*, 6 September 2022
6. *The Times*, 5 September 2022
7. *Sunday Times*, 8 November 2009
8. *The Times*, 5 September 2022
9. *The Times*, 9 June 2012
10. 'Women with Balls', *Spectator*, 8 December 2018
11. *Newscast*, BBC, 16 August 2022
12. *Daily Telegraph*, 3 September 2022
13. 'Women with Balls', *Spectator*, 8 December 2018
14. *The Times*, 23 December 2021
15. *Sunday Times*, 4 September 2022

1996: The Greasy Pole

1. *The Times*, 3 September 2022
2. *Mail on Sunday*, 23 July 2022
3. *Daily Mail*, 3 September 2022
4. *Daily Mail*, 3 September 2022
5. *Guardian*, 26 September 2011
6. *Observer*, 7 October 2001
7. *Daily Telegraph*, 10 October 2002
8. *Guardian*, 13 August 2022
9. The *i*, 22 August 2022
10. *The Times*, 23 December 2021
11. *PR Week*, 25 March 2005
12. *PR Week*, 29 November 2006
13. *The Times*, 30 January 2004
14. 'Women with Balls', *Spectator*, 8 December 2018
15. *Huddersfield Daily Examiner*, 23 May 2006
16. *Halifax Evening Courier*, 8 February 2005
17. *Huddersfield Daily Examiner*, 7 February 2005
18. *Mail on Sunday*, 8 November 2009
19. *Daily Mail*, 20 May 2006
20. *Yorkshire Post*, 2 May 2005
21. *Observer*, 11 July 2009
22. Alex Grant's blog, 13 July 2022
23. *The Times*, 3 September 2022
24. *Independent*, 19 July 2006
25. The *i*, 22 August 2022
26. *Spectator*, 19 April 2009
27. *Mail on Sunday*, 6 January 2008
28. *Evening Standard*, 3 March 2009
29. *Daily Mirror*, 3 June 2008
30. *Western Mail*, 21 August 2009
31. *Daily Express*, 2 September 2008
32. *Spectator*, 10 March 2008
33. ConservativeHome, 20 September 2009

2009: The Turnip Taliban

1. *Mail on Sunday*, 25 October 2009
2. *Daily Mail*, 2 November 2009
3. *Eastern Daily Press*, 31 October 2009

 4. *Mail on Sunday*, 15 November 2009
 5. *Independent*, 27 December 2009
 6. *Mail Online*, 4 November 2009
 7. *Lynn News and Advertiser*, 27 October 2009
 8. *Eastern Daily Press*, 4 November 2009
 9. *Mail on Sunday*, 8 November 2009
10. *Mail on Sunday*, 1 November 2009
11. *Mail Online*, 4 November 2009
12. *Daily Telegraph*, 7 November 2009
13. *Mail on Sunday*, 8 November 2009
14. *Evening Standard*, 20 November 2009
15. *Western Morning News*, 5 November 2009
16. *Mail Online*, 4 November 2009
17. *Daily Telegraph*, 15 November 2009
18. *Daily Mail*, 6 November 2009
19. *Independent*, 16 November 2009
20. ConservativeHome, 5 November 2009
21. *Daily Telegraph*, 31 October 2009
22. *Daily Telegraph*, 13 November 2009
23. *Daily Mail*, 18 November 2009
24. *Lynn News and Advertiser*, 14 November 2009
25. *The Times*, 3 September 2022
26. *Daily Mail*, 18 November 2009
27. *Daily Telegraph*, 21 November 2009
28. *Daily Mail*, 19 November 2009
29. *Observer*, 21 February 2010
30. *Eastern Daily Press*, 16 December 2009
31. ConservativeHome, 30 August 2010
32. *Eastern Daily Press*, 3 May 2010
33. *Eastern Daily Press*, 8 May 2010

2010: Liz Truss, MP

1. *Eastern Daily Press*, 10 June 2010
2. ConservativeHome, 30 August 2010
3. *Bury Free Press*, 2 July 2010
4. *Press and Journal*, 23 November 2010
5. *Eastern Daily Press*, 23 November 2010
6. *Eastern Daily Press*, 19 July 2011
7. *Independent*, 30 June 2012
8. *The Times*, 3 September 2022

9. *The Times*, 31 December 2010
10. *The Times*, 11 February 2011
11. *Daily Mail*, 22 December 2011
12. *Guardian*, 8 December 2011
13. *Sunday Times*, 26 June 2011
14. *Observer*, 7 August 2011
15. *Daily Telegraph*, 12 September 2011
16. *Spectator*, 23 June 2012
17. *Evening Standard*, 6 January 2012
18. *Mail on Sunday*, 29 January 2012
19. *Guardian*, 22 August 2012
20. *The Times*, 9 June 2012
21. *Daily Mail*, 11 August 2012
22. *Daily Mail*, 18 August 2012

2012: The Lowest Rung

1. *Daily Telegraph*, 15 October 2012
2. *Daily Telegraph*, 17 October 2012
3. *The Times*, 3 September 2022
4. *Daily Telegraph*, 30 May 2013
5. *Daily Telegraph*, 26 August 2013
6. *Mail on Sunday*, 25 August 2013
7. *Daily Mail*, 16 July 2014
8. David Laws, *Coalition*, 2016
9. *Daily Telegraph*, 4 March 2014
10. BBC News, 6 June 2014
11. *The Times*, 3 September 2022

2014: 'That Is a Disgrace'

1. Anthony Seldon and Peter Snowdon, *Cameron at Ten*, 2015
2. *Herald*, 16 July 2014
3. *Spectator*, 26 November 2014
4. Dominic Dyer, *Badgered to Death*, 2014
5. *The Rest Is Politics*, 24 August 2022
6. Iain Anderson, *F**k Business*, 2019
7. *Guardian*, 27 August 2022
8. *Spectator*, 20 February 2016
9. *The Times*, 3 September 2022
10. Iain Anderson, *F**k Business*, 2019

2016: Enemies of the People

1. *Sunday Telegraph*, 1 October 2016
2. *Newscast*, BBC, 16 August 2022
3. *Guardian*, 5 November 2016
4. *Guardian*, 10 November 2016
5. *Spectator*, 8 November 2016
6. *Newscast*, BBC, 16 August 2022
7. *The Times*, 19 November 2016
8. Lord Dyson, *A Judge's Journey*, 2019
9. *The Times*, 12 April 2017

2017: Demotion

1. *Spectator*, 13 April 2019
2. *Independent*, 27 June 2018
3. *Eastern Daily Press*, 1 May 2019
4. *Spectator*, 13 April 2019
5. *Spectator*, 8 March 2018
6. *Newscast*, BBC, 16 August 2022
7. *Spectator*, 13 April 2019
8. *Daily Mirror*, 26 June 2018
9. ITV online, 27 June 2018
10. *Independent*, 27 June 2018
11. *The Times*, 3 September 2022
12. Matt Forde's *The Political Party* podcast, 25 January 2019
13. *Peston*, ITV, 17 January 2019
14. The *i*, 10 February 2019
15. *Daily Telegraph*, 20 May 2019
16. Guido Fawkes, 2 April 2019
17. *Spectator*, 16 May 2019
18. *You Magazine, Mail on Sunday*, 12 May 2019
19. *Spectator*, 11 July 2019

2019: Truss Unchained

1. *The Times*, 3 September 2022
2. *Spectator*, 14 September 2021

2021: Diplomacy

1. ConservativeHome, 4 October 2021
2. *The Times*, 3 September 2022
3. *Mail on Sunday*, 27 November 2021
4. Sophie Raworth, BBC, 30 January 2022
5. *Guardian*, 24 February 2022
6. *Guardian*, 21 July 2022

August 2022: Hostile Takeover

1. *Spectator*, 3 September 2022
2. *Guardian*, 21 October 2022

October 2022: Into the Red

1. *Sunday Times*, 23 October 2022
2. *Sunday Times*, 23 October 2022
3. *Mail on Sunday*, 23 October 2022
4. *Sunday Times*, 16 October 2022
5. *The Times*, 22 October 2022
6. *The Times*, 22 October 2022